KU-416-588

RED HOT
CHILLI PEPPER

RED HOT CHILLI PEPPER

Bring a **touch of fire** to your cooking with this **sizzling** collection of more than 140 **chilli-hot recipes**

———

Consultant Editor: Jenni Fleetwood

TED SMART

This edition produced for
The Book People Ltd
Hallwood Avenue
Haydock
St Helens WA11 9UL

© Anness Publishing Limited 2001, 2002
Hermes House, 88–89 Blackfriars Road, London SE1 8HA

All rights reserved. No part of this publication
may be reproduced, stored in a retrieval system, or
transmitted in any way or by any means,
electronic, mechanical, photocopying, recording or
otherwise, without the prior
written permission of the copyright holder.

A CIP catalogue record for this book is
available from the British Library.

ISBN 1 84309 464 9

Publisher: Joanna Lorenz
Managing Editor: Helen Sudell
Project Editor: Valerie Ferguson
Consultant Editor: Jenni Fleetwood
Designer: Nigel Partridge
Typesetter: Diane Pullen
Production Controller: Wendy Lawson
Editorial Reader: Richard McGinlay
Recipes contributed by: Catherine Atkinson, Alex Barker, Angela Boggiano, Carla Capalbo, Kit Chan, Maxine Clark,
Jacqueline Clarke, Trish Davies, Patrizia Diemling, Matthew Drennan,
Tessa Evelegh, Silvano Franco, Shirley Gill, Brian Glover, Rosamund Grant, Nicola Graimes,
Deh-Ta Hsuing, Shehzad Husain, Christine Ingram, Manisha Kanani, Lucy Knox, Lesley Mackley, Sally Mansfield,
Norma Miller, Jane Milton, Sallie Morris, Annie Nichols, Jennie Shapter,
Liz Trigg, Laura Washburn, Jeni Wright
Photography: Karl Adamson, Edward Allwright, Micki Dowie, James Duncan, Ian Garlick,
Michelle Garrett, Amanda Heywood, Ferguson Hill, Janine Hosegood, David Jordan,
Dave King, William Lingwood, Patrick McLeavey, Steve Moss, Thomas Odulate,
Craig Robertson, Simon Smith, Sam Stowell

Printed and bound in Singapore

1 3 5 7 9 10 8 6 4 2

NOTES

Bracketed terms are intended for American readers. For all recipes, quantities are given in both metric and
imperial measures and, where appropriate, measures are also given in standard cups and spoons. Follow
one set, but not a mixture, because they are not interchangeable.

Standard spoon and cup measures are level.
1 tsp = 5ml, 1 tbsp = 15ml, 1 cup = 250ml/8fl oz
Australian standard tablespoons are 20ml. Australian readers should use 3 tsp in place of 1 tbsp for mea-
suring small quantities of gelatine, flour, salt etc.
Medium (US large) eggs are used unless otherwise stated.

The consultant editor would like to thank Christine McFadden and chilli grower
Michael Michaud, fellow members of the Guild of Food Writers, for sharing their knowledge of and enthusiasm
for chillies. Michael and Joy Michaud are market gardeners, and
from July to December each year they can supply fresh chillies by mail order.
Contact them at Peppers by Post, Sea Spring Farm, West Bexington,
Dorchester, Dorset DT2 9DD, UK, tel: 01308 897892.

CONTENTS

INTRODUCTION

There's a ring of fire encircling the globe, and it has nothing to do with volcanic activity. This is fire we're very much in favour of: the warmth that comes from red hot chilli peppers. These powerful little pods originated in South America, but now form a very important part of many of the world's major cuisines.

India is the largest producer and exporter of chillies, with much of the crop used for local consumption. Thailand, Mexico, Japan, Turkey, Nigeria, Ethiopia, Uganda, Kenya and Tanzania are also prime producers, exporting chillies to other countries around the globe.

The word chilli is spelt in different ways. Sometimes it is chile, sometimes chili, sometimes chilli pepper. This last description is accurate insofar as it recognizes that chillies are members of the *Capsicum* family, like the sweet peppers. It also forms a link with all those spicy powders – chilli, cayenne and paprika – which are an essential part of many national dishes.

WHAT'S IN A NAME?

The great explorer Columbus was responsible for confusing chillies with peppers. When he set sail in 1492, hoping to find a sea route to the spice islands, it was a source of black pepper (*Piper nigrum*) he was seeking.

Not only did he fail to find his intended destination, discovering instead the Caribbean island of San Salvador (now Watling Island), but he also made the incorrect assumption that the hot spice flavouring the local food was black pepper. By the time it was realized that the fleshy pods of a fruit were responsible, rather than tiny black peppercorns, it was too late.

Below: Mexican chillies, clockwise from top left: small green chillies, chipotle chillies, mulato chillies, dried habanero chillies, pasilla chillies, green (bell) peppers, green jalapeño chillies, Anaheim chillies, and (centre left) Scotch bonnets, (centre right) red chillies.

Above: Chillies form an important part of many of the world's major cuisines.

The Spanish called the flavouring pimiento (pepper) and the name stuck, and it has led to confusion ever since.

It was the Aztecs who coined the name chilli. Like the Mayas and Incas, they were greatly enamoured of the brightly coloured fruit that had originated in the rainforests of South America, and used chillies both as food and for medicinal purposes. When the Spanish invaded Mexico in 1509, they found many different varieties of both fresh and dried chilli on sale at the market at Tenochtitlan and still more being cultivated in Montezuma's botanical gardens at Huaxtepec.

Mexico remains a mecca for chilli-lovers, with every region having its own special varieties. Chillies are valued for their heat and for their flavour, and accomplished Mexican cooks will often use several different types – fresh and dried – in a single dish.

A CHAIN OF CHILLIES

Columbus is credited with introducing chillies to Europe, bringing back "peppers of many kinds and colours" when he returned to Europe in 1493. Soon after this, Vasco da Gama succeeded in finding the sea route to the spice islands. By the middle of the 16th century, a two-way trade had been established. Spices such as nutmeg, cinnamon and black pepper were brought to Europe from the East, and chillies and other plants from the New World went to Asia.

The spice trade created a culinary explosion, and the chilli rapidly became an important ingredient in the food of

Above: Chillies in all their different guises add both flavour and heat to many kinds of dishes. Here, they are shown fresh and dried, preserved in oil and ground into rich and fragrant powders.

Below: Asian chillies

South-east Asia, India and China. Portuguese and Arab traders introduced it to Africa. It was enthusiastically adopted, and when West African slaves were taken to the Southern States of America to work the cotton plantations, the chillies that were part of their diet went with them.

THE CHILLI IN EUROPE

Although parts of Europe adopted the chilli with great enthusiasm, universal acceptance has been relatively slow. Spain and Portugal use chillies quite extensively, which is not surprising, given the influence of those early explorers, but in France their use is limited to a few signature dishes, like the fiery rouille traditionally served with bouillabaisse.

It used to be the case that the further north you went, the less likely you would be to encounter chilli dishes. All this is changing, however, as Asian food becomes increasingly popular. Don't be surprised if you encounter chilli lollipops (popsicles) or chilli ice cream. The flavour of chillies can be subtle as well as strident, and their affinity for fruit means that, used judiciously, they can make as valuable a contribution to fruit salads as they do to salsas and spicy Mexican dishes.

In response to public demand, most supermarkets stock chillies. Chillies are easy to grow, and many gardeners enjoy cultivating and then cooking them.

Chillies are Good for You

An excellent source of vitamin C, chillies also yield beta carotene, folate, potassium and vitamin E. They stimulate the appetite and improve circulation, but can irritate the stomach if eaten to excess. Chillies are also a powerful decongestant, and can help to clear blocked sinuses.

THE CHILLI FAMILY

There are more than two hundred different types of chilli, all members of the nightshade *(solanacae)* family, like tomatoes and potatoes. Most of those used for culinary purposes belong to the genus *Capsicum annuum*. These were originally thought to be annuals, which explains the name, but can be perennial when cultivated in the tropics. The plants grow to a height of 1m/1yd, and chillies of this type include jalapeños, cayennes, Anaheim chillies and poblanos, as well as the common sweet (bell) peppers.

Tabasco chillies and the very hot Punjab chillies belong to a group called *Capsicum frutescens*, while Scotch bonnets and habaneros – the fragrant hot chillies that look like tam-o'-shanters – are *Capsicum chinense*. Some of the largest chilli plants are *Capsicum baccatum*. Ajis fall into this category, as do peri-peri chillies. Finally, there is a small group called *Capsicum pubescens*. The most notable chilli in this group is the manzano. The name means "apple", and these chillies resemble crab apples in size and shape.

Unless you grow chillies or are lucky enough to live near a farmer's market that features these flavoursome ingredients, you are unlikely to encounter more than a few of the more common varieties, such as serranos, jalapeños

Below: Chillies are members of the nightshade (solanacae) *family, like tomatoes and potatoes.*

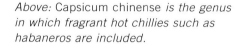

Above: Capsicum chinense is the genus in which fragrant hot chillies such as habaneros are included.

and cayennes, and even these may not be identified as such. Supermarkets have a habit of limiting their labelling to the obvious, like "red chillies" or – one step better – "hot red chillies".

This raises another issue. How do you know whether a chilli is hot or not? Are small chillies hotter than big ones? Or red chillies hotter than green? The answer to the last two questions is no. Although some of the world's hottest chillies are tiny, there are some large varieties that are real scorchers. Colour isn't an infallible indicator either. Most chillies start out green and ripen to red, but some start yellow and become red, and yet others start yellow and stay yellow, and across the spectrum you'll find hot varieties. To confuse the issue still further, chillies on the same plant can have different degrees of heat, and in at least one type of chilli, the top of the fruit is hotter than the bottom. Fortunately for those of us who like to have some warning as to whether the contents of our shopping basket will be fragrant or fiery, there are rating systems for the heat in chillies. The best known of these grades chillies in Scoville units. Until relatively recently, the world's hottest chilli was reckoned to be the Mexican red savina habanero, which scores 557,000 on the Scoville

scale, but a new contender, the tezpur chilli, has been discovered in India. The tezpur registers a blistering 855,000 Scoville units, and is so hot that it is said to have triggered heart attacks in the unwary or novice taster. Scoville units are useful when it comes to fine comparisons such as these, but working with units measured in this way can be unwieldy. For general classification, a simpler system, which rates chillies out of ten, is more often used.

What makes one chilli hotter than another is the amount of the chemical capsaicin contained in the seeds and fibrous white lining. Apart from producing anything from a tingle to a tidal wave of heat, capsaicin also contributes to the feel-good factor by stimulating the brain to produce hormones called endorphins.

A less appealing aspect to capsaicin is that it is an irritant, and can cause severe burning to delicate parts of the face (and other parts of the anatomy) with which it comes into contact. It is therefore vital to handle chillies with care. Wear gloves while preparing them, or cut them up using a knife and fork. If you do handle chillies directly, wash your hands thoroughly in soapy water immediately afterwards (capsaicin does not dissolve in water alone) or use vegetable oil to remove any residue.

THE BURNING QUESTION

If you bite into a chilli that is unpleasantly hot, don't drink a glass of water. That will only spread the discomfort around your mouth making the burning sensation much worse. Instead, try one of these simple solutions:

• Take a large drink of creamy milk, hold it in your mouth for a minute or so, then spit it out discreetly. Repeat as necessary.

• A similar effect can be achieved with water or ice cream, as long as you do not swallow it.

• Eat a piece of fresh bread, a cooked potato or some rice. These will absorb the offending capsaicin oil.

NAMING THE CHILLI

You will find both fresh and dried chillies on sale. Dried chillies can be stored like other spices, and can be rehydrated with excellent results. Some chillies actually taste better when they have been dried. It is well worth getting to know as many different varieties as possible. Then, like a true aficionado, you can start blending several types for the ultimate in chilli pleasure.

The following descriptions of chillies are listed by their heat scale, with 10 being the hottest.

Anaheim

Heat scale 2–3: Their alternative name of "California long green" gives some idea of what these large chillies look like (they are also known as New Mexico). The pods are about 15cm/6in long and about 5cm/2in wide, making them good candidates for stuffing. The flavour is fresh and fruity, like a cross between tart apples and green (bell) peppers. Anaheim skins can be a bit tough, so these chillies are best roasted and peeled. The dried chillies are used to make a mild chilli powder.

Below: Ancho chillies

Ancho

Heat scale 3: Dried poblanos, these are larger than most other dried chillies. Open the packet and savour the wonderful fruity aroma – like dates or dried figs. After rehydration, anchos can be stuffed, and they also taste great sliced or chopped in stir-fries and similar dishes.

Guajillo

Heat scale 3: These dried chillies are about 15cm/6in long, with rough skin. The mature fresh pods are a deep reddish brown and have a smooth texture. It is thought they might be related to Anaheim chillies, as they have a similar look. They have a mild, slightly bitter flavour, suggestive of green tea. Guajillos are used in many classic salsas.

Italia

Heat scale 3: Juicy and refreshing, these dark green chillies ripen to a rich, dark red. They taste great in salads and have an affinity for tropical fruit, especially mangoes.

Below: Mulato chillies

Mulato

Heat scale 3: A dried chilli with a thin, wrinkled, dark brown skin, this is related to the ancho. The flavour is smoky and herby.

Poblano

Heat scale 3: Big and beautiful, poblanos look like sweet (bell) peppers, and are perfect for stuffing. They start off a deep green and ripen to a bright, clear red or rich, dark brown. The flavour is spicier than that of a sweet pepper, with peachy overtones. Poblanos taste wonderful with other chillies, whose flavour they appear to boost.

Below: Poblano chillies

Above: Anaheim chilli

Above: Guajillo chillies

Below: Pasado chillies

Cherry Hot

Heat scale 4: Pungent, with thick walls, these chillies look like large versions of the fruit for which they are named. The skins can be tough, so they are best peeled. Cherry hot chillies have a sweetish flavour and make good pickles.

Below: Cherry hot chillies

Above: Fresno chillies

Fresno

Heat scale 5: Plump and cylindrical, with tapered ends, these fresh chillies are most often sold red, although you will sometimes find green or yellow ones in the shops. They look rather similar to jalapeños, and can be substituted for them if necessary.

Pasado

Heat scale 3–4: Very dark brown, skinny, dried chillies, these are generally about 10cm/4in long. When rehydrated, they taste lemony, with a hint of cucumber and apple. Pasados have an affinity for black beans, and make a fine salsa. Strips taste good on pizzas.

Below: Cascabel chillies

Costeno Amarillo

Heat scale 4: Not to be confused with the much hotter aji amarillo, this is a pale orange dried chilli, which is ideal for use in yellow salsas and Mexican *mole* sauce. It has a citrus flavour and is often used to give depth to the flavour of soups and stews.

Pasilla

Heat scale 4: Open a packet of these deep purple dried chillies and the first thing you notice is their rich liquorice aroma. Quite large at about 15cm/6in in length, pasillas have a spicy, fruity flavour that is good with shellfish, *moles* and mushrooms. Pureés made from rehydrated pasillas do not need to be sieved, as the skin is thin.

Cultivating Chillies

If you can grow tomatoes, then you'll be able to try your luck with chillies. They enjoy similar conditions, prefer higher temperatures, need watering more often and like slightly acid soils. You can grow them in tubs, hanging baskets or pots on the windowsill. Raise the plants under glass in spring, or buy them from a good plantsman. Plant out when frost is no longer a problem and the first flowers are visible. Water well in dry weather, mulch thickly and feed fortnightly with a high-potash fertilizer. Stake taller varieties. Pinch out growing tips if sideshoots are not being made and stop these once they have set fruit. During the growing season, watch for aphids, cutworms or slugs, and treat. Harvest about 12–16 weeks after planting out. Pull up plants and hang under glass in a sunny place when frost threatens to encourage the fruit to continue ripening.

Cascabel

Heat scale 4: The name translates as "little rattle", and refers to the sound the seeds make inside this round dried chilli. The woody, nutty flavour is best appreciated when the skin is removed. Soak them, then either scrape the flesh off the skin or sieve it. Cascabels are great in stews, soups and salsas.

Chilli Boost

For an instant lift, sprinkle some dried crushed chilli on your food.

Above: Pasilla chillies

Above: Jalapeño chillies

Hungarian Wax Chillies

Heat scale 5: These really do look waxy, like novelty candles. Unlike many chillies, they start off yellow, not green. It is not necessary to peel them, and they are often used in salads and salsas.

Aji Amarillo

Heat scale 6–7: There are several different varieties of this chilli, including one that is yellow when fully ripe, and a large brown aji that is frequently dried. The chillies average about 10cm/4in in length and look rather like miniature windsocks. Red ajis originated in Peru, and were popular among the Incas.

Above: Chipotle chillies

Chipotle

Heat scale 6–10: This smoke-dried jalapeño has wrinkled, dark red skin and thick flesh. Chipotles need long, slow cooking to soften them and bring out their full flavour, which is hot and tasty with a deep intriguing smokiness.

Jalapeño

Heat scale 4–7: These are frequently seen in supermarkets. Plump and stubby, like fat fingers, they have shiny skins. They are sold at both the green and the red stage, although the former seem to be marginally more popular. Jalapeños have a piquant, grassy flavour, and are widely used in salsas, salads, dips and stews; they are also canned and bottled. Their fame is due to the fact that they are the best known and most commonly used chilli in Mexican food. A heat-free jalapeño has been developed in the US. Too thick-skinned to be sun-dried, jalapeños are generally smoke-dried and acquire a name change. In this form they are known as chipotle chillies.

Below: Pickled jalapeño chillies

Below: Cayenne chillies

Cayenne

Heat scale 6–8: There are several varieties of this very popular chilli, including the familiar "long hot reds". They range from 7.5cm/3in to 17cm/6½ in in length, and have a sweet yet fiery flavour. The basis of cayenne pepper, these chillies are also used in sauces.

Serrano

Heat scale 7: Usually sold green, these are small (about 4cm/1½in long) and quite slender. Serranos are the classic Mexican green chilli (*chiles verdes*), and are an important ingredient in guacamole. The flavour is clean and crisp, with a suggestion of citrus. Serranos are thin-skinned and do not need to be peeled. They dry well, but are seldom sold that way, although you may come across them occasionally for sale in a Mexican or Spanish market.

Above: Serrano chillies

Left: Bird's eye chillies

Bird's Eye

Heat scale 8: Small and extremely hot, these come from a highly volatile family of chillies that are found in Africa, Asia, the United States and the Caribbean, and often labelled simply as "Thai chillies". Thin-fleshed and explosively hot, they are sold green and red, often with the stems still attached. Dried, they are widely available in jars. They are called bird's eyes because they are much liked by mynah birds.

Below: Dried bird's eye chillies

Tiny Terrors

Thailand grows many different varieties of chillies. The smallest are so tiny they are popularly referred to as *prik kee noo* (mouse droppings). Use cautiously as they are fiery hot.

De Arbol

Heat scale 8: More often sold dried than fresh, these smooth cayenne-type chillies are slim and curvacious. A warm orange-red, they are about 7.5cm/3in long. De arbols combine blistering heat with a clean, grassy flavour. Add them to soups or use to enliven vinegar or oil. Unlike most dried chillies, which must be soaked in hot water for 20–30 minutes before use, dry de arbol pods can be crumbled and added straight to stews or similar dishes. To reduce the heat, slit them and shake out the seeds first.

Above: Dried de arbol chillies

Manzano

Heat scale 9: This delicious chilli is very hot and fruity. About the size of a crab apple, it is the only chilli to have purple/black seeds.

Habanero

Heat scale 10: Don't imagine that intense heat is the only defining feature of this lantern-shaped chilli. Habaneros have a wonderful, fruity flavour, and a surprisingly delicate aroma. Some say it

Above: Dried habanero chillies

reminds them of chardonnay wine; others that it is redolent of sun-warmed apricots. Don't sniff them too enthusiastically, however, and be ultra-cautious when handling habaneros, for they are excessively hot. Always wear strong gloves when preparing them, and don't stand over a food processor or blender when using them to make a paste, or the fumes may burn your face. When cooking with habaneros, a little goes a long way. They are very good with fruit and in salsas. Dried habaneros have medium-thick flesh and wrinkled skins. When rehydrated, they have a rich tropical-fruit flavour.

Scotch Bonnets

Heat scale 10: Often confused with habaneros, which they closely resemble. Scotch bonnets are grown in Jamaican and are the principal ingredient of jerk seasoning.

Below: Scotch bonnet chillies

Use Scotch bonnets very cautiously as they are one of the hottest chillies. It is advisable to deseed them before use unless you can tolerate their intense and lingering flavour.

CHILLI PRODUCTS

Specialist shops, devoted to chillies and chilli products, are springing up all over the world. Alongside mugs, plates, bowls and aprons rioting with chilli motifs, you'll find an astonishing array of powders, pastes, sauces and oils.

POWDERS

Anything connected with chillies tends to be confusing, and chilli powder is no exception. The name suggests that this product is simply powdered chilli, but it is in fact a blend of several ingredients, designed specifically for making chilli con carne. In addition to ground hot chillies, it typically contains cumin, oregano, salt and garlic powder.

Pure powders – the whole chilli and nothing but the chilli – are less easy to come by, but are available from specialist shops and by mail order. Ancho, caribe and Anaheim (New Mexico) red powders are mild (heat scale 3). Pasilla, a rich, dark powder, registers 4 on the heat scale, while chipotle is a little hotter still.

Right: Chilli powder

Left: Ancho powder

Right: Pasilla powder

Left: Paprika

Right: Cayenne pepper

Convenient Chillies

Jars of whole chillies in white wine vinegar are handy for the home cook. Also look out for minced (ground) chillies. After opening, jars must be tightly closed, kept in the refrigerator and the contents consumed by the use-by date.

Cayenne pepper is a very fine ground powder from the *Capsicum frutescens* variety of chilli. The placenta (the fibrous white inner lining) and seeds are included, so it is very hot. Tiny amounts of cayenne are often added to cheese and egg dishes, and it is sprinkled over smoked fish and prawns (shrimp). It is also added to some curries.

Paprika is a fine, rich red powder made from mild chillies. The core and seeds are removed, but the flavour can still be quite pungent. Hungarians have adopted this as their national spice, but it is also widely used in Spanish and Portuguese cooking. Look out for *pimentón dulce*, a delicious smoked paprika from Estramadura in Spain.

Right: Crushed chilli flakes

CRUSHED CHILLIES

Dried chilli flakes are widely available. Italians call them *peperoncini* and add them to their famous arrabiata sauce. Sprinkle them on pizzas or add to cooked dishes for a last-minute lift. Crushed dried green jalapeños are a useful pantry item, combining considerable heat with a delicious, melting sweetness.

CHILLI PASTE

It is worth keeping a few jars of ready-made chilli paste, such as harissa or *ras-el-hanout*, on your shelves. A hot chilli paste is quite easy to make at home. Simply seed fresh chillies, then purée them in a blender or food processor until smooth. Store small amounts in the refrigerator for up to 1 week, or freeze for up to 6 months. Chilli paste can also be made from dried chillies. Having rehydrated them, purée as for fresh chillies. You may have to sieve tough-skinned varieties.

Below: Hot chilli paste

Left: Red Tabasco sauce

Left: Green Tabasco sauce

CHILLI SAUCES

There are many varieties of these and the names appear to prove that chillies stimulate the imagination as well as the appetite. Some of the printable ones include Endorphin Rush, Lethal Weapon and Global Warming, along with the unforgettable Scorned Woman Hot Sauce.

The most famous chilli sauce, however, is Tabasco, developed in

Louisiana by E. McIlhenny in the latter half of the 19th century. Chillies are matured in oak barrels to develop the sauce's unique flavour. Try mixing a few drops with fresh lime juice as a baste next time you grill salmon steaks, or add to sauces, soups or casseroles. Also available is Tabasco Jalapeño Sauce – often referred to as green Tabasco sauce. Milder in flavour than the red version, it is good with nachos, hamburgers or on pizza.

Chilli sauces are also widely used in Asia. Chinese chilli sauce is quite hot and spicy, with a hint of fruitiness thanks to the inclusion of apples or plums. For an even milder flavour, look out for sweet chilli sauce, which is a blend of red chillies, sugar and tamarind juice from Sichuan. There is also a thick Chinese sauce made solely from chillies and salt. This is usually sold in jars, and is much hotter than the bottled version. Vietnamese chilli sauce is very hot, while the Thai sauce tends to be thicker and more spicy. Bottled chilli sauces are used both for cooking and as a dip.

CHILLI OILS

Various types of chilli oil are on sale. Toss them with pasta, add a dash to a stir-fry, or drizzle them over pizzas.

Chilli oils also make a good basis for salad dressings. You can make your own chilli oil by heating chillies in oil, or use a ready-made mixture. Olive oil, flavoured with chipotle and de arbol chillies, with a hint of rosemary, is a particularly good blend. It can also be used for light cooking.

Chilli oil is seldom used for cooking in China and South-east Asia, but is a popular dipping sauce. Two types are widely sold. The first is a simple infusion of dried chillies, onions, garlic and salt in

vegetable oil. The second, XO chilli oil, is flavoured with dried scallops and costs considerably more. Chilli oil has a pleasant smell, and a concentrated flavour, much stronger than chilli sauce. It is often drizzled over fish and shellfish just before serving. It should be used sparingly.

Below: Chilli oil

Chilli and Tomato Oil

Heating oil with chillies intensifies the rich flavour. This tastes great sprinkled over pasta.

1 Heat 150ml/¼ pint/⅔ cup olive oil in a pan. When it is very hot, but not smoking, stir in 10ml/2 tsp tomato purée (paste) and 15ml/1 tbsp dried red chilli flakes.

2 Leave to cool, then pour into an airtight jar and store in the refrigerator for up to 2 months.

Above: Sweet chilli sauce (top) and chilli sauce

CHOOSING, STORING AND EQUIPMENT

Below is some helpful advice on selecting and storing chillies and tips on equipment that will make their preparation simpler.

CHOOSING AND STORING CHILLIES

• When buying fresh chillies, apply the same criteria as when buying sweet (bell) peppers. The fruit should look bright and unblemished.
• Some chillies are naturally wrinkled when ripe, however, so a smooth skin is not essential.

Above: Chillies dried on string or canes will keep well for many months.

• Avoid any chillies that seem limp or dry, or that have bruising on the skin.
• In the supermarket, wrap your hand in a plastic bag when picking out chillies, or you may have an unpleasant surprise if you later touch your face.
• To store chillies, wrap them in kitchen paper, place in a plastic bag and keep in the salad compartment of the refrigerator for a week or more.
• Chillies can also be frozen. There is no need to blanch them if you plan to use them fairly soon.
• Frozen chillies are a huge boon to the busy cook, as they can be sliced when only partially thawed, and crushed with garlic and ginger to make a fragrant spice paste.
• To dry chillies, thread them on a string, hang them in a warm place until dry, then crush them and store in a sealed jar.

EQUIPMENT

Gloves may not seem obvious pieces of equipment, but they are invaluable for the dedicated chilli cook. The fine disposable gloves used in hospitals can be used for most chillies, but you need the heavy-duty type for really hot varieties such as habaneros. Of course, you can prepare chillies without wearing gloves, either by using a knife and fork for cutting, or by taking a chance and washing your hands in soapy water afterwards, but burns from capsaicin, the chemical found in the seeds and fibrous white lining, can be very unpleasant.

A mortar and pestle is ideal for grinding chillies and making chilli pastes, but it does involve a fair amount of hard work. Traditional Indian or Asian granite or stone sets are generally fairly large, with deep, pitted or ridged bowls. The rough surface acts like pumice, increasing the grinding effect. Porous volcanic rock is also used for the Mexican mortar – the *molcajete* – which traditionally stands on wide legs, and is very sturdy. The Mexican *tejolote* tends to be shorter

Left: A smooth mortar and pestle for crushing dry ingredients.

Above: A rough mortar and pestle for making wet pastes.

Left: If you like to make your own spice mixtures, then a spice or coffee grinder kept solely for this purpose is very useful.

than the traditional pestle, and fits neatly into the hand. *Molcajetes* must be tempered before being used. To do this, a mixture of dry rice and salt is spooned into the bowl, then ground into the surface to remove any loose sand or grit before being discarded.

A food processor is faster and easier, if less satisfying, than a mortar and pestle, especially for pastes, but must be very carefully cleaned after use. If you intend preparing chillies and spice pastes frequently, it may be worth investing in a mini food processor, and reserving it for spices.

A spice grinder, or coffee grinder kept specifically for spices, is handy when making dry spice mixtures.

Left: A food processor or a blender will process chillies very efficiently, and is especially useful for large quantities.

PREPARATION AND COOKING TECHNIQUES

Every cook handling chillies has had the same experience, that unthinking moment when the hand goes to the face and the burning, tingling sensation of chilli oil is experienced, especially around the sensitive areas of the eyes, nose and mouth. It's not worth it! So be warned, be careful. Wear rubber gloves or wash your hands thoroughly in plenty of hot soapy water when handling chillies. Water alone will not remove the chemical capsaicin, and even after using soap, traces may remain. Baby oil or olive oil can be used to remove it from sensitive areas. This advice applies to dried and fresh chillies as the burning properties are equally strong for both.

Preparing Fresh Chillies

1 If the chilli is to be stuffed, and kept whole, merely slit it without separating the 2 halves. For all other purposes, hold the chilli firmly at the stalk end, and cut it neatly in half lengthwise with a sharp knife.

2 Cut off the stalk from both halves of the chilli, removing a thin slice containing the stalk from the top of the chilli at the same time. This will help to free the white membrane (placenta) and make it easier to scrape out the seeds to be discarded.

3 Carefully scrape out all the seeds and discard them. Remove the core with a small sharp knife.

4 Cut out any white membrane from the centre of each chilli half. Keep the knife blade close to the flesh so that all the membrane is removed. This is usually easy to do. Discard the membrane.

5 Slice each piece of chilli into thin strips. If diced chilli is needed, bunch the strips together and cut across them to produce tiny pieces.

COOK'S TIP
Much of the capsaicin, the fiery oil in chillies, is concentrated in the fibrous white section that contains the seeds. Many recipes suggest removing and discarding this, but true chilli lovers usually leave it in.

Soaking Dried Chillies

Most dried chillies must be rehydrated before being used. In some instances, a recipe will recommend toasting as a first step, to intensify the flavour. This can be done by putting the seeded chillies in a roasting pan in the oven for a few minutes, or by pressing them on to the surface of a hot, dry, heavy frying pan. Do not let them burn, or they could become bitter. Once this is done, continue as below.

1 Wipe the chillies to remove any surface dirt. If you like, you can slit them and shake out the seeds before soaking. Alternatively, just brush away any seeds you can see.

2 Put the chillies in a bowl and pour over hot water to cover. If necessary, fit a saucer in the bowl to keep the chillies submerged. Soak for 20–30 minutes (up to 1 hour if possible), until the colour is restored and the chillies have softened and swelled.

3 Drain the chillies, cut off the stalks if necessary, then slit them and scrape out the seeds. Slice or chop the flesh. If the chillies are to be puréed, process them with a little of the soaking water. Sieve the purée if necessary.

Roasting Fresh Chillies

There are several ways of roasting fresh chillies. You use the grill, roast in the oven, dry-fry as explained below, or hold them over a gas flame.

1 Put the chillies in a dry frying pan and place over the heat until the skins are charred and blistered. Alternatively, roast the chillies in a griddle pan.

2 For larger chillies that are to be stuffed, make a neat slit down the side of each one. Place in a dry frying pan over a moderate heat, turning frequently until the skins blister.

3 To roast chillies on a skewer over a flame, spear them on a long-handled metal skewer and roast them over the flame of a gas burner until the skins blister and darken.

4 Slip the roasted chillies into a strong plastic bag and tie the top to keep the steam in.

5 Set aside for 20 minutes. Take the chillies out of the bag and remove the skins, either by peeling them off, or by rubbing the chillies with a clean dishtowel. Cut off the stalks, then slit the chillies and, using a sharp knife, scrape out and discard the seeds.

Grinding Chillies

When making chilli powder, this method gives a distinctive and smoky taste.

1 Soak the chillies, if dried, pat dry and then dry fry in a heavy pan until crisp. You can also do this on a griddle. In either case, watch the chillies carefully because they can suddenly burn, and then you have to start all over again!

2 Transfer to a mortar and grind to a fine powder with a pestle. Store in an airtight container.

Making a Chilli Flower

This makes a very attractive garnish for a special dish.

1 Wearing rubber gloves and using a small pair of scissors or a slim-bladed knife, cut a chilli carefully lengthwise from the tip to within 1cm/½in of the stem end. Repeat this at regular intervals around the chilli – more cuts will produce more petals.

2 Rinse the chilli in cold water and remove all the seeds. Place in a bowl of iced water and chill for at least 4 hours. For very curly flowers, leave the chilli overnight. When ready to use, lift the chilli out and drain it on kitchen paper.

SPICE POWDERS

The name "curry powder" used to be attached to any ground spice mixture used for making hot or highly flavoured foods. It isn't an authentic term, but is a corruption of the Tamil word "karhi", which simply means a food cooked in a sauce. During the days of the Raj, British merchants and soldiers returning home were eager to continue enjoying the flavours they had encountered in India, and demand for a commercial curry powder was the result. The first of these were crude mixtures, bearing little resemblance to the sophisticated and often subtle blends that Indian cooks produced every day. These differed according to whether they were to be used for meat, poultry, fish or vegetables, and reflected the personal tastes of the maker.

Above: Ancho powder

Today, although bought curry powders have improved greatly, many individuals prefer to make their own spice mixtures in the traditional fashion, roasting and grinding whole spices and savouring the wonderful aroma that is part and parcel of the procedure.

Chillies do not feature in all spice blends, but are typical of those that originated in hot spots such as Madras, Mysore or Goa (the home of vindaloo).

Dry spice mixes – or curry powders – are popular in India, Pakistan and Sri Lanka. Each region has its own favourite blend of spices. When making your own spice powders and pastes, feel free to experiment with different types of dried or fresh chillies. Where chilli powder is listed in recipes, you can opt for the blended spice or a pure powder from a specific type of chilli.

Classic Curry Powder

This mixture can be modified to suit your own personal taste. Try not to keep it too long, or it will lose its aroma.

MAKES ABOUT 115G/4OZ/1 CUP

INGREDIENTS
    6–8 dried red chillies
    105ml/7 tbsp coriander seeds
    60ml/4 tbsp cumin seeds
    10ml/2 tsp fenugreek seeds
    10ml/2 tsp black mustard seeds
    10ml/2 tsp black peppercorns
    15ml/1 tbsp ground turmeric
    5ml/1 tsp ground ginger

1 Unless you like a fiery mixture, snap off the stalks from the dried chillies and shake out and discard most of the seeds and all the stalks.

2 Heat a heavy pan and dry-fry the chillies with the seeds and black peppercorns over a medium heat until they give off a rich aroma. Shake the pan constantly so that the spices are evenly roasted.

3 Tip the roasted spices into a mortar and grind them to a smooth powder. Alternatively, use a spice grinder or a coffee grinder reserved for spices.

4 Stir in the ground turmeric and the ginger. Use immediately or store in an airtight jar protected from strong light.

Below: Classic curry powder

Mild Curry Powder

This is a basic recipe for a mild Indian curry powder, but you can adjust the quantities to suit your taste.

MAKES ABOUT 115G/4OZ/1 CUP

INGREDIENTS
Whole spices
    50g/2oz/½ cup coriander seeds
    60ml/4 tbsp cumin seeds
    30ml/2 tbsp fennel seeds
    30ml/2 tbsp fenugreek seeds
    4 dried red chillies
    5 curry leaves
Ground spices
    15ml/1 tbsp chilli powder
    15ml/1 tbsp ground turmeric
    2.5ml/½ tsp salt

1 Dry-roast the whole spices in a large heavy-based frying pan for 8–10 minutes, shaking the pan from side to side until the spices begin to darken and release a rich aroma. Allow them to cool slightly.

2 Put the spices in a spice grinder or mini food processor and process gently to achieve a fine powder.

3 Add the remaining ground spices and store in an airtight jar.

Garam Masala

Garam means "hot" and masala means "spices" so the spices used are those that "heat" the body, such as chillies, black peppercorns, cinnamon and cloves. Garam masala is added at the end of cooking and sprinkled over dishes as a garnish.

Below: Garam masala

MAKES ABOUT 50G/2OZ/½ CUP

INGREDIENTS
    10 dried red chillies
    2 × 2.5cm/1in cinnamon sticks
    2 curry leaves
    30ml/2 tbsp coriander seeds
    30ml/2 tbsp cumin seeds
    5ml/1 tsp black peppercorns
    5ml/1 tsp cloves
    5ml/1 tsp fenugreek seeds
    5ml/1 tsp black mustard seeds
    1.5ml/¼ tsp chilli powder

1 Dry-fry the chillies, cinnamon sticks and curry leaves in a large heavy frying pan for 2 minutes until you smell the spices as they roast.

2 Add the coriander and cumin seeds, peppercorns, cloves, fenugreek and mustard seeds, and dry-fry for a further 8–10 minutes, shaking the pan from side to side until the spices begin to darken and release a rich aroma.

3 Allow the mixture to cool slightly before grinding. Put the mixture into a spice grinder or electric coffee grinder, kept for spice grinding, or use a pestle and mortar. Grind to a fine powder. Add the chilli powder, mix together and store the powder in an airtight jar.

COOK'S TIP
Garam masala will keep for 2–4 months in an airtight container and the flavours will mature during storage.

Keep a lid on it
If your pan is a fairly shallow one, put a lid over it when frying the mustard seeds. When they pop, they can travel a surprising distance. Shiver the pan from side to side while the seeds are frying, so that they do not stick to the base. Fry over a gentle heat. You can use this technique for other small seeds, such as cumin.

Sambaar Powder

This blend of spices and dhal is used in South Indian cooking to flavour vegetable and lentil combinations, braised dishes and spicy broths. The powder also acts as a thickening agent.

MAKES ABOUT 105ML/7 TBSP

INGREDIENTS
    8–10 dried red chillies
    90ml/6 tbsp coriander seeds
    30ml/2 tbsp cumin seeds
    10ml/2 tsp black peppercorns
    10ml/2 tsp fenugreek seeds
    10ml/2 tsp urad dhal (white split
      gram beans)
    10ml/2 tsp channa dhal (yellow
      split peas)
    10ml/2 tsp mung dhal (yellow
      mung beans)
    25ml/1½ tbsp ground turmeric

1 Snap off the stalks from the dried chillies and shake out most of the seeds. Heat a heavy frying pan and add the first 5 ingredients.

2 Toss all the spices together over a medium heat until they give off a rich aroma, then turn into a bowl.

3 Repeat the process with the pulses, to toast them without letting them burn.

4 Mix the spices and pulses together, then grind them to a fine powder. Stir in the turmeric. Use immediately or store in an airtight jar away from strong light.

Below: Sambaar powder

Sri Lankan Curry Powder

This has totally different characteristics from Indian curry powders. The spices are roasted separately, and chilli powder is used instead of whole dried chillies. The result is a rich, dark curry powder that is ideal for fish, poultry, meat and vegetable curries.

In Sri Lanka, coriander, cumin, fennel and fenugreek seeds are roasted separately before being combined with roasted cinnamon, cloves and cardamom seeds. After grinding, chilli powder is stirred into the mixture, which is aromatic, rather than fiery. Colour and presentation are key features of Sri Lankan cuisine, and you will often find red, yellow and even black curries artistically arranged around a central bowl of rice.

MAKES ABOUT 75G/3OZ/¾ CUP

INGREDIENTS
  90ml/6 tbsp coriander seeds
  45ml/3 tbsp cumin seeds
  15ml/1 tbsp fennel seeds
  5ml/1 tsp fenugreek seeds
  5cm/2in piece cinnamon stick
  5ml/1 tsp cloves
  8 green cardamom pods
  6 dried curry leaves
  5–10ml/1–2 tsp chilli powder

1 Dry-fry or roast the coriander seeds, cumin seeds, fennel seeds and fenugreek seeds separately, because they all turn dark at different stages. Do not let the spices burn; remove them as soon as they give off a rich aroma.

2 Dry-fry the cinnamon stick, cloves and cardamom pods together for a few minutes until they give off a pungent aroma.

Above: Sri Lankan Curry powder

3 As soon as they are cool enough to handle, remove the seeds from the cardamom pods and place them in a mortar. Add the remaining dry-fried ingredients, then the curry leaves. Grind to a smooth powder. Alternatively, use a spice grinder.

4 Stir in the chilli powder. Use immediately or store in an airtight jar away from strong light.

Singapore-style Curry Powder

Chillies are a key ingredient in this curry powder for poultry and meat dishes.

MAKES ABOUT 75G/3OZ/¾ CUP

INGREDIENTS
  3–4 dried red chillies
  90ml/6 tbsp coriander seeds
  15ml/1 tbsp cumin seeds
  15ml/1 tbsp fennel seeds
  10ml/2 tsp black peppercorns
  2.5cm/1in piece cinnamon stick
  4 green cardamom pods
  6 cloves
  10ml/2 tsp ground turmeric

1 Unless you like a fiery mixture, snap off the stalks from the dried chillies and shake out most of the seeds.

2 Heat a heavy pan and add all the seeds, with the chillies, peppercorns, cinnamon stick, cardamoms and cloves. Dry-fry over a medium heat, stirring, until the spices give off a rich aroma.

Above: Singapore-style curry powder

3 When cool enough to handle, break the cinnamon stick into small pieces and remove the seeds from the cardamom pods.

4 Grind all the roasted spices to a fine powder in a mortar. Alternatively, use a spice grinder or an electric coffee grinder reserved for spices.

5 Stir in the ground turmeric. Use immediately or store in an airtight jar away from strong light.

VARIATION
To adapt Singapore-style curry powder for using with fish and shellfish, use only 2–3 chillies and 5ml/1 tsp black peppercorns, but increase the fennel seeds to 30ml/ 2 tbsp. Add 5ml/1 tsp fenugreek seeds. Leave out the cinnamon stick, cardamom pods and cloves.

Seven-seas Curry Powder

Like Sri Lankan Curry Powder, this uses chilli powder rather than whole dried chillies. Milder than some of the other mixtures, it combines the fiery taste of chilli with the warm flavours of cumin, cinnamon and cloves. It is widely used in Indonesian and Malaysian cooking.

MAKES ABOUT 90G/3½OZ/SCANT 1 CUP

INGREDIENTS
    6–8 white cardamom
      pods, bruised
    90ml/6 tbsp coriander seeds
    45ml/3 tbsp cumin seeds
    25ml/1½ tbsp celery seeds
    5cm/2in piece cinnamon stick
      or cassia
    6–8 cloves
    15ml/1 tbsp chilli powder

1 Put the cardamom pods in a heavy frying pan with all the other whole spices. Dry-fry the mixture, stirring it and shaking the pan constantly, until the spices give off a rich, heavy aroma.

2 When they are cool enough to handle, remove the cardamom seeds from the pods, then grind them finely with all the other roasted ingredients.

3 Add the chilli powder and mix. Use immediately or store in an airtight jar.

Below: Seven-seas curry powder

Malayan-Chinese Curry Powder

This is good for poultry, especially chicken, and robust fish curries. You can double or even treble the quantities, but it is better to make a smaller amount and use it fairly quickly, as curry powder will stale if stored for too long.

MAKES ABOUT 60ML/4 TBSP

INGREDIENTS
    2 dried red chillies
    6 whole cloves
    1 small cinnamon stick
    5ml/1 tsp coriander seeds
    5ml/1 tsp fennel seeds
    10ml/2 tsp Sichuan peppercorns
    2.5ml/½ tsp grated nutmeg
    2.5ml/½ tsp ground star anise
    5ml/1 tsp ground turmeric

1 Snap or cut the tops off the dried chillies and shake out most of the seeds. Use a small, sharp knife to remove any remaining seeds.

2 Put the chillies, cloves, cinnamon stick, coriander seeds and fennel seeds in a wok or heavy frying pan. Add the Sichuan peppercorns. Dry-fry over a medium heat, tossing the spices frequently, until they give off a rich, spicy aroma.

3 Tip the spices into a mortar and grind them to a smooth powder. Alternatively, use a spice grinder or an electric coffee grinder reserved for spices.

4 Stir in the grated nutmeg, star anise and turmeric. Use immediately or store in an airtight jar away from strong light to keep its flavour.

COOK'S TIPS

• When you are buying spices, always go to stores where there will be a good turnover. Indian or Asian speciality stores would be ideal. Whole spices do not have an indefinite shelf life, and you want to get the best flavour from your spice mix. Buy individual spices in small quantities and write the date of purchase on the packet if you are buying them loose and they do not have a "best before" date stamped on them. Then you can check them regularly and throw out any that have been stored for more than a couple of months.

• Although it is best to make curry powder and similar spice mixes in small quantities, a trip to a market with a fine selection of fresh spices might tempt you to make a large amount. Put some of the surplus in small jars as gifts for friends who like to cook, and store the rest in airtight tubs in the freezer.

SPICE PASTES

Unlike powdered blends, pastes are made from what are called "wet spices": lemon grass, fresh ginger, garlic, galangal, shallots, tamarind and chillies. These are traditionally ground using a mortar and pestle, but today a food processor is often used for convenience and speed. Supermarkets stock some excellent ready-made spice pastes, but making your own is simple and highly satisfying. Any surplus paste can be stored in a tub in the freezer.

Thai cooking is based on curry pastes. Thai cooks strive to create a balance between spicy hot, sweet, sour and salty tastes, and their curries reflect this. There are three principal types of curry paste – red, green and sour. Fresh ingredients such as chillies, lemon grass and shallots are given a salty tang with shrimp paste, while citrus juice and rind adds a touch of sourness. Fresh pastes can be bought from any Thai market, but most cooks prefer to make their own as needed. You will find commercial curry powder in Thailand – used in dishes such as stir-fried crab in curry sauce – but pastes are preferred.

Madrasi Masala

Masalas can be dry mixes or pastes. This one belongs to the latter category, and is a blend of dry and wet spices. The paste is cooked in oil to develop the flavours.

MAKES ABOUT 450G/1LB/2½ CUPS

INGREDIENTS
    120ml/8 tbsp coriander seeds
    60ml/4 tbsp cumin seeds
    15ml/1 tbsp black peppercorns
    15ml/1 tbsp black mustard seeds
    165ml/11 tbsp ground turmeric
    45–60ml/3–4 tbsp chilli powder
    15ml/1 tbsp salt
    8 garlic cloves, crushed
    7.5cm/3in piece fresh root ginger,
        peeled and finely grated (shredded)
    about 60ml/4 tbsp cider vinegar
    175ml/6fl oz/¾ cup sunflower oil

1 Heat a heavy frying pan and dry-fry the coriander seeds, cumin seeds and peppercorns for 1–2 minutes, stirring.

Above: Madrasi masala

2 Add the mustard seeds and toss constantly over the heat until they start to pop and the mixture gives off a rich aroma. Do not let the spices become too dark.

3 Grind the mixture to a fine powder, then add the turmeric, chilli and salt. Stir in the garlic, ginger and enough of the vinegar to make a paste.

4 Heat the oil in a large frying pan and fry the paste, stirring and turning it constantly, until the oil begins to separate from the spicy mixture.

5 Spoon the masala into a clean jar. Make sure that there is a film of oil floating on top. This will form an airtight seal and act as a preservative, ensuring that the paste keeps its colour. Store in the refrigerator for 2–3 weeks.

Thai Red Curry Paste

Some excellent versions of this classic paste are now produced commercially, but if you prefer to make your own, here's how.

MAKES ABOUT 175G/6OZ/1 CUP

INGREDIENTS
    3 lemon grass stalks
    10 fresh red chillies, seeded
        and sliced
    115g/4oz dark red onions or
        shallots, chopped
    4 garlic cloves
    1cm/½in piece fresh galangal,
        peeled, sliced and bruised
    stems from 4 fresh coriander
        (cilantro) sprigs
    15–30ml/1–2 tbsp groundnut
        (peanut) oil
    5ml/1 tsp grated (shredded) dried
        citrus rind
    1cm/½in cube of shrimp paste,
        wrapped in foil and warmed in a
        frying pan
    15ml/1 tbsp coriander seeds
    10ml/2 tsp cumin seeds
    5ml/1 tsp salt

1 Slice the tender lower portion of the lemon grass stalks and bruise them with a cleaver. Put them in a large mortar and add the chillies, onions or shallots, garlic, galangal and coriander stems.

2 Grind with a pestle, gradually adding the oil until the mixture forms a paste. Alternatively, purée the ingredients in a food processor or blender. Add the citrus rind and the shrimp paste. Mix well.

3 Dry-fry the coriander seeds and cumin seeds in a frying pan, then tip them into a large mortar and grind to a powder. Stir into the spice paste, with the salt.

4 Use the paste immediately, or scrape it into a glass jar. Cover with clear film (plastic wrap) and an airtight lid, then store in the refrigerator for 3–4 weeks.

Left: Thai red curry paste

Green Curry Paste

This medium-hot curry paste with its vivid green colour is based on chillies. It is good used with lamb, beef or chicken.

MAKES ABOUT 75G/3OZ/½ CUP

INGREDIENTS
  2 lemon grass stalks
  15 fresh hot green chillies
  3 shallots, sliced
  2 garlic cloves
  15ml/1 tbsp chopped fresh galangal
  4 kaffir lime leaves, chopped
  2.5ml/½ tsp grated (shredded) kaffir
    lime rind
  5ml/1 tsp chopped coriander
    (cilantro) root
  6 black peppercorns
  5ml/1 tsp coriander seeds, roasted
  5ml/1 tsp cumin seeds, roasted
  15ml/1 tbsp granulated sugar
  5ml/1 tsp salt
  15–30ml/1–2 tbsp groundnut
    (peanut) oil

1 Slice the tender lower portion of the lemon grass and bruise with a cleaver. Put them in a large mortar and add all the remaining ingredients except the oil. Grind to a paste. Add the oil, a little at a time, blending between each addition.

2 Use the paste immediately, or scrape it into a glass jar. Cover with clear film (plastic wrap) and an airtight lid. Store in the refrigerator for 3–4 weeks.

Below: Green curry paste

Thai Mussaman Curry Paste

Originating from the Malaysian border area, this paste can be used with beef, chicken or duck.

MAKES ABOUT 175G/6OZ/1 CUP

INGREDIENTS
  12 large dried red chillies
  1 lemon grass stalk
  60ml/4 tbsp chopped shallots
  5 garlic cloves, roughly chopped
  10ml/2 tsp chopped fresh galangal
    or fresh root ginger
  5ml/1 tsp cumin seeds
  15ml/1 tbsp coriander seeds
  2 cloves
  6 black peppercorns
  1cm/½ in cube of shrimp paste,
    wrapped in foil and warmed in a
    frying pan
  5ml/1 tsp salt
  5ml/1 tsp granulated sugar
  30ml/2 tbsp oil

1 Snap the dried chillies and shake out most of the seeds. Discard the stems. Soak the chillies in a bowl of hot water for 20–30 minutes.

2 Cut the tender lower portion of the lemon grass stalk into small pieces, using a small sharp knife. Place in a dry wok. Add the chopped shallots, roughly chopped garlic and galangal or ginger and dry-fry for a moment or two until the mixture gives off an aroma.

3 Stir in the whole cumin seeds, coriander seeds, cloves and peppercorns, and continue to dry-fry over a low heat for 5–6 minutes, stirring constantly. Spoon the mixture into a large mortar.

Above: Thai Mussaman curry paste

4 Drain the chillies and add them to the mortar. Use a pestle to grind the mixture finely, then add the prepared shrimp paste with the salt, granulated sugar and oil. Pound to form a rough paste. Use as required, then spoon any leftover paste into a jar, seal tightly and store in the refrigerator for up to 4 months.

COOK'S TIP
Shrimp paste is made from fermented shrimps. Also known as blachan, terasi, kapi or ngapi, it is widely used in the cooking of South-east Asia. It is available from Asian food stores and comes in block form, or packed in tiny tubs or jars. It smells rather vile because it is fermented, but the odour vanishes as soon as the paste is cooked. Warming it tempers the raw taste; the easiest way to do this is to wrap a small cube in foil and dry-fry it in a frying pan for about 5 minutes, turning it occasionally to heat evenly.

SAMBALS

When Westerners speak of sambals, they are usually referring to the side dishes served with curry – diced cucumber, sliced bananas and yogurt. These dishes are designed to cool the palate, but true sambals are something else entirely. They are extremely hot sauces or relishes based on chillies. Traditionally, they are served in small bowls, and used like mustard, to pep up other dishes. A sambal can also be a dish cooked with a hot chilli paste.

Chilli Sambal

This Indonesian speciality – *sambal oelek* – is a very simple mixture, made by pounding hot chillies with salt. Tamarind water is sometimes added, and Asian cooks will occasionally temper its heat by stirring ground roasted peanuts into the mixture.

MAKES 450G/1LB/2½ CUPS

INGREDIENTS
    450g/1lb fresh red chillies, seeded
    10ml/2 tsp salt

1 Cut the chillies in half and remove the stems. Using a sharp knife, scrape out and discard the seeds. Bring a pan of water to the boil, add the chillies and cook for 5–8 minutes.

2 Drain the chillies and tip them into a food processor or blender. Process to a rough paste.

3 Add the salt, process briefly to mix, then scrape the paste into a glass jar. Cover with clear film (plastic wrap) and a lid and store in the refrigerator. To serve, spoon into small dishes and offer the sambal as an accompaniment, or use it as suggested in recipes.

Sambal Blachan

Hot chillies can hold their own against strong flavours, as this sambal proves. The shrimp paste gives it a pungent quality, while the lemon or lime juice adds a welcome sharpness. Sambal blachan is frequently served with rice dishes. The rice tempers the heat.

MAKES ABOUT 30ML/2 TBSP

INGREDIENTS
    2–4 fresh red chillies, seeded
    salt
    1cm/½in cube of shrimp paste
    juice of ½ lemon or lime

1 Chop the chillies roughly and place them in a mortar. Add a little salt, then use a pestle to pound them to a paste.

2 Warm the shrimp paste, either by moulding it on to the end of a metal skewer and heating it in a gas flame until the outside begins to look dry, or by wrapping the paste in foil and heating it in a dry frying pan for about 5 minutes.

3 Add the shrimp paste to the chillies and pound to mix well. Stir in lemon or lime juice to taste.

Above: Sambal kecap

Sambal Kecap

Frequently served as a dip with chicken or beef satays, instead of the more usual peanut sauce, this is also delicious with deep-fried chicken.

MAKES ABOUT 150ML/¼ PINT/⅔ CUP

INGREDIENTS
    1 fresh red chilli, seeded and
      finely chopped
    2 garlic cloves, crushed
    60ml/4 tbsp dark soy sauce
    20ml/4 tsp lemon juice or 15ml/
      1 tbsp tamarind juice
    30ml/2 tbsp hot water
    30ml/2 tbsp deep-fried onion
      slices (optional)

1 Place the chopped chilli, crushed garlic and soy sauce in a small bowl. Stir in the lemon or tamarind juice, mix well, then thin with the hot water.

2 Stir in the deep-fried onion slices, if using. Cover and leave the sambal to stand for about 30 minutes before using.

COOK'S TIP
Deep-fried onion slices are very easy to make. Cut 2–3 onions in half, then into very thin slices. Blot these dry on kitchen paper, then add them to hot oil. Lower the heat slightly and cook until the onions have firmed up and browned. Lift out with a slotted spoon, drain on kitchen paper and leave until cold.

Above: Chilli sambal and sambal blachan (right)

Nam Prik Sauce

This is the universal Thai sauce, served solo, with rice or as a dip for fresh vegetables. The quantities can be varied.

MAKES ABOUT 275G/10OZ/1½–2 CUPS

INGREDIENTS
    50g/2oz dried prawns (shrimp)
    1cm/½in cube of shrimp paste,
      wrapped in foil and warmed in a
      frying pan
    3–4 garlic cloves, crushed
    3–4 fresh red chillies, seeded
      and sliced
    50g/2oz peeled cooked
      prawns (shrimp)
    a few coriander (cilantro) sprigs
    8–10 tiny baby aubergines (eggplant)
    45–60ml/3–4 tbsp lemon or
      lime juice
    30ml/2 tbsp Thai fish sauce (*nam
      pla*) or to taste
    10–15ml/2–3 tsp soft light
      brown sugar

1 Soak the dried prawns in water for 15 minutes. Drain and put in a mortar with the shrimp paste, garlic and chillies. Pound to a paste with a pestle, or process in a food processor. Add the cooked prawns and coriander. Pound or process again until combined.

2 Chop the aubergines roughly and gradually pound them into the sauce. Add the lemon or lime juice, fish sauce and sugar to taste.

Below: Nam prik sauce

Above: Sambal Salamat

Sambal Salamat

This hot tomato sambal is very popular in Indonesia. It has a very strong flavour and should be used sparingly.

MAKES ABOUT 120ML/4FL OZ/½ CUP

INGREDIENTS
    3 ripe tomatoes
    2.5ml/½ tsp salt
    5ml/1 tsp chilli sauce
    60ml/4 tbsp Thai fish sauce
      (*nam pla*)
    15ml/1 tbsp chopped fresh coriander
      (cilantro) leaves

1 Cut a small cross in the base of each tomato. Place them in a heatproof bowl and pour over boiling water to cover. Leave the tomatoes in the water for 30 seconds.

2 Lift out the tomatoes with a slotted spoon and plunge them into a bowl of cold water. The skins will have begun to peel back from the crosses. Remove the skins completely, cut the tomatoes in half and squeeze out the seeds. Chop the flesh finely and put it in a bowl.

3 Add the salt, chilli sauce, fish sauce and coriander. Mix well. Set aside for at least 2 hours before serving, so that the flavours can blend.

VARIATION
Use a fresh red chilli instead of chilli sauce, if you prefer. Slit it, remove the seeds and then chop the flesh finely. To give the sambal a slightly smoky flavour, roast the chilli under the grill (broiler) until the skin blisters and begins to blacken, then remove the skin and seeds before chopping the flesh.

Above: Nuoc Cham

Nuoc Cham

In Vietnam, this fiery sauce is used as a condiment, and serves much the same purpose as salt and pepper does in the West. It tastes good with fried spring rolls. Chillies are widely used in Vietnamese cooking, especially in the centre of the country, where it is believed that eating them frequently keeps mosquitoes away and malaria at bay.

MAKES ABOUT 105ML/7 TBSP

INGREDIENTS
    2 fresh red chillies, seeded
    2 garlic cloves, crushed
    15ml/1 tbsp granulated sugar
    45ml/3 tbsp Thai fish sauce
      (*nam pla*)
    juice of 1 lime or ½ lemon

1 Chop the chillies roughly, place them in a large mortar and use a pestle to pound them to a paste.

2 Scrape the paste into a bowl and add the garlic, sugar and fish sauce. Stir in lime or lemon juice to taste.

AFRICAN SPICE MIXTURES

Chillies are not native to Africa. They were introduced by Portuguese and Arab traders, but Africans really warmed to them, partly for the flavour they brought to a diet that was sometimes rather bland, and partly for the cooling effect they had on the skin by promoting perspiration. Today, Africa is an important chilli producer, with Nigeria, Ethiopia, Uganda, Kenya and Tanzania leading the field.

One of the world's most famous chilli pastes – harissa – comes from North Africa. A spicy blend of red chillies, coriander and cumin, it has a host of uses. Moroccan and Tunisian cooks serve it solo or with puréed tomatoes as a side dish for dipping pieces of barbecue-cooked meat. It is wonderful for adding to soups and stews and also serves as the basis of a sauce for serving over couscous.

Right: Large dried red chillies are used in harissa.

Dried chilli spice mixes are also popular in Africa. They invariably include warm spices such as cardamom, cumin, coriander and ginger, and are used with fish, meat and vegetables. The best-known spice mixes are Berbere, which comes from Ethiopia, and *Ras-el-hanout*, a Moroccan chilli powder that can include upwards of 20 different spices. This also comes as a paste. Tsire powder is a simple peanut and spice mixture used in West Africa for coating kebabs.

Harissa

Serve this hot, spicy condiment as a dipping sauce, or stir it into soups or stews. When added to natural (plain) yogurt, it makes a very good marinade for pork or chicken.

MAKES ABOUT 120ML/4FL OZ/½ CUP

INGREDIENTS
    12 dried red chillies
    15ml/1 tbsp coriander seeds
    10ml/2 tsp cumin seeds
    2 garlic cloves
    2.5ml/½ tsp salt
    60–90ml/4–6 tbsp olive oil

1 Snap the chillies and shake out some, but not all, of the seeds. Discard the stems, then put the chillies in a bowl and pour over warm water to cover. Soak for 20–30 minutes, until softened.

2 Meanwhile, dry-fry the coriander seeds and cumin seeds in a frying pan until they give off a rich aroma. Tip them into a mortar and grind them to a powder with a pestle. Tip them into a bowl and set them aside.

3 Put the garlic in the mortar, sprinkle it with the salt, and pound to a paste. Drain the chillies, add them to the paste and pound until it is smooth.

4 Add the spices, then gradually work in the oil, trickling it in and mixing until the sauce is well blended and has a consistency like that of mayonnaise.

Below: Harissa

Above: Tsire powder

Tsire Powder

This simple spice mixture is used as a coating for kebabs throughout West Africa. Cubes of raw meat are first dipped in oil or beaten egg and then coated in the powder. The cooked kebabs are dusted with a little more tsire powder before being served.

MAKES ABOUT 60ML/4 TBSP

INGREDIENTS
    50g/2oz/½ cup salted peanuts
    5ml/1 tsp mixed spice or apple
      pie spice
    2.5–5ml/½–1 tsp chilli powder
    salt

1 Grind the peanuts to a coarse powder in a mortar, blender or food processor.

2 Add the mixed spice or apple pie spice, chilli powder and a little salt. Mix or process until well blended.

3 Use immediately or transfer to an airtight container, close tightly and store in a cool place for up to 6 weeks.

COOK'S TIP
Mixed spice is a commercial mixture of ready ground spices. It typically contains allspice, cinnamon, cloves, ginger and nutmeg. Similar blends are marketed as apple pie spice or pumpkin pie spice. It is best used within 6 months of purchase to enjoy the best flavour.

Above: Berbere

Berbere

Ethiopia produces some of Africa's most delicious food. Dishes, such as the spicy stews, fuelled by the fire of this hot spice mixture, are served on large discs of bread, called *injera*.

MAKES ABOUT 50G/2OZ/SCANT ½ CUP

INGREDIENTS
    10 dried red chillies
    8 white cardamom pods
    5ml/1 tsp cumin seeds
    5ml/1 tsp coriander seeds
    5ml/1 tsp fenugreek seeds
    8 cloves
    5ml/1 tsp allspice berries
    10ml/2 tsp black peppercorns
    5ml/1 tsp ajowan seeds
    5ml/1 tsp ground ginger
    2.5ml/½ tsp grated nutmeg
    30ml/2 tbsp salt

1 Snap the chillies and shake out some of the seeds. Remove the stalks. Heat a heavy frying pan. Bruise the cardamom pods and add them to the pan with the chilli, cumin, coriander, fenugreek, cloves, allspice berries, peppercorns and ajowan seeds. Roast the spices, shaking the pan over a medium heat, until they give off a rich aroma.

2 Seed the cardamoms, then tip all the roasted spices into a large mortar, spice mill or coffee grinder kept specifically for spices. Grind to a fine powder. Stir in the ginger, nutmeg and salt. Use immediately or transfer to an airtight jar.

Baharat

Variations on this spice are to be found in all the countries that border the eastern Mediterranean, from Egypt and Jordan to the Lebanon and Syria. Its use has also spread south, to the Sudan and Ethiopia. An indication of just how fundamental it is to the cooking of these areas is to be found in its Arabic name, which simply translates as "spice". The recipe here is a basic one, but there are umpteen variations, some including cassia bark.

MAKES ABOUT 115G/4OZ/1 CUP

INGREDIENTS
    1 cinnamon stick
    30ml/2 tbsp coriander seeds
    30ml/2 tbsp cumin seeds
    90ml/6 tbsp cardamom seeds
    30ml/2 tbsp cloves
    30ml/2 tbsp black peppercorns
    60ml/4 tbsp paprika
    5ml/1 tsp ground allspice
    10ml/2 tsp grated nutmeg
    10ml/2 tsp chilli powder

1 Grind the cinnamon stick in a spice mill or a coffee grinder kept especially for spices. Tip the ground cinnamon into a bowl.

2 Heat a frying pan. Add the coriander seeds, cumin seeds, cardamom seeds, cloves and peppercorns. Roast the spices, shaking the pan over a medium heat, until they give off a rich aroma and just begin to change colour.

3 Grind the whole roasted spices, in batches if necessary, until they form a fine powder. This can be done using a mortar and pestle. Alternatively use an electric spice mill or coffee grinder.

4 Add the ground spice mixture to the cinnamon and mix well to blend the flavours.

5 Stir in the paprika, ground allspice, grated nutmeg and chilli powder. Use immediately, or transfer to an airtight jar and store out of the light to retain its colour and strength.

COOK'S TIPS
• Ajowan seeds resemble cumin seeds in appearance. When crushed, they release a powerful aroma reminiscent of thyme. If you can't locate these seeds, use extra cumin instead, or stir in a little dried thyme just before using the spice.
• If you are unlikely to use the Berbere spice mix quickly, store it in an airtight plastic container in the freezer where it will keep for several months.

Ras-el-hanout
What distinguishes this traditional Moroccan spice mixture is its complexity. It can contain more than 20 different ingredients, including dried rose petals. Every spice merchant seems to have a different blend, and recipes are jealously guarded. Chillies are usually in there somewhere, along with cinnamon, cardamom, coriander seeds, cloves, salt, peppercorns, ginger, nutmeg, turmeric, but it is the secret extras – some of which are rumoured to have aphrodisiac qualities – that really set it apart.

BARBECUE SPICE MIXTURES

Spice rubs and marinades are a boon to the barbecue cook, improving the appearance and flavour of cooked meats, poultry and fish while filling the air with a tantalizing aroma. Many of the mixtures are also delicious on roast chicken; just brush the bird lightly with olive oil before cooking, sprinkle the barbecue spice over it and rub in.

Basic Barbecue Spice Mix

Rub this on chops, steaks or portions of chicken. To make a marinade, add the mixture to a glass of red or white wine. Add a few slices of onion and stir in 60ml/4 tbsp of garlic-flavoured oil (or chilli oil if you are feeling adventurous).

MAKES ABOUT 60ML/4 TBSP

INGREDIENTS
  10ml/2 tsp celery seeds
  5ml/1 tsp paprika
  5ml/1 tsp grated nutmeg
  5ml/1 tsp chilli powder
  5ml/1 tsp garlic powder
  5ml/1 tsp onion salt
  10ml/2 tsp dried marjoram
  5ml/1 tsp salt
  5–10ml/1–2 tsp soft light brown sugar
  5ml/1 tsp lightly ground black pepper

1 Put the celery seeds in a mortar and grind to a powder with a pestle, or use a spice mill. Tip the powder into a bowl and stir in the remaining ingredients. Use the spice mixture immediately or store in an airtight jar.

Below: Basic barbecue spice mix

Above: Old-fashioned Philadelphia spice powder

Old-fashioned Philadelphia Spice Powder

This only has a trace of chilli, but the taste combines well with the warm, rounded flavours of the nutmeg and mace. The mixture makes a truly great seasoning for a pork joint, or can be rubbed both on steaks and chops. Do this in plenty of time before you plan to roast or cook on the barbecue, to allow the flavours to develop.

MAKES ABOUT 30–45ML/2–3 TBSP

INGREDIENTS
  8 cloves
  5ml/1 tsp chilli powder
  2.5ml/½ tsp grated nutmeg
  1.5ml/¼ tsp ground mace
  5ml/1 tsp dried basil
  5ml/1 tsp dried thyme
  2 dried bay leaves
  salt

1 Grind the cloves to a coarse powder, then add the other ingredients and continue grinding until fine.

2 Use immediately or store in an airtight container, away from strong light.

COOK'S TIP
All spices and spice mixtures start to deteriorate soon after being ground, so try to use them as soon as possible. Store in airtight and preferably tinted glass jars in a cool place, away from direct light, or keep them in the freezer.

Jamaican Jerk Paste

Give pork chops or chicken pieces a taste-lift with this delectable paste. Scotch bonnet chillies would be used in Jamaica, but they are extremely hot, so unless you are a devout chilli-head, you might prefer to substitute a milder variety, or reduce the quantity.

SUFFICIENT FOR FOUR MEAT PIECES

INGREDIENTS
  15ml/1 tbsp oil
  2 onions, finely chopped
  2 fresh red chillies, seeded and
    finely chopped
  1 garlic clove, crushed
  2.5cm/1in piece of fresh root
    ginger, grated (shredded)
  5ml/1 tsp dried thyme
  5ml/1 tsp ground allspice
  5ml/1 tsp Tabasco sauce or other
    hot pepper sauce
  30ml/2 tbsp rum
  grated (shredded) rind and juice
    of 1 lime
  salt and ground black pepper

1 Heat the oil in a frying pan. Add the onions and cook for 10 minutes until soft. Stir in the chillies, garlic, ginger, thyme and allspice, and fry for 2 minutes more. Stir in the Tabasco sauce or hot pepper sauce, rum, lime rind and juice.

2 Simmer until the mixture forms a dark paste with a rich aroma. Season with salt and pepper, and leave to cool.

3 To use, rub over chops or chicken pieces, place in a shallow dish, cover and chill for 8 hours or overnight before barbecuing (grilling) or roasting.

Chermoula

This Moroccan mixture makes a very good marinade for meaty fish, but you can also use it as a cold sauce for fried fish. It is important to not use too much onion.

SUFFICIENT FOR 675G/1½LB FISH FILLETS

INGREDIENTS
 1 small red onion, finely chopped
 2 garlic cloves, crushed
 1 fresh red chilli, seeded and
  finely chopped
 30ml/2 tbsp chopped fresh
  coriander (cilantro)
 15ml/1 tbsp chopped fresh mint
 5ml/1 tsp ground cumin
 5ml/1 tsp paprika
 generous pinch of saffron threads
 60ml/4 tbsp olive oil
 juice of 1 lemon
 generous pinch of salt

1 Mix the onion, garlic, chilli, coriander, mint, cumin, paprika and saffron threads in a bowl. Add the olive oil, lemon juice and the salt. Mix well.

2 To use, add cubed fish to the bowl and toss until coated. Cover and leave in a cool place to marinate for 1 hour. Thread onto skewers and barbecue or grill (broil).

Thai Chilli and Citrus Marinade

This delectable combination of hot and sour flavours is perfect for chicken and seafood. Marinate fish or shellfish for about 1 hour; chicken for 3–4 hours.

MAKES ABOUT 175ML/6FL OZ/¾ CUP

INGREDIENTS
 2 small fresh red chillies
 15ml/1 tbsp granulated sugar
 2 garlic cloves, crushed
 white parts of 3 spring onions
  (scallions), chopped
 2.5cm/1in piece of fresh galangal or
  ginger, peeled and finely chopped
 grated (shredded) rind and juice of
  1 mandarin
 15ml/1 tbsp tamarind juice
 15ml/1 tbsp Thai fish sauce
  (*nam pla*)
 30ml/2 tbsp light soy sauce
 juice of 1 lime
 15ml/1 tbsp vegetable oil

1 Slit the chillies and scrape out the seeds. Chop the flesh roughly and put it in a mortar. Add the sugar and grind to a paste with a pestle.

2 Add the crushed garlic, chopped spring onions and chopped fresh galangal or ginger. Add the grated rind of the mandarin to the mortar. Grind to a paste.

3 Scrape the paste into a bowl. Squeeze the juice from the mandarin and add it to the paste, with the tamarind juice, fish sauce and soy sauce. Stir in the lime juice and oil, mixing well. Set the marinade aside for 30 minutes, to allow the flavours to blend before using as a marinade.

Peri-peri Barbecue Marinade

Peri-peri is a hot chilli sauce that originated in Portugal, but which is now popular wherever there are large Portuguese communities. It is widely used in South Africa and Mozambique, and makes a marvellous marinade that is particularly good with shellfish.

MAKES ABOUT 75ML/5 TBSP

INGREDIENTS
 1 fresh red chilli
 2.5ml/½ tsp paprika
 2.5ml/½ tsp ground coriander
 1 garlic clove, crushed
 juice of 1 lime
 30ml/2 tbsp olive oil
 salt and ground black pepper

1 Slit the chilli using a small sharp knife and scrape out and discard the seeds. Chop the flesh finely and put it in a small bowl.

2 Stir in the paprika, ground coriander, crushed garlic and lime juice, then whisk in the olive oil, using a fork or salad dressing whisk. Season to taste with salt and pepper. This makes an excellent marinade for prawns (shrimp) and can also be used with chicken. Marinate prawns for about 30 minutes; chicken for several hours. When cooking the shellfish or chicken on the barbecue, baste it with any of the remaining marinade.

COOK'S TIP
Tamarind pods yield a sour, fruity pulp that is as widely used in South-east Asia as lemon is in the West. Buy tamarind as a compressed block, in slices or as a concentrate. To use block tamarind, pinch off the equivalent of 15ml/1 tbsp and soak this in 150ml/¼ pint/⅔ cup warm water for 10 minutes. Swirl the tamarind with your fingers to release the pulp from the seeds, then strain the liquid through a nylon sieve into a bowl. Tamarind slices must also be soaked in warm water, while the concentrate is mixed with warm water in the ratio of 15ml/1 tbsp concentrate to 75ml/ 5 tbsp water.

CAJUN SPICE MIXTURES AND BASTES

Louisiana is home to some of the world's most exciting food, the marriage of French and Creole cooking with Spanish and African influences. The more sophisticated, cosmopolitan style is called Creole, while Cajun cooking is the food of rustic, country people; the trappers and fishers descended from the French who were exiled from Nova Scotia by the British in 1765. They like their food hot and spicy.

Cajun Spice Mix

This can be used as a seasoning for fish steaks, chicken or meat. It can also be used for gumbo, a thick soup or stew that generally contains okra, and for jambalaya.

MAKES ABOUT 150ML/¼ PINT/⅔ CUP

INGREDIENTS
    1 onion
    2 garlic cloves
    5ml/1 tsp black peppercorns
    5ml/1 tsp cumin seeds
    5ml/1 tsp white mustard seeds
    10ml/2 tsp paprika
    5ml/1 tsp chilli powder or
      cayenne pepper
    5ml/1 tsp dried oregano
    10ml/2 tsp dried thyme
    5ml/1 tsp salt

1 Finely chop the onion. Press the garlic firmly with the flat side of a wide-bladed knife to release the skin, then peel and chop it very finely. Set aside until ready to use.

2 Dry-fry the peppercorns, cumin and mustard seeds over a medium heat, to release their flavours, but do not allow them to burn.

3 Grind the dry-fried spices to a fine powder, then add the paprika, chilli powder or cayenne, oregano, thyme and salt. Grind again to achieve a uniformly fine mixture.

4 If the mix is to be used immediately, add the spices to the finely chopped garlic and onion in a blender or food processor and process until well combined. Alternatively, store the dry mixture in an airtight container, and add the garlic and onion only when ready to use the spice mix.

Below: Cajun spice mix

COOK'S TIP
A simple way to use this spice mix is as a coating for fish steaks, chicken pieces, pork chops or beef steaks that have been dipped in melted butter to help the spices adhere to the flesh. Fry the coated fish or meat in a large frying pan in hot oil or butter in a kitchen that has a good extractor fan, because the cooking process will produce a lot of smoke that can sting the eyes and produce unpleasant smells.

Chilli Pepper Baste

This sauce was developed by the McIlhenny family, producers of Tabasco sauce, and is quite fiery. Cautious cooks should start off by using less Tabasco in the mixture, adding an extra dash or two at the end if necessary rather than making the sauce too hot initially. It is sufficient to baste four pork chops, duck breast portions or lamb steaks.

MAKES ABOUT 115G/4OZ/½ CUP

INGREDIENTS
    115g/4oz/½ cup butter
    juice of 1 lemon
    15ml/1 tbsp Worcestershire sauce
    7.5ml/1½ tsp Tabasco sauce
    1 garlic clove, finely chopped
    salt and ground black pepper

1 Melt the butter in a small non-aluminium pan. Add the lemon juice and bring the mixture to simmering point over a low heat. Do not let the butter burn or it will taste bitter.

2 Add the Worcestershire and Tabasco sauces and the chopped garlic. Continue cooking over a low heat, without letting the garlic brown, for another 5 minutes. Season with salt and pepper. Meanwhile, preheat the grill (broiler) until hot.

3 Use the baste immediately it is ready, otherwise the butter will solidify, preventing application. Using a large pastry brush, spread the baste over the top of the chosen meat or poultry, grill (broil) for about 5 minutes, then turn over and brush the other side with more baste. Grill until the meat or poultry is cooked to your liking.

CHILLI PASTA

Making your own pasta is great fun, and when you add chillies to the dough, it not only looks good, but it tastes excitingly different, too. A flavoured pasta such as this needs to be served with a simple sauce, or stuffed with crab meat for a special treat.

SERVES FOUR TO SIX

INGREDIENTS
  300g/11oz/2¾ cups flour
    (see Cook's Tip)
  3 eggs
  5–10ml/1–2 tsp dried red
    chilli flakes
  5ml/1 tsp salt

1 Mound the flour on a clean work surface and make a large, deep well in the centre with your hands. Keep the sides of the well quite high, so that when the eggs are added they will not run out. Crack the eggs into the well, then add the chilli flakes and salt.

2 With a table knife or fork, mix the eggs, chilli and salt together, then gradually start incorporating the flour from the sides of the well. Try not to break the sides of the well or the runny mixture will escape and quickly spread over the work surface.

3 As soon as the egg mixture is no longer liquid, dip your fingers in the flour and use them to work the ingredients together until they form a rough and sticky dough. Scrape up any dough that sticks to the work surface with a knife, then scrape this off the knife with your fingers. If the dough is too dry, add a few drops of cold water; if it is too moist, sprinkle a little flour over it.

4 Press the dough into a rough ball and knead it as you would bread. Push it away from you with the heel of your hand, then fold the end of the dough back on itself so that it faces towards you and push it out again. Continue folding the dough back a little further each time and pushing it out until you have folded it back all the way towards you.

5 Give the dough a quarter turn anti-clockwise, then continue kneading, folding and turning for 5 minutes if you intend shaping the dough in a pasta machine, or for 10 minutes if you will be rolling it out by hand. Wrap the kneaded dough in clear film (plastic wrap) and leave to rest for about 15–20 minutes at room temperature before rolling and shaping for cooking.

Making Pasta in a Food Processor

This is a quick and simple way of making pasta.

1 Sift the flour into the bowl of the food processor and add the salt and chilli flakes.

2 Crack the eggs into the flour and process the mixture until the dough begins to come together. Tip it out and knead until smooth. Wrap in clear film (plastic wrap) and leave for 30 minutes.

Rolling and Shaping Pasta

For rounded spaghetti shapes, you need a machine, but you can easily make flat shapes or filled pasta by hand.

After the dough has rested, sprinkle plenty of flour over your work surface and begin rolling the dough, rotating it in quarter turns. Roll out until you have a sheet 3mm/⅛in thick. Fold into a wide, flat sausage.

For tagliatelle, cut the rolled pasta into 5mm/¼in strips. For ravioli, cut out two equally sized pieces 35 x 23cm/ 14 x 9in. Space the filling evenly across the pasta and moisten with egg to make the seal. Place the second piece on top, pressing down around the filling to push out the air. Divide using a serrated pastry wheel.

COOK'S TIP

The best flour to use is Farina Bianca 00 or Tipo 00, which is available from some larger supermarkets and good Italian delicatessens. Imported from Italy, this is a fine, soft white wheat flour. If you use ordinary plain (all-purpose) flour, you will find the dough quite difficult to knead and roll, especially by hand. If you can't get 00 flour, use a strong white (bread) flour.

CHILLI GIFTS

Bright and colourful, chillies make beautiful gifts. For a simple "thank you" to a friend who loves cooking spicy foods, simply tie a bunch of chillies together with a raffia bow. When the occasion calls for a more elaborate present, fill a basket with spices, including bunches of small red and green chillies. Chilli oils and vinegars are always welcome, and you can include a pot of chilli mustard as a special treat.

Above: A decorative chilli and cinnamon rope

Chilli Rope

To make a dried chilli rope, thread red chillies on a long piece of fine string and hang in a cool, airy place. They should retain their rich colour and can be used when quite dry. If you are making the rope as a gift, add a little label with the above instructions.

Chilli Spice Basket

The perfect gift for a house-warming! Choose a pretty basket, preferably a coloured one that will set off the contents. Fill with any or all of the following, or make up your own selection of spices.

    6–7 fresh red chillies, tied
      with ribbon
    6–7 fresh green chillies, tied
      with ribbon
    cinnamon sticks, tied with ribbon
    whole nutmegs
    cardamom pods packed in a muslin
      or cheesecloth bag
    lemon grass sticks wrapped in kaffir
      lime leaves and tied with raffia
    dried pomegranates
    vanilla pods (beans) tied with raffia
    dried orange peel
    coriander seeds and cumin seeds
                packed in muslin or
        cheesecloth "purses"

Right: Chilli spice basket

Right: Chilli spice oil

Chilli Spice Oil

This looks very pretty on the kitchen shelf and makes a thoughtful gift. The quantities given are just a guide – use your own artistic flair!

MAKES ABOUT 600ML/1 PINT/2½ CUPS

    600ml/1 pint/2½ cups extra virgin
      olive oil
    1 garlic clove, peeled and halved
    3 dried red chillies
    5ml/1 tsp coriander seeds
    3 allspice berries
    6 black peppercorns
    4 juniper berries
    2 bay leaves

1 Pour oil into a sterilized bottle, filling it three-quarters full. Add the garlic, chillies, coriander, allspice, peppercorns, juniper and bay, then top up with more oil to fill the bottle. Seal tightly and label clearly. Leave in a cool, dark place for 2 weeks. If the flavour is not sufficiently pronounced, leave for another week.

COOK'S TIP
Moulds can grow in oil, so long-term storage is not recommended.

Chilli Spirit

For a drink with a real kick, steep chillies in sherry or vodka. Choose a pale spirit to show off the chillies.

MAKES 1 LITRE/1¾ PINTS/4 CUPS

INGREDIENTS
  25–50g/1–2oz small fresh
    red chillies
  1 litre/1¾ pints/4 cups pale dry
    sherry or vodka

1 Wash and dry the chillies thoroughly with kitchen paper, discarding any that are less than perfect, as these will look unsightly in the bottle. Using a fine cocktail stick or toothpick, prick the chillies all over to release their flavours into the alcohol.

2 Sterilize an attractive glass bottle with a wide enough neck to allow the chillies to pass easily. Pack the chillies tightly in the bottle, pushing them down with a metal or wooden skewer.

3 Top up with sherry or vodka to reach almost to the top of the bottle. Cork tightly and leave in a dark, cool place for at least 10 days, or up to 2 months, shaking the bottle occasionally for the chilli flavour to mingle evenly.

Right: Chilli vinegar

Chilli Vinegar

Pep up soups and sauces with this spicy vinegar, or use to deglaze a pan after cooking beef steaks.

MAKES ABOUT 600ML/1 PINT/2½ CUPS

  8 dried red chillies
  600ml/1 pint/2½ cups red wine
    vinegar or sherry vinegar

1 Place the chillies in a sterilized preserving jar or heatproof bottle. Pour the vinegar into a pan and bring to the boil. Carefully pour the vinegar into the jar or bottle. Cool, cover tightly, and leave to steep for 2 weeks, shaking the jar occasionally.

2 Taste for flavour and strain when sufficiently strong, pouring the vinegar into a clean, sterilized bottle, filled right to the top. Cover tightly, label and store.

VARIATION
Chilli Ho Ho Fill a sterilized bottle with small whole chillies. Top up with sherry vinegar, or spirits such as gin or vodka. Cover tightly or seal with a cork, label clearly and leave for 2 weeks, shaking occasionally.

Chilli and Garlic Mustard

A jar of this makes a great gift to add to a basket of mixed chilli goodies.

MAKES ABOUT 300ML/½ PINT/1¼ CUPS

INGREDIENTS
  1 dried red chilli
  40g/1½oz/¼ cup white mustard seeds
  40g/1½oz/¼ cup black mustard seeds
  50g/2oz/¼ cup soft light brown sugar
  5ml/1 tsp salt
  5ml/1 tsp whole peppercorns
  10ml/2 tsp tomato purée (paste)
  1 large garlic clove
  200ml/7fl oz/scant 1 cup distilled
    malt vinegar

1 Snap the top off the chilli and shake out the seeds. Discard the stem. Put the chilli in a food processor or blender with the mustard seeds, sugar, salt, peppercorns, tomato purée and garlic.

2 Whizz until mixed. Add 15ml/1 tbsp vinegar at a time, processing the mixture until it forms a coarse paste.

3 Leave to stand for 10–15 minutes, to thicken slightly. Spoon into a 300ml/½ pint/1¼ cup jar or several smaller jars. Cover the surface of the mustard with clear film (plastic wrap) or a waxed paper disc, seal tightly and label.

Below: Chilli and garlic mustard

Turn up the heat with these sizzling sauces, selected to show just how versatile chillies can be in a supporting role. A spoonful of Mango and Chilli Salsa adds sweetness and spice to all sorts of dishes, from baked ham to crackers and cheese. Hot Hot Habanero Salsa stokes the fire, while Guacamole cools and comforts. Some sauces are based on specific chillies, like chipotle and guajillo, while others leave the choice to you. Add chutneys, relishes, breads and nibbles, and it's easy to see why this chapter is your passport to chilli heaven.

Scorching Salsas, Dips and Extras

GREEN FIRE

ALSO KNOWN AS SALSA VERDE, THIS IS A CLASSIC GREEN SALSA IN WHICH CAPERS PLAY AN IMPORTANT PART. MAKE IT WITH GREEN CAYENNE CHILLIES OR THE MILDER JALAPEÑOS.

SERVES FOUR

INGREDIENTS
    2–4 fresh green chillies
    8 spring onions (scallions)
    2 garlic cloves
    50g/2oz/½ cup salted capers
    1 fresh tarragon sprig
    bunch of fresh parsley
    grated (shredded) rind and juice
      of 1 lime
    juice of 1 lemon
    90ml/6 tbsp olive oil
    15ml/1 tbsp green Tabasco sauce
    ground black pepper

1 Cut the chillies in half and scrape out and discard the seeds. Trim the spring onions and cut them into short lengths. Cut the garlic in half. Mix in a food processor and pulse until chopped.

2 Use your fingertips to rub the excess salt off the capers but do not rinse them (see Cook's Tip). Add the capers, tarragon and parsley to the food processor and pulse again until they are quite finely chopped.

3 Transfer the mixture to a small bowl. Stir in the lime rind and juice, lemon juice and olive oil. Stir lightly so the citrus juice and oil do not emulsify.

4 Add green Tabasco and black pepper to taste. Chill until ready to serve but do not prepare more than 8 hours in advance.

COOK'S TIP
If you can only find capers pickled in vinegar, they must be rinsed well in cold water before using.

AVOCADO AND SWEET RED PEPPER SALSA

THIS SIMPLE SALSA IS A FIRE-AND-ICE MIXTURE THAT COMBINES HOT CHILLI WITH COOLING AVOCADO. SERVE IT WITH CORN CHIPS FOR DIPPING.

SERVES FOUR

INGREDIENTS
    2 ripe avocados
    1 red onion
    1 sweet red (bell) pepper
    4 fresh green chillies
    30ml/2 tbsp chopped fresh
      coriander (cilantro)
    30ml/2 tbsp sunflower oil
    juice of 1 lemon
    salt and ground black pepper

1 Cut the avocados in half and remove the stone (pit) from each. Scoop out the flesh and dice it. Finely chop the red onion.

2 Slice the top off the sweet red pepper and pull out the central core. Shake out any remaining seeds. Cut the pepper into thin strips, then into dice.

3 Cut the chillies in half lengthways, scrape out and discard the seeds and finely chop the flesh. Put it in a jug (pitcher) and mix in the coriander, oil, lemon juice and salt and pepper to taste.

4 Place the avocado, red onion and pepper in a bowl. Pour in the chilli dressing and toss well. Serve immediately.

COOK'S TIP
Serrano chillies would be a good choice, or moderate them with the milder Anaheim if you like.

CHILLI AND PESTO SALSA

USE LONG SLIM RED CHILLIES TO MAKE THIS AROMATIC SALSA, WHICH IS DELICIOUS OVER FISH AND CHICKEN. IT IS ALSO GOOD TOSSED WITH PASTA RIBBONS OR USED TO DRESS A FRESH AVOCADO AND TOMATO SALAD. YOU CAN MAKE IT INTO A DIP BY MIXING IT WITH A LITTLE MAYONNAISE OR SOUR CREAM.

SERVES FOUR

INGREDIENTS
    50g/2oz/1⅓ cups fresh coriander
      (cilantro) leaves
    15g/½oz/¼ cup fresh parsley
    2 fresh red chillies
    1 garlic clove, halved
    50g/2oz/½ cup shelled pistachio nuts
    25g/1oz/⅓ cup freshly grated
      (shredded) Parmesan cheese
    90ml/6 tbsp olive oil
    juice of 2 limes
    salt and ground black pepper

1 Process the coriander and parsley in a food processor until finely chopped. Cut the chillies in half, scrape out and discard seeds. Add to the herbs, with the garlic and process until finely chopped.

2 Add the pistachio nuts to the herb mixture and pulse until they are roughly chopped. Scrape the mixture into a bowl and stir in the Parmesan cheese, olive oil and lime juice.

3 Add salt and pepper to taste. Spoon the mixture into a serving bowl, cover and chill until ready to serve.

FIERY CITRUS SALSA

THIS VERY UNUSUAL SALSA, WHICH COMBINES FRUIT WITH CHILLIES, MAKES A FANTASTIC MARINADE FOR SHELLFISH AND IT IS ALSO DELICIOUS DRIZZLED OVER BARBECUE-COOKED MEAT.

SERVES FOUR

INGREDIENTS
    1 orange
    1 green apple
    2 fresh red chillies
    1 garlic clove
    8 fresh mint leaves
    juice of 1 lemon
    salt and ground black pepper

1 Slice the base off the orange so that it will stand firmly on a chopping board. Using a sharp knife, remove the peel and pith in sections.

2 Holding the orange over a bowl to catch the juices, cut away the segments from the membrane, letting them fall into the bowl. Squeeze any juice from the remaining membrane into the bowl.

3 Peel, quarter and core the apple. Put it in a food processor. Cut the chillies in half and scrape out and discard the seeds. Add them to the food processor with the orange segments and juice, garlic and fresh mint.

4 Process until smooth. Then, with the motor running, pour in the lemon juice through the feeder tube. Season to taste. Pour into a bowl and serve immediately.

VARIATION
If you're feeling really daring, don't seed the chillies! They will make the salsa particularly hot and fierce.

CLASSIC MEXICAN TOMATO SALSA

THERE ARE VERY MANY RECIPES FOR THIS TRADITIONAL SALSA, BUT ONION, TOMATO, CHILLI AND CORIANDER ARE COMMON TO ALL OF THEM.

SERVES SIX

INGREDIENTS
  3–6 fresh serrano chillies
  1 large white onion
  grated (shredded) rind and juice
    of 2 limes, plus strips of lime
    rind, to garnish
  8 ripe, firm tomatoes
  large bunch of fresh
    coriander (cilantro)
  1.5ml/¼ tsp sugar
  salt

1 Use 3 chillies for a salsa of medium heat; up to 6 if you like it hot. To peel the chillies, spear them on a long-handled metal skewer and roast them over the flame of a gas burner until the skins blister and darken. Do not let the flesh burn. Alternatively, dry-fry them until the skins are scorched.

2 Place the roasted chillies in a strong plastic bag and tie the top of the bag. Set aside for about 20 minutes.

3 Meanwhile, chop the onion finely, put it in a bowl with the lime rind and juice, and stir the mixture lightly. The lime juice will soften the onion.

4 Remove the chillies from the bag and peel off the skins. Cut off the stalks, slit the chillies and scrape out all the seeds with a knife. Discard the seeds. Chop the flesh and set it aside.

VARIATION
For a smoky flavour, use chipotle chillies instead of fresh serrano chillies.

5 Cut a small cross in the base of each tomato. Place the tomatoes in a heatproof bowl and pour over boiling water to cover.

6 Leave the tomatoes in the water for 30 seconds, then lift them out using a slotted spoon and plunge them into a bowl of cold water to prevent them cooking further. Drain. The skins will have begun to peel back from the crosses. Remove the skins completely.

7 Dice the peeled tomatoes and put them in a bowl. Add the onion and lime mixture. Chop the coriander finely.

8 Add the coriander to the salsa, with the chillies and the sugar. Mix gently until the sugar has dissolved. Season to taste with salt. Cover and chill for 2–3 hours to allow the flavours to blend. The salsa will keep for 3–4 days in the refrigerator. Garnish with the strips of lime rind just before serving.

ROASTED TOMATO SALSA

SLOW ROASTING THESE TOMATOES TO A SEMI-DRIED STATE RESULTS IN A VERY RICH, FULL-FLAVOURED SWEET SAUCE. THE COSTENO AMARILLO CHILLI IS MILD AND HAS A FRESH LIGHT FLAVOUR, MAKING IT THE PERFECT PARTNER FOR THE RICH TOMATO TASTE.

SERVES SIX

INGREDIENTS
   500g/1¼lb tomatoes
   8 small shallots
   5 garlic cloves·
   1 fresh rosemary sprig
   2 dried costeno amarillo chillies
   grated (shredded) rind and juice of
      ½ small lemon
   30ml/2 tbsp extra virgin olive oil
   1.5ml/¼ tsp soft dark brown sugar
   sea salt

1 Preheat the oven to 160°C/325°F/ Gas 3. Cut the tomatoes into quarters and place them on a baking tray.

2 Peel the shallots and garlic cloves, and add them to the baking tray. Sprinkle with sea salt. Roast in the oven for 1¼ hours or until the tomatoes are beginning to dry. Do not let them burn or they will have a bitter taste.

3 Leave the tomatoes to cool, then peel off the skins and chop the flesh finely. Place in a bowl. Remove the tough outer layer of skin from any shallots.

4 Using a large, sharp knife, chop the shallots and garlic roughly, place them with the tomatoes in a bowl and mix.

5 Strip the rosemary leaves from the woody stem and chop them finely. Add half to the tomato and shallot mixture and mix lightly.

COOK'S TIP
This salsa is great with tuna or sea bass and makes a marvellous sandwich filling when teamed with creamy cheese.

6 Soak the chillies in hot water for about 10 minutes until soft. Drain, remove the stalks, slit them and scrape out the seeds with a sharp knife. Chop the chilli flesh finely and add it to the tomato mixture.

7 Stir in the lemon rind and juice, the olive oil and the sugar. Mix well, taste and add more salt if needed. Cover and chill for at least 1 hour before serving, sprinkled with the remaining rosemary. It will keep for 1 week, refrigerated.

CHUNKY CHERRY CHILLI AND TOMATO SALSA

PUNGENT CHERRY CHILLIES AND SWEET CHERRY TOMATOES ARE MIXED WITH COOLING CUCUMBER IN THIS DELICIOUS DILL-SEASONED SALSA.

SERVES FOUR

INGREDIENTS

1 ridge cucumber
5ml/1 tsp sea salt
500g/1¼lb cherry tomatoes
1–2 fresh hot cherry chillies
1 lemon
1 garlic clove, crushed
45ml/3 tbsp chilli oil
30ml/2 tbsp chopped fresh dill
salt and ground black pepper

1 Trim the ends off the cucumber and cut it into 2.5cm/1in lengths, then cut each piece lengthways into thin slices.

2 Spread out the cucumber slices in a colander and sprinkle them with the sea salt. Leave for 5 minutes until the cucumber has wilted.

COOK'S TIPS
• Cherry chillies are usually only moderately hot, but have quite a pungent, biting flavour. One could easily be sufficient to flavour the salsa.
• If you do not have gas roast the chillies under a hot grill (broiler) until blistered and blackened.

3 Wash the cucumber slices well under cold water and pat them dry with kitchen paper.

4 Quarter the cherry tomatoes and place in a bowl with the wilted cucumber. Skewer the chilli (or chillies) on a metal fork and hold in a gas flame for 2–3 minutes, turning often, until blistered and blackened. Slit, scrape out the seeds, then finely chop the flesh. Add it to the bowl.

5 Grate the lemon rind finely and place in a small bowl. Squeeze the lemon and add the juice to the bowl, with the garlic, chilli oil and dill. Add salt and pepper to taste, and whisk the ingredients together with a fork.

6 Pour the chilli oil dressing over the tomato and cucumber and toss well. Leave the salsa to marinate at room temperature for at least 2–3 hours before serving.

DEMON SALSA

THIS IS A SCORCHINGLY HOT SALSA MADE WITH TWO TYPES OF CHILLIES, AND SHOULD BE TREATED WITH THE UTMOST CAUTION. SPREAD IT SPARINGLY ON COOKED MEATS AND BURGERS.

3 Use a clean dishtowel to rub the skins off the blistered chillies.

4 Try not to touch the chillies with your bare hands: use a fork to hold them and slice them open with a sharp knife. Scrape out and discard the seeds, then finely chop the flesh.

5 Cut the jalapeño chillies in half lengthways, remove the seeds, then finely slice them into tiny strips. Mix both types of chilli, the tomatoes and the chopped parsley in a bowl.

SERVES FOUR TO SIX

INGREDIENTS
    6 fresh habanero chillies or
      Scotch bonnets
    2 ripe tomatoes
    4 fresh green jalapeño chillies
    30ml/2 tbsp chopped fresh parsley
    30ml/2 tbsp olive oil
    15ml/1 tbsp balsamic or
      sherry vinegar
    salt

1 Skewer a habanero or Scotch bonnet chilli on a metal fork and hold it in a gas flame for 2–3 minutes, turning until the skin darkens and blisters. Repeat with the remaining chillies. Set aside.

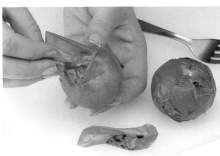

2 Skewer the tomatoes one at a time and hold in a gas flame for 1–2 minutes, until the skin splits and wrinkles. Slip off the skins, halve the tomatoes, then use a teaspoon to scoop out and discard the seeds. Chop the flesh very finely.

6 Make a dressing by mixing the olive oil and vinegar with a little salt, pour this over the salsa and toss to mix. Cover the bowl. Chill for up to 3 days.

MANGO AND CHILLI SALSA

THIS HAS A FRESH, FRUITY TASTE AND IS PERFECT WITH FISH OR AS A CONTRAST TO RICH, CREAMY DISHES. THE BRIGHT COLOURS MAKE IT AN ATTRACTIVE ADDITION TO ANY TABLE.

SERVES FOUR

INGREDIENTS
    2 fresh red fresno chillies
    2 ripe mangoes
    ½ white onion
    small bunch of fresh
       coriander (cilantro)
    grated (shredded) rind and juice
       of 1 lime

1 To peel the chillies, spear them on a long-handled metal skewer and roast them over the flame of a gas burner, turning the chillies continually, until the skins blister and darken. Do not let the flesh burn. Alternatively, dry-fry them in a frying pan until the skins are scorched.

2 Place the roasted chillies in a strong plastic bag and tie the top. Set aside.

VARIATION
For a refreshing change, look out for juicy Italia chillies, which have a wonderful affinity for mangoes.

3 Meanwhile, put one of the mangoes on a board and cut off a thick slice close to the flat side of the stone (pit). Turn the mango round and repeat on the other side. Score the flesh on each thick slice with criss-cross lines at 1cm/½in intervals, taking care not to cut through the skin. Repeat with the second mango.

4 Fold the mango halves inside out so that the mango flesh stands proud of the skin, in neat dice. Carefully slice these off the skin and into a bowl. Cut off the flesh adhering to each stone, dice it and add it to the bowl.

5 Remove the roasted chillies from the bag and carefully peel off the skins. Cut off the stalks, then slit the chillies and scrape out the seeds with a sharp knife. Discard the seeds.

6 Chop the white onion and the coriander finely and add them to the diced mango. Chop the chilli flesh finely and add it to the mixture in the bowl, together with the lime rind and juice. Toss the ingredients in the bowl thoroughly, then cover and chill for at least 1 hour before serving. The salsa will keep for 2–3 days in the refrigerator.

ROASTED SERRANO AND TOMATO SALSA

ROASTING THE CHILLIES GIVES A GREATER DEPTH TO THE TASTE OF THIS SALSA, WHICH ALSO BENEFITS FROM THE ROUNDED FLAVOUR OF ROASTED TOMATOES.

SERVES SIX

INGREDIENTS
    500g/1¼lb tomatoes
    2 fresh serrano chillies
    1 onion
    juice of 1 lime
    large bunch of fresh
       coriander (cilantro)
    salt

1 Preheat the oven to 200ºC/400ºF/ Gas 6. Cut the tomatoes into quarters and place them in a roasting pan. Add the chillies. Roast for 45–60 minutes, until charred and softened.

2 Place the roasted chillies in a strong plastic bag. Tie the top to keep the steam in and set aside for 20 minutes. Leave the tomatoes to cool slightly, then remove the skins and dice the flesh.

3 Chop the onion finely, then place in a bowl and add the lime juice and the diced tomatoes.

4 Remove the chillies from the bag and peel off the skins. Cut off the stalks, then slit the chillies and scrape out the seeds with a sharp knife. Chop the chillies roughly and add them to the onion mixture. Mix well.

5 Chop the coriander and add most to the salsa. Add salt, cover and chill for at least 1 hour before serving, sprinkled with the remaining coriander. This salsa will keep in the refrigerator for 1 week.

SWEET POTATO AND JALAPEÑO SALSA

COLOURFUL AND SWEET, WITH JUST A HINT OF HEAT, THIS SALSA MAKES THE PERFECT ACCOMPANIMENT TO HOT, SPICY MEXICAN DISHES.

SERVES FOUR

INGREDIENTS
  675g/1½lb sweet potatoes
  juice of 1 small orange
  5ml/1 tsp crushed dried
    jalapeño chillies
  4 small spring onions (scallions)
  juice of 1 small lime (optional)
  salt

COOK'S TIP
This fresh and tasty salsa is also very good served with a simple grilled (broiled) salmon fillet or other fish dishes, and makes a delicious accompaniment to veal escalopes (scallops) or chicken breast portions.

1 Peel the sweet potatoes and dice the flesh finely. Bring a pan of water to the boil. Add the sweet potato and cook for 8–10 minutes, until just soft. Drain off the water, cover the pan and put it back on the stove top, having turned off the heat.

2 Leave for 5 minutes to dry out, tip it into a bowl and set aside.

3 Mix the orange juice and crushed dried chillies in a bowl. Chop the spring onions finely and add them to the juice and chillies.

4 When the sweet potatoes are cool, add the orange juice mixture and toss carefully until all the pieces are coated. Cover the bowl and chill for 2 hours.

5 Taste the salsa and season with salt. Stir in the lime juice if you think the mixture needs to be sharpened slightly. The salsa will keep for 2–3 days in a covered bowl in the refrigerator.

HOT HOT HABANERO SALSA

THIS IS A VERY FIERY SALSA WITH AN INTENSE HEAT LEVEL. A DAB ON THE PLATE ALONGSIDE A MEAT OR FISH DISH ADDS A FRESH, CLEAN TASTE, BUT THIS IS NOT FOR THE FAINT-HEARTED.

3 Put the chillies in a food processor and add a little of the soaking liquid. Purée to a fine paste. Do not lean over the processor – the fumes may burn your face. Remove the lid and scrape the mixture into a bowl.

4 Put the chopped spring onions in another bowl and add the grapefruit or orange juice, with the lime rind and juice. Roughly chop the coriander.

SERVE SPARINGLY

INGREDIENTS
    5 dried roasted habanero chillies
    4 dried costeno amarillo chillies
    3 spring onions (scallions), chopped
    juice of ½ large grapefruit or
      1 Seville (Temple) orange
    grated (shredded) rind and juice
      of 1 lime
    small bunch of fresh
      coriander (cilantro)
    salt

COOK'S TIP
Dried habanero chillies are just as hot as when fresh. Lantern shaped and deep orange in colour, they release a lovely fruity aroma when reconstituted, and go very well with the milder, citrus-flavoured costeno amarillo chillies.

1 Soak the habanero and costeno amarillo chillies in hot water for about 20 minutes until softened. Drain, reserving the soaking water.

2 Wear rubber gloves to handle the habaneros. Remove the stalks from all the chillies, then slit them and scrape out the seeds with a small sharp knife and discard. Chop the flesh roughly.

5 Carefully add the chopped coriander to the chilli mixture and then combine the ingredients very thoroughly. Add salt to taste. Cover the bowl and chill for at least 1 day before use. Serve this salsa very sparingly and warn your guests that it is hot.

BLACK BEAN SALSA

THIS SALSA HAS A VERY STRIKING APPEARANCE. IT IS RARE TO FIND A BLACK SPICE AND IT PROVIDES A WONDERFUL CONTRAST TO THE MORE COMMON REDS AND GREENS ON THE PLATE.

SERVES FOUR

INGREDIENTS
    130g/4½oz/generous ½ cup black
      beans, soaked overnight in water
    1 pasado chilli
    2 fresh red fresno chillies
    1 red onion
    grated (shredded) rind and juice
      of 1 lime
    30ml/2 tbsp Mexican beer (optional)
    15ml/1 tbsp olive oil
    small bunch of fresh coriander
      (cilantro), chopped
    salt

1 Drain the beans, rinse them thoroughly and put them in a large pan. Pour in water to cover. Do not add salt as this toughens the outside skin and prevents the bean from cooking properly. Place the lid on the pan and bring to the boil. Lower the heat slightly and simmer the beans for about 40 minutes or until tender. They should still have a little bite and should not have begun to disintegrate. Drain, rinse under cold water, then drain again and leave the beans until cold.

2 Soak the pasado chilli in hot water for about 20 minutes until softened. Drain, remove the stalk, then slit the chilli and, using a small sharp knife, scrape out the seeds and discard them. Chop the flesh finely.

COOK'S TIP
Pasado chillies are always sold in their dried, roasted form. Dark, almost black, in colour, they have a subtle citrus flavour and are only mildly hot.

3 Spear the fresno chillies on a long-handled metal skewer and roast them over the flame of a gas burner, turning the chillies all the time, until the skins blister and darken. Do not let the flesh burn. Alternatively, dry-fry them in a griddle pan until the skins are scorched.

4 Place the roasted chillies in a strong plastic bag and tie the top to keep the steam in. Set aside for 20 minutes.

5 Meanwhile, chop the red onion finely. Remove the chillies from the bag and peel off the skins. Slit them, remove and discard the seeds, and chop them finely.

6 Tip the beans into a bowl and add the onion and both types of chilli. Stir in the lime rind and juice, and beer, if using, then add the oil and coriander. Season with salt and mix well. Leave the salsa for a day or two to allow the flavours to develop fully. Serve chilled.

SPICY TOMATO AND CHILLI DIP

GET YOUR TASTE BUDS TINGLING WITH THIS TANGY DIP, SPIKED WITH FRESH GREEN CHILLIES. IT IS DELICIOUS SERVED WITH DEEP-FRIED POTATO SKINS OR HASH BROWNS.

SERVES FOUR

INGREDIENTS
1 shallot, halved
2 garlic cloves, halved
handful of fresh basil leaves, plus
  extra, to garnish
500g/1¼lb ripe tomatoes
30ml/2 tbsp olive oil
2 fresh green chillies
salt and ground black pepper

COOK'S TIP
Use green serrano or jalapeño chillies. Anaheims are also suitable, and will give a milder result.

1 Place the shallot and garlic in a blender or food processor. Add the basil leaves and process until very finely chopped. You may need to scrape down the sides of the bowl with a spatula.

2 Cut the tomatoes in half and add them to the shallot mixture. Pulse until the mixture is well blended and the tomatoes are finely chopped.

3 With the motor still running, slowly pour in the olive oil through the feeder tube. Add salt and pepper to taste and pulse briefly to mix. Spoon the mixture into a bowl.

4 Cut the chillies lengthways and scrape out the seeds with a sharp knife and discard. Finely slice across the chillies, cutting them into tiny strips and stir them into the tomato mixture. Garnish with a few torn basil leaves. Serve the dip at room temperature. Refrigerated, this will keep for 3–4 days.

GUACAMOLE

ONE OF THE BEST-LOVED MEXICAN SALSAS, THIS BLEND OF CREAMY AVOCADO, TOMATOES, CHILLIES, CORIANDER AND LIME NOW APPEARS ON TABLES THE WORLD OVER.

SERVES SIX TO EIGHT

INGREDIENTS

    4 medium tomatoes
    4 ripe avocados, preferably fuerte
    juice of 1 lime
    ½ small onion
    2 garlic cloves
    small bunch of fresh coriander
      (cilantro), chopped
    3 fresh red fresno chillies
    salt
    tortilla chips, to serve

1 Cut a cross in the base of each tomato. Place the tomatoes in a heatproof bowl and pour over boiling water to cover.

2 Leave the tomatoes in the water for 30 seconds, then lift them out using a slotted spoon and plunge them into a bowl of cold water. Drain. The skins will have begun to peel back from the crosses. Remove the skins completely. Cut the tomatoes in half, remove the seeds with a teaspoon, then chop the flesh roughly and set it aside.

3 Cut the avocados in half and remove the stones (pits). Scoop the flesh into a food processor or blender. Process until almost smooth, then scrape into a bowl and stir in the lime juice.

4 Chop the onion finely, then crush the garlic. Add both to the avocado and mix well. Stir in the coriander.

5 Remove the stalks from the chillies, slit them and scrape out and discard the seeds. Chop the chillies finely and add them to the avocado mixture, with the chopped tomatoes. Mix well.

6 Check the seasoning and add salt to taste. Cover closely with clear film (plastic wrap) or a tight-fitting lid and chill for 1 hour before serving as a dip with tortilla chips. If it is well covered, guacamole will keep in the refrigerator for 2–3 days.

COOK'S TIP
Smooth-skinned fuerte avocados are native to Mexico, so would be ideal for this dip. If they are not available, use any avocados, but make sure they are ripe. To test, gently press the top of the avocado; it should give a little.

CHILLI BEAN DIP

SUBSTANTIAL ENOUGH TO SERVE FOR SUPPER ON A BAKED POTATO, THIS CREAMY BEAN DIP ALSO TASTES GREAT WITH TRIANGLES OF LIGHTLY TOASTED PITTA BREAD OR A BOWL OF CRUNCHY TORTILLA CHIPS. SERVE IT WARM TO ENJOY IT AT ITS BEST.

SERVES FOUR

INGREDIENTS
2 fresh green chillies
2 garlic cloves
1 onion
30ml/2 tbsp vegetable oil
5–10ml/1–2 tsp hot chilli powder
400g/14oz can kidney beans
75g/3oz/¾ cup grated (shredded)
  mature (sharp) Cheddar cheese
1 fresh red chilli, seeded
salt and ground black pepper

1 Slit the green chillies and use a sharp knife to scrape out the seeds. Chop the flesh finely, then crush the garlic and finely chop the onion.

2 Heat the oil in a large pan and add the garlic, onion, green chillies and chilli powder. Cook gently for 5 minutes, stirring, until the onions have softened and are transparent, but not browned.

COOK'S TIP
Fresh green chillies provide the heat in this dip. You can substitute sweet red (bell) pepper for the garnish.

3 Drain the kidney beans, reserving the liquid in which they were canned. Set aside 30ml/2 tbsp of the beans and purée the remainder in a food processor or blender.

4 Spoon the puréed beans into the pan and stir in 30–45ml/2–3 tbsp of the reserved can liquid. Heat gently, stirring to mix well.

5 Stir in the reserved whole kidney beans and the Cheddar cheese. Cook gently for 2–3 minutes, stirring regularly until the cheese melts. Add salt and pepper to taste.

6 Cut the red chilli into tiny strips. Spoon the dip into 4 individual serving bowls and sprinkle the chilli strips over the top. Serve warm.

CHILLI AND RED ONION RAITA

RAITA IS A TRADITIONAL INDIAN ACCOMPANIMENT, A COOLING AGENT TO SERVE WITH HOT CURRIES. IT IS ALSO DELICIOUS SERVED WITH POPPADUMS AS A DIP.

SERVES FOUR

INGREDIENTS
5ml/1 tsp cumin seeds
1 large red onion
1 small garlic clove
1 small fresh green chilli, seeded
150ml/¼ pint/⅔ cup natural
  (plain) yogurt
30ml/2 tbsp chopped fresh coriander
  (cilantro), plus extra, to garnish
about 2.5ml/½ tsp granulated sugar
salt

1 Heat a small pan and dry-fry the cumin seeds for 1–2 minutes, until they release their aroma and begin to pop.

2 Let the seeds cool for a few minutes, then tip them into a mortar. Crush them with a pestle or flatten them with the heel of a heavy-bladed knife.

COOK'S TIPS
• For an extra tangy raita, stir in 15ml/ 1 tbsp lemon juice.
• For a thicker consistency, drain off any liquid from the yogurt before adding the ingredients.

3 Cut the red onion in half. Cut a few thin slices for the garnish and chop the rest finely. Crush the garlic, then finely chop the chilli. Stir the onion, garlic and chilli into the yogurt with the crushed cumin seeds and coriander.

4 Add sugar and salt to taste. Spoon the raita into a small bowl, cover and chill until ready to serve. Garnish with the reserved onion slices and extra coriander before serving. The dip will keep for 2 days in the refrigerator.

THAI RED CURRY SAUCE

SERVE THIS WITH MINI SPRING ROLLS OR SPICY INDONESIAN CRACKERS, OR TOSS IT INTO FRESHLY COOKED RICE NOODLES FOR A DELICIOUS MAIN-MEAL ACCOMPANIMENT.

SERVES FOUR

INGREDIENTS

200ml/7fl oz/scant 1 cup creamed coconut (coconut cream)
10–15ml/2–3 tsp Thai red curry paste
4 spring onions (scallions), plus extra, to garnish
30ml/2 tbsp chopped fresh coriander (cilantro)
1 fresh red chilli, seeded and thinly sliced into rings
5ml/1 tsp soy sauce
juice of 1 lime
granulated sugar, to taste
25g/1oz/¼ cup dry-roasted peanuts
salt and ground black pepper

1 Pour the creamed coconut into a small bowl and stir in the curry paste.

COOK'S TIP
The dip may be prepared in advance up to the end of step 3. Cover and keep in the refrigerator for up to 4 hours.

2 Trim the spring onions and finely slice them on the diagonal. Stir into the creamed coconut with the chopped fresh coriander and chilli.

3 Stir in the soy sauce and fresh lime juice, with sugar, salt and pepper to taste. Pour the sauce into a small serving bowl.

4 Finely chop the dry-roasted peanuts and sprinkle them over the sauce. Garnish with spring onions sliced lengthways into thin curls. Serve immediately.

VARIATION
As an alternative to spring onions, try using baby leeks. You may need only one or two and they can be prepared in the same way.

CHIPOTLE SAUCE

THE SMOKY FLAVOUR OF THIS RICH SAUCE MAKES IT IDEAL FOR BARBECUE-COOKED FOOD, EITHER AS A MARINADE OR AS AN ACCOMPANIMENT. IT IS ALSO WONDERFUL STIRRED INTO CREAM CHEESE AS A SANDWICH FILLING WITH CHICKEN. CHIPOTLE CHILLIES ARE SMOKE-DRIED JALAPEÑOS.

SERVES SIX

INGREDIENTS
    500g/1¼lb tomatoes
    5 chipotle chillies
    3 garlic cloves, roughly chopped
    150ml/¼ pint/⅔ cup red wine
    5ml/1 tsp dried oregano
    60ml/4 tbsp clear honey
    5ml/1 tsp American mustard
    2.5ml/½ tsp ground black pepper
    salt

1 Preheat the oven to 200°C/400°F/ Gas 6. Cut the tomatoes into quarters and place them in a roasting pan. Roast for 45–60 minutes, until they are charred.

2 Meanwhile, soak the chillies in a bowl of cold water to cover for about 20 minutes or until soft. Remove the stalks, slit the chillies and scrape out the seeds with a small sharp knife. Discard the seeds. Chop the flesh roughly.

3 Remove the tomatoes from the oven, let them cool slightly, then remove the skins. If you prefer a smooth sauce, remove the seeds. Chop the tomatoes in a blender or food processor. Add the chillies, garlic and red wine. Process until smooth, then add the oregano, honey, mustard and black pepper. Process briefly to mix, then taste and season with salt.

4 Pour the mixture into a small pan. Bring to the boil, lower the heat and simmer the sauce for about 10 minutes, stirring occasionally, until it has reduced and thickened. Spoon into a bowl and serve hot or cold.

GUAJILLO CHILLI SAUCE

THIS SAUCE CAN BE SERVED OVER ENCHILADAS OR STEAMED VEGETABLES. IT IS ALSO GOOD EATEN HOT OR COLD WITH MEATS SUCH AS PORK, AND A LITTLE MAKES A FINE SEASONING FOR SOUPS OR STEWS.

SERVES FOUR

INGREDIENTS
    2 tomatoes
    2 red (bell) peppers, cored, seeded
      and quartered
    3 garlic cloves, in their skins
    2 ancho chillies
    2 guajillo chillies
    30ml/2 tbsp tomato purée (paste)
    5ml/1 tsp dried oregano
    5ml/1 tsp soft dark brown sugar
    300ml/½ pint/1¼ cups chicken stock

1 Preheat the oven to 200°C/400°F/ Gas 6. Cut the tomatoes into quarters and place them in a roasting pan with the peppers and whole garlic cloves. Roast for 45–60 minutes, until the tomatoes and peppers are slightly charred.

COOK'S TIP
Like chipotle chillies, guajillos are dried. They give the sauce a well-rounded, fruity flavour and do not make it too hot.

2 Put the peppers in a strong plastic bag and tie the top to keep the steam in. Set aside for 20 minutes. Remove the skin from the tomatoes. Soak the chillies in boiling water for 20 minutes.

3 Remove the peppers from the bag and rub off the skins. Cut them in half, remove the cores and seeds, then chop the flesh roughly and put it in a food processor or blender. Drain the chillies, remove the stalks, then slit them and scrape out and discard the seeds. Chop them roughly and add to the peppers.

4 Add the roasted tomatoes to the food processor. Squeeze the roasted garlic out of the skins and add to the tomato mixture, with the tomato purée, oregano, sugar and stock. Process until smooth.

5 Pour the mixture into a pan, place over a medium heat and bring to the boil. Lower the heat and simmer for 10–15 minutes until the sauce has reduced to about half. Transfer to a bowl and serve. Or leave to cool, then chill until required. The sauce will keep in the refrigerator for up to 1 week.

ADOBO SEASONING

ADOBO MEANS VINEGAR SAUCE, AND THIS ONE IS A PASTE MADE FROM DRIED CHILLIES, WHICH IS USED FOR MARINATING PORK CHOPS OR STEAKS. ADOBOS ARE WIDELY USED IN MEXICAN COOKING.

MAKES ENOUGH TO MARINATE
SIX CHOPS OR STEAKS

INGREDIENTS
   1 small head of garlic
   5 ancho chillies
   2 pasilla chillies
   15ml/1 tbsp dried oregano
   5ml/1 tsp cumin seeds
   6 cloves
   5ml/1 tsp coriander seeds
   10cm/4in piece of cinnamon stick
   10ml/2 tsp salt
   120ml/4fl oz/½ cup white
     wine vinegar

1 Preheat the oven to 180°C/350°F/ Gas 4. Cut a thin slice off the top of the head of garlic, so that the inside of each clove is exposed. Wrap the head of garlic in foil. Roast for 45–60 minutes or until the garlic is soft.

2 Meanwhile, slit the chillies and shake out most of the seeds. Break up the dried chillies a little and put them in a food processor, spice mill or mortar. Add the oregano, cumin seeds, cloves, coriander seeds, cinnamon stick and salt. Process or grind to a fine powder.

3 Remove the garlic from the oven. When it is cool enough to handle, squeeze the pulp out of each clove.

4 Add the garlic and white wine vinegar to the spice mixture and process or grind to a smooth paste. Scrape into a bowl and leave to stand for 1 hour, to allow the flavours to blend. Spread over pork chops or steaks as a marinade, before cooking.

COOK'S TIP
You can buy wild Mexican oregano from Mexican food stores or by mail order.

CHILLI RELISH

FOR INSTANT HEAT, KEEP A POT OF THIS SPICY RELISH. IT TASTES GREAT WITH SAUSAGES, BURGERS AND CHEESE. IT WILL KEEP IN THE REFRIGERATOR FOR UP TO TWO WEEKS.

SERVES EIGHT

INGREDIENTS

6 tomatoes
1 onion
1 sweet red (bell) pepper, seeded
2 garlic cloves
30ml/2 tbsp olive oil
5ml/1 tsp ground cinnamon
5ml/1 tsp dried chilli flakes
5ml/1 tsp ground ginger
5ml/1 tsp salt
2.5ml/½ tsp ground black pepper
75g/3oz/scant ⅔ cup light muscovado (brown) sugar
75ml/5 tbsp cider vinegar
handful of fresh basil leaves

COOK'S TIP
This relish thickens slightly on cooling, so do not worry if the mixture seems a little sloppy when it is first made.

1 Skewer each of the tomatoes in turn on a metal fork and hold in a gas flame for 1–2 minutes, turning until the skin splits and wrinkles. Place the tomatoes on a chopping board, slip off the skins, then roughly chop.

2 Roughly chop the onion, red pepper and garlic. Gently heat the oil in a pan. Tip in the onion, red pepper and garlic, stirring lightly.

3 Cook gently for 5–8 minutes, until the pepper has softened. Add the chopped tomatoes, cover and cook for 5 minutes.

4 Stir in the cinnamon, chilli flakes, ginger, salt, pepper, sugar and vinegar. Bring gently to the boil, stirring until the sugar dissolves.

5 Simmer, uncovered, for 20 minutes, until the mixture is pulpy. Stir in the basil leaves and check the seasoning.

6 Allow to cool completely, then spoon into a glass jar or a plastic tub with a tightly fitting lid. Store, covered, in the refrigerator. This relish will keep in the refrigerator for up to a fortnight. Stir before using.

CHILLI STRIPS WITH LIME

THIS FRESH RELISH IS IDEAL FOR SERVING WITH STEWS, RICE DISHES OR BEAN DISHES. THE OREGANO ADDS A SWEET NOTE WHILE THE ABSENCE OF SUGAR OR OIL MAKES THIS A VERY HEALTHY CHOICE.

MAKES ABOUT 60ML/4 TBSP

INGREDIENTS
    10 fresh green chillies
    ½ white onion
    4 limes
    2.5ml/½ tsp dried oregano
    salt

COOK'S TIP
This method of roasting chillies is ideal if you need more than one or two, or if you do not have a gas burner. To roast over a burner, spear the chillies, four or five at a time, on a long-handled metal skewer and hold them over the flame, turning them round frequently, until the skins blister.

1 Roast the chillies in a griddle pan over a medium heat until the skins are charred and blistered but not blackened, as this might make the salsa bitter. Place the roasted chillies in a strong plastic bag and tie the top to keep the steam in. Set aside for 20 minutes.

2 Meanwhile, slice the onion very thinly and put it in a large bowl. Squeeze the limes and add the juice to the bowl, with any pulp that gathers in the strainer. The lime juice will have the effect of softening the onion. Stir in the oregano.

3 Remove the chillies from the bag and peel off the skins. Slit them, then scrape out and discard all the seeds. Cut the chillies into long strips using a sharp knife. These are called "rajas".

4 Add the chilli strips to the onion mixture and season lightly with salt. Cover the bowl and chill for at least 1 day before serving, to allow the flavours to blend. Taste the salsa and add more salt at this stage if necessary. The salsa will keep for up to 2 weeks in a covered bowl in the refrigerator.

VARIATION
White onions have a mild sweet flavour, as do red onions, which could equally well be used in their place. The colour combination of red and green would look particularly good with rice dishes.

SPICY SWEETCORN RELISH

A TOUCH OF HEAT TEMPERS THE SWEETNESS OF THIS DELICIOUS RELISH. TRY IT WITH CRISP ONION BHAJIS OR SLICES OF HONEY-ROAST HAM FOR A SPICY SNACK.

SERVES FOUR

INGREDIENTS

1 large onion
1 fresh red chilli, seeded
2 garlic cloves
30ml/2 tbsp vegetable oil
5ml/1 tsp black mustard seeds
10ml/2 tsp hot curry powder
320g/11¼oz can sweetcorn
grated rind and juice of 1 lime
45ml/3 tbsp chopped fresh
 coriander (cilantro)
salt and ground black pepper

1 Chop the onion, chilli and garlic. Heat the vegetable oil in a large frying pan and cook the onion, chilli and garlic over a high heat for 5 minutes, until the onions are just beginning to brown.

2 Stir in the mustard seeds and curry powder. Cook for a further 2 minutes, stirring, until all the seeds start to splutter and the onions have browned.

COOK'S TIP
Opt for canned rather than frozen sweetcorn if possible, as the kernels are plump, moist and ready to eat.

3 Remove the fried onion mixture from the heat and allow to cool. Place in a glass bowl. Drain the sweetcorn and stir it into the onion mixture.

4 Add the lime rind and juice, coriander and salt and pepper to taste. Cover and refrigerate until needed. The relish is best served at room temperature.

RED ONION, GARLIC AND CHILLI RELISH

THIS POWERFUL RELISH IS FLAVOURED WITH NORTH AFRICAN SPICES AND PUNCHY PRESERVED LEMONS, AVAILABLE FROM DELICATESSENS AND LARGER SUPERMARKETS OR FROM MIDDLE EASTERN FOOD STORES.

2 Add the garlic cloves and coriander seeds. Cover and cook gently for another 5–8 minutes, stirring occasionally to prevent the onions from browning, until the garlic is beginning to soften.

3 Add a pinch of salt, lots of pepper and the sugar, and cook, uncovered, for 5 minutes. Meanwhile, soak the saffron in the warm water for 5 minutes. Then add the saffron mixture (including the saffron threads) to the onions. Add the cinnamon, chillies and bay leaves. Stir in 30ml/2 tbsp of the sherry vinegar and the orange juice.

4 Cook gently, uncovered, until the onions are very soft and most of the liquid has evaporated. Stir in the preserved lemon and cook gently for 5 minutes. Taste and adjust the seasoning, adding sugar and/or vinegar to balance the flavours. You may not need to add more salt, since the lemons are preserved in it.

5 Serve warm or at room temperature, but not hot or chilled. The relish tastes best the day after it is made. Remove the cinnamon stick before serving.

SERVES SIX

INGREDIENTS
45ml/3 tbsp olive oil
3 large red onions, sliced
2 heads of garlic, separated into
  cloves and peeled
10ml/2 tsp coriander seeds, crushed
  but not finely ground
10ml/2 tsp light muscovado (brown)
  sugar, plus a little extra
pinch of saffron threads
45ml/3 tbsp warm water
10cm/2in piece of cinnamon stick
2–3 small whole dried red chillies
2 fresh bay leaves
30–45ml/2–3 tbsp sherry vinegar
juice of ½ small orange
30ml/2 tbsp chopped
  preserved lemon
salt and ground black pepper

1 Heat the oil in a heavy pan. Add the onions and stir, then cover and reduce the heat to the lowest setting. Cook for 10–15 minutes, stirring occasionally, until the onions are very soft but not browned.

COOK'S TIPS
• Although you can use any type of dried chilli in this relish, it is worth looking out for the sweet, mild choricero chillies, which impart a lovely, fruity flavour but no heat. Alternatively, use a combination of dried hot and mild chillies.
• If you do not have a pestle and mortar with which to crush the coriander, put the seeds into a small, strong plastic bag and crush under a rolling pin or heavy object.
• Saffron has a strong, slightly bitter flavour, a pungent sweet scent, and is brilliant yellow when soaked.

HOT THAI PICKLED SHALLOTS <u>WITH</u> CHILLIES

THAI PINK SHALLOTS REQUIRE LENGTHY PREPARATION, BUT THEY LOOK EXQUISITE WITH WHOLE CHILLIES IN THIS SPICED PICKLE. SERVE THEM FINELY SLICED.

MAKES TWO TO THREE JARS

INGREDIENTS
    5–6 small red or green bird's
      eye chillies
    500g/1¼lb Thai pink shallots, peeled
    2 large garlic cloves, halved
For the vinegar
    600ml/1 pint/2½ cups cider vinegar
    45ml/3 tbsp granulated sugar
    10ml/2 tsp salt
    5cm/2in piece fresh root
      ginger, sliced
    15ml/1 tbsp coriander seeds
    2 lemon grass stalks, trimmed and
      cut in half lengthways
    4 kaffir lime leaves or strips of
      lime rind
    15ml/1 tbsp chopped fresh
      coriander (cilantro)

4 Pack the shallots into sterilized jars, distributing the lemon grass, lime leaves, chillies and garlic between them. Pour over the hot vinegar. Cool, then seal and leave in a dark place for 2 months before eating.

COOK'S TIPS
• When making pickles, see that bowls and pans used for the vinegar are not chemically affected by the acid of the vinegar. China and glass bowls and stainless steel pans are suitable.
• Ensure that metal lids do not come in contact with the pickle. The acid in the vinegar would corrode the metal. Use plastic-coated lids or glass lids with rubber rings. Or, when using metal lids, cover the top of each jar with a circle of waxed paper to prevent direct contact.
• Let hot jars cool slightly after sterilizing. But do not let them cool completely, or they might crack when the hot vinegar is poured in.

1 Prick the chillies several times with a cocktail stick or toothpick. Bring a large pan of water to the boil. Blanch the chillies, shallots and garlic for 1–2 minutes, then drain. Rinse all the vegetables under cold water, then drain again thoroughly in a colander.

2 To prepare the vinegar, put the cider vinegar, sugar, salt, ginger, coriander seeds, lemon grass and lime leaves or lime rind in a pan and bring to the boil. Reduce the heat and simmer for 3–4 minutes, then leave to cool.

3 Scoop out the ginger, then bring the vinegar back to the boil. Add the fresh coriander, garlic and chillies (leave the shallots in the colander) and cook for 1 minute.

COCONUT CHUTNEY WITH ONION AND CHILLI

SERVE THIS REFRESHING COCONUT CHUTNEY AS AN ACCOMPANIMENT TO INDIAN-STYLE DISHES OR AT THE START OF A MEAL, WITH POPPADUMS, A RAITA AND OTHER CHUTNEYS.

SERVES FOUR TO SIX

INGREDIENTS
  200g/7oz fresh coconut, grated
  3–4 fresh green chillies, seeded
    and chopped
  60ml/4 tbsp chopped fresh
    coriander (cilantro)
  30ml/2 tbsp chopped fresh mint
  30–45ml/2–3 tbsp lime juice
  about 2.5ml/½ tsp salt
  about 2.5ml/½ tsp granulated sugar
  15–30ml/1–2 tbsp coconut milk
  30ml/2 tbsp groundnut
    (peanut) oil
  5ml/1 tsp kalonji (nigella seeds)
  1 small onion, very finely chopped
  fresh coriander (cilantro) sprigs,
    to garnish

1 Place the coconut, chillies, coriander and mint in a food processor. Add 30ml/2 tbsp of the lime juice, then process until thoroughly chopped.

2 Scrape the mixture into a bowl. Stir in more lime juice to taste, with the salt, sugar and coconut milk.

3 Heat the oil in a small pan and fry the kalonji until they begin to pop. Reduce the heat and add the onion. Fry, stirring frequently, until the onion is soft.

4 Stir the spiced onions into the coconut mixture and cool. Garnish with coriander sprigs before serving.

ONION, MANGO AND CHILLI CHAAT

CHAATS ARE SPICED RELISHES OF VEGETABLES AND NUTS SERVED WITH INDIAN MEALS. USE GREEN JALAPEÑOS OR SERRANOS FOR MEDIUM HEAT, OR GREEN CAYENNE CHILLIES IF YOU WANT IT HOT.

SERVES FOUR

INGREDIENTS
  15ml/1 tbsp groundnut (peanut) oil
  90g/3½oz/1 cup unsalted peanuts
  1 onion, chopped
  10cm/4in piece cucumber, seeded
    and cut into 5mm/¼in dice
  1 mango, peeled, stoned (pitted)
    and diced
  1–2 fresh green chillies, seeded and
    finely chopped
  30ml/2 tbsp chopped fresh
    coriander (cilantro)
  15ml/1 tbsp chopped fresh mint
  15ml/1 tbsp lime juice
  pinch of granulated sugar
For the chaat masala
  10ml/2 tsp ground toasted
    cumin seeds
  2.5ml/½ tsp cayenne pepper
  5ml/1 tsp mango powder (amchoor)
  2.5ml/½ tsp garam masala
  salt and ground black pepper

1 To make the chaat masala, grind all the spices together, then season with 2.5ml/½ tsp each of salt and pepper.

2 Heat the oil in a small pan and fry the peanuts until lightly browned, then drain on kitchen paper and set aside until cool.

COOK'S TIP
Mango powder (amchoor) is made by grinding sun-dried mango slices and mixing the powder with a little turmeric.

3 Mix the onion, cucumber, mango, chilli, fresh coriander and mint. Sprinkle in 5ml/1 tsp of the chaat masala. Stir in the peanuts and then add the lime juice and sugar to taste. Set the mixture aside for 20–30 minutes for the flavours to mature.

4 Spoon the mixture into a serving bowl, sprinkle another 5ml/1 tsp of the chaat masala over and serve. Any remaining chaat masala will keep in a sealed jar for 4–6 weeks.

CHILLI POORIS

THESE SMALL DISCS OF DOUGH PUFF UP INTO LIGHT AIRY BREADS WHEN FRIED. LIGHTLY STUDDED WITH PIECES OF CHILLI, THEY MELT IN YOUR MOUTH AND LEAVE YOU WITH A WARM GLOW.

MAKES TWELVE

INGREDIENTS
    115g/4oz/1 cup unbleached plain
        (all-purpose) flour
    115g/4oz/1 cup wholemeal
        (whole-wheat) flour
    2.5ml/½ tsp salt
    2.5ml/½ tsp mild chilli powder
    30ml/2 tbsp vegetable oil
    1 fresh red chilli, seeded and finely
        chopped (optional)
    100–120ml/3½–4fl oz/
        scant ½ cup–½ cup water
    oil, for frying

VARIATION
To make spinach-flavoured pooris, omit the fresh chilli. Thaw 50g/2oz/⅓ cup frozen chopped spinach, drain and add to the dough with 5ml/1 tsp grated fresh ginger and 2.5ml/½ tsp ground cumin.

1 Sift the flours, salt and chilli powder into a large bowl. Add the vegetable oil then mix in enough water to make a dough. Turn the dough out on a lightly floured surface and knead for 8–10 minutes until it is smooth, elastic and springy.

2 Place in a lightly oiled bowl and cover with lightly oiled clear film (plastic wrap). Leave to rest for 30 minutes.

3 Turn out on to a lightly floured surface. Knead in the chopped fresh chilli, if using, then divide the dough into 12 equal pieces. Keeping the rest of the dough covered, roll one piece into a 13cm/5in round. Repeat with the remaining dough. Stack the pooris, layered between clear film.

4 Pour oil into a deep pan to a depth of 2.5cm/1in. Heat it to 180°C/350°F or until a cube of day-old bread, added to the oil, browns in about 45 seconds. Using a spatula, lift one poori and slide it into the oil; it will sink but will rise and begin to sizzle. Press the poori into the oil. It will puff up. Turn it over after a few seconds and cook for 20–30 seconds. Remove the poori from the pan and drain on kitchen paper. Keep warm in a preheated low oven while cooking the remaining pooris.

MISSI ROTIS

THESE FLAVOUR-PACKED UNLEAVENED BREADS ARE POPULAR IN NORTHERN INDIA. THEY ARE MADE WITH GRAM FLOUR, WHICH IS MILLED FROM CHANA DHAL, A TYPE OF CHICKPEA.

2 Mix in enough water to make a pliable, soft dough. Place the dough on a lightly floured surface and knead it until smooth, then place it in a lightly oiled bowl, cover with lightly oiled clear film (plastic wrap) and rest for 1 hour.

3 Transfer the dough to a lightly floured surface. Divide into 4 equal pieces and shape into balls. Roll out each ball of dough into a thick round, about 15–18cm/6–7in in diameter. Heat a griddle or heavy frying pan over a medium heat for a few minutes until it is hot.

4 Brush both sides of one roti with a little of the remaining oil or melted butter. Add it to the griddle or frying pan and cook for about 2 minutes, turning after 1 minute. Brush the cooked roti lightly with oil or melted butter again, slide it on to a plate and keep warm in a preheated low oven while cooking the remaining rotis in the same way. Serve warm.

MAKES FOUR

INGREDIENTS
115g/4oz/1 cup gram flour
115g/4oz/1 cup wholemeal (whole-wheat) flour
1 fresh green chilli, seeded and chopped
½ onion, finely chopped
15ml/1 tbsp chopped fresh coriander (cilantro)
2.5ml/½ tsp ground turmeric
2.5ml/½ tsp salt
45ml/3 tbsp oil or melted butter
120–150ml/4–5fl oz/½–⅔ cup lukewarm water

1 Mix the gram and wholemeal flours, chopped chilli, onion and coriander, ground turmeric and salt well together in a large bowl. Stir in 15ml/1 tbsp of the oil or melted butter.

VARIATION
Use 1.5–2.5ml/¼–½ tsp chilli powder instead of the fresh chilli.

MIXED SPICED NUTS

SPICE UP YOUR VERY OWN HAPPY HOUR WITH THESE SUPERB SNACKS. THEY ARE EXCELLENT WITH DRINKS.

SERVES FOUR TO SIX

INGREDIENTS
  75g/3oz/1 cup dried unsweetened
    coconut flakes
  75ml/5 tbsp groundnut (peanut) oil
  2.5ml/½ tsp hot chilli powder
  5ml/1 tsp paprika
  5ml/1 tsp tomato purée (paste)
  225g/8oz/2 cups unsalted
    cashew nuts
  225g/8oz/2 cups whole
    blanched almonds
  60ml/4 tbsp granulated sugar
  5ml/1 tsp ground cumin
  2.5ml/½ tsp salt
  ground black pepper
  fresh herbs, to garnish

1 Heat a wok, add the coconut flakes
and dry-fry until golden. Tip out on to a
plate and leave to cool.

COOK'S TIP
The nuts can be stored separately for up
to 1 month in an airtight tub.

2 Heat the wok again and add 45ml/
3 tbsp of the oil. When it is hot, add the
chilli powder, paprika and tomato purée.
Stir well, add the cashew nuts and
gently stir-fry until well coated. Drain,
season with pepper and leave to cool.

3 Wipe out the wok with kitchen paper,
heat it, then add the remaining oil.
When the oil is hot, add the almonds
and sprinkle in the sugar. Stir-fry gently
until the almonds are golden brown and
the sugar has caramelized. Place the
cumin and salt in a bowl. Add the hot
almonds, toss well, then leave to cool.

4 Either mix the cashew nuts, almonds
and coconut flakes together or serve
them in separate bowls. Garnish with
sprigs of fresh herbs such as parsley
and coriander.

RED-HOT ROOTS

*COLOURFUL AND CRISP CHIPS, MADE FROM A SELECTION OF ROOT VEGETABLES, TASTE DELICIOUS
WITH A LIGHT DUSTING OF CHILLI SEASONING. SERVE AS AN ACCOMPANIMENT OR AS A TASTY SNACK.*

SERVES FOUR TO SIX

INGREDIENTS
  1 carrot
  2 parsnips
  2 raw beetroot (beets)
  1 sweet potato
  groundnut (peanut) oil, for
    deep-frying
  1.5ml/¼ tsp hot chilli powder
  5ml/1 tsp sea salt flakes

1 Peel all the vegetables, then slice the
carrot and parsnips into long, thin
ribbons and the beetroot and sweet
potato into thin rounds. Pat dry all the
vegetable ribbons and rounds on
kitchen paper.

2 Half-fill a wok with oil. Heat it to
180°C/350°F or until a cube of day-old
bread, added to the oil, browns in about
45 seconds. Add the vegetable slices in
batches and deep-fry for 2–3 minutes
until golden and crisp. Remove and
drain on kitchen paper.

3 Place the chilli powder and sea salt in
a mortar and grind with a pestle to a
coarse powder. Pile up the vegetable
chips on a serving plate, sprinkle over
the spiced salt and serve immediately.

COOK'S TIP
To save time, you can slice the
vegetables using a mandoline or a food
processor fitted with a thin slicing disc.

CHILLI-SPICED PLANTAIN CHIPS

THIS SNACK HAS A LOVELY SWEET TASTE, WHICH IS BALANCED BY THE HEAT FROM THE CHILLI POWDER AND SAUCE. COOK THE CHIPS JUST BEFORE YOU INTEND TO SERVE THEM.

SERVES FOUR

INGREDIENTS
    2 large plantains with very
      dark skins
    groundnut (peanut) oil, for
      shallow-frying
    2.5ml/½ tsp hot chilli powder
    5ml/1 tsp ground cinnamon
    hot chilli sauce, to serve

1 Peel the plantains. Cut off and throw away the ends, then slice the fruit diagonally into rounds; do not make them too thin.

2 Pour the oil for frying into a small frying pan, to a depth of about 1cm/½in. Heat the oil until it is very hot, watching it closely all the time. Test by carefully adding a slice of plantain; it should float and the oil should immediately bubble up around it.

3 Fry the plantain slices in small batches or the temperature of the oil will drop. When they are golden brown, remove from the oil with a slotted spoon and drain on kitchen paper.

4 Mix the chilli powder with the cinnamon. Put the plantain chips on a serving plate, sprinkle them with the chilli and cinnamon mixture and serve immediately, with a small bowl of hot chilli sauce for dipping.

COOK'S TIP
Plantains are more starchy than the bananas to which they are related, and must be cooked before being eaten. When ready to eat, the skin is almost black.

POPCORN WITH LIME AND CHILLI

IF THE ONLY POPCORN YOU'VE HAD CAME OUT OF A CARTON AT THE CINEMA, TRY THIS MEXICAN SPECIALITY. THE LIME JUICE AND CHILLI POWDER ARE INSPIRED ADDITIONS, AND THE SNACK IS QUITE A HEALTHY CHOICE TO SERVE WITH DRINKS.

MAKES ONE LARGE BOWL

INGREDIENTS
    30ml/2 tbsp vegetable oil
    225g/8oz/1¼ cups corn kernels
      for popcorn
    10ml/2 tsp mild or hot chilli powder
    juice of 2 limes

1 Heat the oil in a large, heavy frying pan until it is very hot. Add the popcorn and immediately cover the pan with a lid and reduce the heat.

2 After a few minutes, the corn should start to pop. Resist the temptation to lift the lid to check. Shake the pan occasionally so that all the corn will be cooked and lightly browned.

3 When the sound of popping corn has stopped, quickly remove the pan from the heat and allow to cool slightly. Take off the lid and use a spoon to lift out and discard any corn kernels that have not popped. Any uncooked corn will have fallen to the base of the pan and will be inedible.

4 Add the chilli powder to the pan. Replace the lid firmly and shake the pan repeatedly to make sure that all of the corn is covered with a colourful dusting of chilli powder.

5 Tip the popcorn into a large bowl and keep warm. Sprinkle over the juice of the limes immediately prior to serving the popcorn.

Dips and snacks may whet the appetite, but it's the first

course that really determines whether a meal will go

with a swing. Play safe with a humdrum appetizer, and

you set the scene for a staid and sensible evening;

introduce chillies and there's no telling what could

happen! Whether you select a soup with a teasing

warmth that keeps everyone guessing as to its source, or

make a more blatant statement with something like

Peri-peri Prawns, conversation – and compliments –

will flow like wine.

Spicy Soups,
Appetizers
and Snacks

PROVENÇAL FISH SOUP WITH ROUILLE

AN AUTHENTIC CHILLI-SPIKED ROUILLE LIFTS THIS EXCELLENT SOUP INTO THE REALMS OF THE SUBLIME. A GOOD SOUP FOR A PARTY BECAUSE YOU CAN PREPARE IT ALL IN ADVANCE.

SERVES FOUR TO SIX

INGREDIENTS
    30ml/2 tbsp olive oil
    1 leek, sliced
    2 celery sticks, chopped
    1 onion, chopped
    2 garlic cloves, chopped
    4 ripe tomatoes, chopped
    15ml/1 tbsp tomato purée (paste)
    150ml/¼ pint/⅔ cup dry white wine
    1 bay leaf
    5ml/1 tsp saffron threads
    fish trimmings, bones and heads
    1kg/2¼lb mixed fish fillets and
       prepared shellfish
    salt and ground black pepper
    croûtons and grated (shredded)
       Gruyère cheese, to serve
For the rouille
    1 slice of white bread,
       crusts removed
    1 red (bell) pepper, cored, seeded
       and quartered
    1–2 fresh red chillies, seeded
       and chopped
    2 garlic cloves, roughly chopped
    olive oil (optional)

1 Make the rouille. Soak the bread in 30–45ml/2–3 tbsp cold water for 10 minutes. Meanwhile, grill (broil) the red pepper, skin side up, until the skin is charred and blistered. Put into a plastic bag and tie the top to keep the steam in. Leave until cool enough to handle. Peel off the skin. Drain the bread and squeeze out excess water.

2 Roughly chop the pepper quarters and place in a blender or food processor with the bread, chillies and garlic. Process to a fairly coarse paste, adding a little olive oil, if necessary. Scrape the rouille into a small bowl and set it aside.

COOK'S TIP
If you are preparing this soup in advance, cook it for the time stated then cool and chill as rapidly as possible. A fish soup should not be left simmering on top of the stove.

3 Heat the olive oil in a large pan. Add the leek, celery, onion and garlic. Cook gently for 10 minutes until soft. Add the tomatoes, tomato purée, wine, bay leaf, saffron and the fish trimmings. Bring to the boil, reduce the heat, cover and simmer for 30 minutes.

4 Strain through a colander into a clean pan, pressing out all the liquid. Cut the fish fillets into large chunks and add to the liquid, with the shellfish. Cover and simmer for 5–10 minutes until cooked.

5 Strain through a colander into a clean pan. Put half the cooked fish into a blender or food processor with about 300ml/½ pint/1¼ cups of the soup. Process for just long enough to blend, while retaining some texture.

6 Stir the processed mixture back into the remaining soup, then add the fish and shellfish from the colander, with salt and pepper to taste. Reheat gently. Serve the soup with the rouille, croûtons and cheese.

WARMING SPINACH AND RICE SOUP

THE CHILLI ADDS JUST A FLICKER OF FIRE TO THIS LIGHT AND FRESH-TASTING SOUP, MADE USING VERY YOUNG SPINACH LEAVES AND RISOTTO RICE.

SERVES FOUR

INGREDIENTS
   675g/1½lb fresh spinach, washed
   45ml/3 tbsp extra virgin olive oil
   1 small onion, finely chopped
   2 garlic cloves, finely chopped
   1 small fresh red chilli, seeded and
     finely chopped
   115g/4oz/generous ½ cup risotto rice
   1.2 litres/2 pints/5 cups
     vegetable stock
   60ml/4 tbsp grated (shredded)
     Pecorino cheese
   salt and ground black pepper

1 Place the spinach in a large pan with just the water that clings to its leaves. Add a pinch of salt. Heat until the spinach has wilted, then remove from the heat and drain, reserving any liquid.

2 Either chop the spinach finely using a large knife or place in a food processor and process briefly to achieve a fairly coarse purée.

3 Heat the oil in a large pan and gently cook the onion, garlic and chilli for 4–5 minutes until softened but not browned. Stir in the risotto rice until well coated with the mixture.

4 Pour in the stock and reserved spinach liquid. Bring to the boil, reduce the heat and simmer for 10 minutes.

5 Add the spinach, with salt and pepper to taste. Cook for 5–7 minutes more, until the rice is tender. Check the seasoning and serve in heated soup plates or bowls, with the Pecorino cheese sprinkled over.

PUMPKIN SOUP WITH ANIS

USE MILD CHILLIES FOR THIS TASTY SOUP, SO THAT THEY ACCENTUATE THE PUMPKIN FLAVOUR AND DO NOT MASK THE LIQUORICE TASTE OF THE ANISEED-FLAVOURED APERITIF.

SERVES FOUR

INGREDIENTS

    1 pumpkin, about 675g/1½lb
    30ml/2 tbsp olive oil
    2 large onions, sliced
    1 garlic clove, crushed
    2 fresh red chillies, seeded
      and chopped
    5ml/1 tsp curry paste
    1 litre/1¾ pints/4 cups vegetable or
      chicken stock
    15ml/1 tbsp Anis, Pernod, or aniseed
      (anise seed)-flavoured aperitif
    150ml/¼ pint/⅔ cup single
      (light) cream
    salt and ground black pepper

1 Peel the pumpkin with a sturdy knife, cutting the skin away from the flesh, remove the seeds and then chop the flesh roughly.

2 Heat the oil in a pan and fry the onions until golden. Stir in the garlic, chillies and curry paste. Cook for 1 minute, then add the chopped pumpkin and cook for 5 minutes more, stirring frequently to prevent browning.

3 Pour over the stock and season with salt and pepper. Bring to the boil, reduce the heat, cover and simmer for about 25 minutes.

4 Spoon about one-third of the soup into a blender or food processor, process until smooth, then scrape into a clean pan. Repeat with the remaining soup, processing it in 2 batches.

5 Add the anis and reheat. Taste and season if necessary with salt and pepper. Serve the soup in individual heated bowls, adding a spoonful of cream to each portion.

SPICED MUSSEL SOUP

CHUNKY AND COLOURFUL, THIS FISH SOUP HAS THE CONSISTENCY OF A CHOWDER. THE CHILLI FLAVOUR COMES FROM HARISSA, A SPICY SAUCE THAT IS POPULAR IN NORTH AFRICAN COOKING.

SERVES SIX

INGREDIENTS
  1.6kg/3½lb live mussels
  150ml/¼ pint/⅔ cup white wine
  3 tomatoes
  30ml/2 tbsp olive oil
  1 onion, finely chopped
  2 garlic cloves, crushed
  2 celery sticks, thinly sliced
  bunch of spring onions (scallions),
    thinly sliced
  1 potato, diced
  7.5ml/1½ tsp harissa
  45ml/3 tbsp chopped fresh parsley
  ground black pepper
  thick yogurt, to serve (optional)

1 Scrub the mussels and remove the beards, discarding any mussels that are damaged or that fail to close when tapped with a knife.

2 Bring the wine to the boil in a large pan. Add the mussels and cover tightly with a lid. Cook for 4–5 minutes until the mussels have opened. Drain the mussels, reserving the cooking liquid. Discard any mussels that remain closed. Reserve a few mussels in their shells for the garnish. Shell the rest.

3 Cut a small cross in the base of each tomato. Put them in a heatproof bowl and pour over boiling water. Leave for 30 seconds, then lift out and plunge into cold water. Drain, peel off the skins and dice the flesh. Heat the oil in a pan and fry the onion, garlic, celery and spring onions for 5 minutes.

COOK'S TIP
Harissa can be bought in tubes or jars. Stir it into salads or cooked vegetable dishes to give them a spicy lift.

4 Add the shelled mussels, reserved liquid, potato, harissa and tomatoes. Bring just to the boil, reduce the heat and cover. Simmer gently for about 25 minutes, or until the potatoes are beginning to break up.

5 Stir in the parsley and pepper, and add the reserved mussels, in their shells. Heat through for 1 minute. Serve with a spoonful of yogurt if you like.

SPICED RED LENTIL AND COCONUT SOUP

HOT, SPICY AND RICHLY FLAVOURED, THIS SUBSTANTIAL SOUP IS ALMOST A MEAL IN ITSELF. IF YOU ARE REALLY HUNGRY, SERVE IT WITH CHUNKS OF WARMED NAAN BREAD OR THICK SLICES OF TOAST.

SERVES FOUR

INGREDIENTS

   30ml/2 tbsp sunflower oil
   2 red onions, finely chopped
   1 bird's eye chilli, seeded and
     finely sliced
   2 garlic cloves, chopped
   1 lemon grass stalk, outer layers
     removed and inside finely sliced
   200g/7oz/scant 1 cup red lentils,
     rinsed and drained
   5ml/1 tsp ground coriander
   5ml/1 tsp paprika
   400ml/14fl oz/1⅔ cups
     coconut milk
   900ml/1½ pints/3¾ cups water
   juice of 1 lime
   3 spring onions (scallions), chopped
   20g/¾oz/½ cup fresh coriander
     (cilantro), finely chopped
   salt and ground black pepper

1 Heat the oil in a large pan and add the onions, chilli, garlic and lemon grass. Cook for 5 minutes or until the onions have softened but not browned, stirring occasionally.

COOK'S TIP
Bird's eye chillies may look insubstantial, but they pack quite a punch. Don't be tempted to add more unless you are a real chilli head!

2 Add the lentils and spices. Pour in the coconut milk and water, and stir. Bring to the boil, stir, then reduce the heat and simmer for 40–45 minutes or until the lentils are soft and mushy.

3 Stir in the lime juice and add the spring onions and fresh coriander, reserving a little of each for the garnish. Season, then ladle into heated bowls. Top with the reserved garnishes.

GAZPACHO WITH AVOCADO SALSA

CHILLIES IN A CHILLED SOUP MAKES AN UNUSUAL COMBINATION. CLASSIC GAZPACHO TASTES DELICIOUS WITH THE ADDITION OF CHILLI AND TABASCO. THE FLAVOURS ARE ECHOED IN THE SALSA.

SERVES FOUR

INGREDIENTS
    2 slices day-old bread
    600ml/1 pint/2½ cups chilled water
    1kg/2¼lb tomatoes
    1 cucumber
    1 red (bell) pepper, seeded
      and chopped
    1 fresh green chilli, seeded
      and chopped
    2 garlic cloves, chopped
    30ml/2 tbsp extra virgin olive oil
    juice of 1 lime and 1 lemon
    a few drops Tabasco sauce
    salt and ground black pepper
    8 ice cubes, to serve
    a handful of basil leaves, to garnish
For the croûtons
    2 slices day-old bread,
      crusts removed
    1 garlic clove, halved
    15ml/1 tbsp olive oil
For the avocado salsa
    1 ripe avocado
    5ml/1 tsp lemon juice
    2.5cm/1in piece cucumber, diced
    ½ fresh red chilli, seeded and
      finely chopped

1 Soak the bread in 150ml/¼ pint/ ⅔ cup of the chilled water for 5 minutes. Meanwhile, place the tomatoes in a bowl and cover with boiling water. Leave for 30 seconds, then peel, seed and chop the flesh.

2 Thinly peel the cucumber, then cut it in half lengthways and scoop out the seeds with a teaspoon. Discard the seeds and chop the flesh.

3 Place the bread (with any free liquid) in a food processor or blender. Add the tomatoes, cucumber, red pepper, chilli, garlic, olive oil, citrus juices and Tabasco then pour in the remaining 450ml/¾ pint/scant 2 cups chilled water. Blend until well combined but still chunky. Season to taste, pour into a bowl and chill in the refrigerator for 2–3 hours.

4 To make the croûtons, rub the slices of bread with the garlic clove. Cut the bread into cubes and place in a plastic bag with the olive oil. Seal the bag and shake until the bread cubes are evenly coated. Heat a large non-stick frying pan and fry the croûtons over a medium heat until crisp and golden.

5 Just before serving, make the salsa. Cut the avocado in half, remove the stone (pit), then peel and dice the flesh. Put it in a small bowl. Add the lemon juice, toss to prevent browning, then mix with the cucumber and chilli.

6 Ladle the soup into chilled bowls, add the ice cubes, and top each portion with a spoonful of the avocado salsa. Garnish with the basil and hand round the croûtons separately.

TORTILLA SOUP

THE SOUTH-WESTERN UNITED STATES STAKES ITS CLAIM TO THIS SIMPLE AND DELICIOUS SOUP, BUT IT PROBABLY ORIGINATED IN MEXICO, WHERE CONSIDERABLY HOTTER VERSIONS ARE POPULAR.

SERVES FOUR TO SIX

INGREDIENTS
    15ml/1 tbsp vegetable oil
    1 onion, finely chopped
    1 large garlic clove, crushed
    2 medium tomatoes, peeled, seeded
      and chopped
    2.5ml/½ tsp salt
    2 litres/3½ pints/8 cups
      chicken stock
    1 carrot, diced
    1 courgette (zucchini), diced
    1 skinless, boneless chicken breast
      portion, cooked and shredded
    1 fresh green chilli, seeded
      and chopped
To garnish
    4 corn tortillas
    oil, for frying
    1 small ripe avocado, peeled, stoned
      (pitted) and diced
    2 spring onions (scallions),
      finely chopped
    chopped fresh coriander (cilantro)
    grated Cheddar or Monterey Jack
      cheese (optional)

1 Heat the oil in a large pan and fry the onion and garlic over a medium heat for 5–8 minutes until softened. Stir in the tomatoes and salt, and cook for 5 minutes more.

2 Stir in the stock. Bring to the boil, then cover, reduce the heat and simmer for about 15 minutes.

COOK'S TIP
To make stock, put a chicken carcass in a large pan, add water to cover, 2 chopped onions, a stick of celery and some peppercorns. Bring to the boil, cover, simmer for 40 minutes then strain.

3 Meanwhile, for the garnish, trim the tortillas into squares, then cut into strips.

4 Pour oil into a frying pan to a depth of about 1cm/½in. Heat until hot but not smoking. Add the tortilla strips, in batches, and fry until just beginning to brown. Remove with a slotted spoon and drain on kitchen paper.

5 Add the carrot to the soup. Cook, covered, for 10 minutes. Add the courgette, chicken and chilli, and continue cooking for about 5 minutes, until the vegetables are just tender.

6 Divide the tortilla strips among 4–6 heated soup bowls. Sprinkle with the avocado. Ladle in the soup, then arrange spring onions and coriander on top. Serve with grated cheese if you like.

VARIATION
Parmesan balls make a nice alternative to shredded cheese. Grate 25g/1oz Parmesan and mix well with 2 egg yolks. When the soup is ready to serve, drop half teaspoons of the mixture all over the surface. Leave for 2–3 minutes or until just firm, then serve.

VEGETABLE SOUP WITH CHILLI AND COCONUT

ALL OVER AFRICA, CHILLIES PLAY AN IMPORTANT PART IN THE CUISINE. IN THIS HEARTY VEGETABLE SOUP, CHILLI IS PARTNERED WITH OTHER WARMING SPICES.

SERVES FOUR

INGREDIENTS
 ½ red onion
 175g/6oz each of turnip, sweet
  potato and pumpkin
 30ml/2 tbsp butter
 5ml/1 tsp dried marjoram
 2.5ml/½ tsp ground ginger
 1.5ml/¼ tsp ground cinnamon
 15ml/1 tbsp chopped spring
  onion (scallion)
 1 litre/1¾ pint/4 cups well-flavoured
  vegetable stock
 30ml/2 tbsp flaked (sliced) almonds
 1 fresh red chilli, seeded
  and chopped
 5ml/1 tsp granulated sugar
 25g/1oz creamed coconut
  (coconut cream)
 salt and ground black pepper
 chopped fresh coriander (cilantro),
  to garnish (optional)

1 Finely chop the onion, then peel the turnip, sweet potato and pumpkin and cut into 1cm/½in dice.

2 Melt the butter in a large non-stick pan. Fry the onion for 4–5 minutes. Add the diced vegetables and fry for 3–4 minutes.

3 Stir in the marjoram, ginger, cinnamon and spring onion with salt and pepper to taste. Fry over a low heat for about 10 minutes, stirring frequently.

COOK'S TIP
Choose young small turnips. The flavour will have a nutty sweetness.

4 Pour in the vegetable stock and add the almonds, chopped chilli and sugar. Stir well to mix, then cover and simmer gently for 10–15 minutes until the vegetables are just tender.

5 Grate the creamed coconut into the soup and stir gently to mix. Sprinkle with the chopped coriander, if you like, and spoon into heated bowls and serve.

Thai Chicken <u>and</u> Chilli Soup

This aromatic soup is rich with coconut milk and intensely flavoured with galangal, which is mildly peppery and gingery, together with lemon grass and kaffir lime leaves.

SERVES FOUR TO SIX

INGREDIENTS

   4 lemon grass stalks, trimmed and
     outer leaves discarded
   2 × 400ml/14fl oz/1⅔ cup cans
     coconut milk
   475ml/16fl oz/2 cups chicken stock
   2.5cm/1in piece galangal
   2 fresh red chillies
   10 black peppercorns, crushed
   10 kaffir lime leaves, torn
   300g/11oz skinless, boneless chicken
     breast portions, cut into thin strips
   115g/4oz/1½ cups button
     (white) mushrooms
   50g/2oz/½ cup baby corn cobs,
     quartered lengthways
   60ml/4 tbsp lime juice
   45ml/3 tbsp Thai fish sauce (*nam pla*)
   chopped spring onions (scallions)
     and fresh coriander (cilantro)
     leaves, to garnish

1 Cut off the lower 5cm/2in from each lemon grass stalk and chop it finely. Bruise the remaining pieces of stalk. Bring the coconut milk and chicken stock to the boil in a large pan. Peel and thinly slice the galangal. Seed and finely chop the chillies. Add all the lemon grass, the galangal and half the chopped chillies, then stir in the peppercorns and half the lime leaves, lower the heat and simmer gently for 10 minutes. Strain into a clean pan.

2 Return the soup to the heat, then add the chicken, mushrooms and the quartered baby corn cobs. Bring to the boil, then lower the heat and simmer for 5–7 minutes or until the chicken is cooked.

3 Stir in the lime juice and fish sauce, then add the remaining lime leaves. Serve hot, garnished with the remaining chopped chillies and the spring onions and coriander.

Hot-and-sour Shellfish Soup

This is a classic Thai shellfish soup – Tom Yam Kung. The balance of flavours is what counts, so you may want to start with half the chillies and add more to taste.

SERVES FOUR TO SIX

INGREDIENTS

   450g/1lb raw king prawns (jumbo
     shrimp), thawed if frozen
   1 litre/1¾ pints/4 cups chicken stock
     or water
   3 lemon grass stalks, trimmed
   10 kaffir lime leaves, torn in half
   225g/8oz can straw mushrooms
   45ml/3 tbsp Thai fish sauce
     (*nam pla*)
   60ml/4 tbsp lime juice
   30ml/2 tbsp chopped spring
     onion (scallion)
   15ml/1 tbsp fresh coriander
     (cilantro) leaves
   4 fresh red chillies, seeded and
     thinly sliced
   salt and ground black pepper

1 Shell the prawns, putting the shells in a colander. Devein the prawns and set them aside. Rinse the shells under cold water, drain, then put in a large pan with the stock or water. Bring to the boil.

2 Bruise the lemon grass stalks and add them to the stock with half the lime leaves. Simmer gently for 5–6 minutes.

3 Strain the stock, return it to the clean pan and reheat. Drain the straw mushrooms and add them with the prawns. Cook until the prawns turn pink. Stir in the fish sauce, lime juice, spring onion, coriander, chillies and the remaining lime leaves. Taste and adjust the seasoning. The soup should be sour, salty, spicy and hot.

PIQUANT PUMPKIN AND COCONUT SOUP

WHEN THERE ARE PLENTY OF PUMPKINS ABOUT, SOUP SEEMS THE OBVIOUS ANSWER. THIS THAI VERSION IS A LITTLE OUT-OF-THE-ORDINARY AND TASTES SUPERB.

2 Pour the chicken stock into a large pan. Bring it to the boil, add the ground paste and stir gently to blend it into the stock.

3 Add the pumpkin and simmer for about 10–15 minutes or until the pumpkin is tender.

4 Stir in the creamed coconut, then bring back to a simmer. Add the Thai fish sauce, sugar and ground black pepper to taste.

5 Add the prawns and cook until they are heated through. Serve in heated soup bowls, each one garnished with the finely sliced red chillies and whole basil leaves.

SERVES FOUR TO SIX

INGREDIENTS
    1 lemon grass stalk
    2 garlic cloves, crushed
    4 shallots, finely chopped
    2.5ml/½ tsp shrimp paste
    15ml/1 tbsp dried shrimps, soaked in
      water for 10 minutes and drained
    2 fresh green chillies, seeded
    salt, to taste
    600ml/1 pint/2½ cups chicken stock
    450g/1lb pumpkin, cut into
      2cm/¾ in chunks
    600ml/1 pint/2½ cups creamed
      coconut (coconut cream)
    30ml/2 tbsp Thai fish sauce
      (*nam pla*)
    5ml/1 tsp granulated sugar
    8–12 small cooked peeled
      prawns (shrimp)
    ground black pepper
    2 fresh red chillies, seeded and
      finely sliced, to garnish
    10–12 fresh basil leaves, to garnish

1 Cut off the lower 5cm/2in of the lemon grass stalk and chop it roughly. Put it in a mortar and add the garlic, shallots, shrimp paste, dried shrimps, green chillies and salt. Grind to a paste.

COOK'S TIPS
• Chillies freeze very well and break down much more easily than fresh ones, so are perfect for pastes.
• Add salt to this soup with care. The shrimps will have been lightly salted before drying, and the shrimp paste and fish sauce may also be salty.

HOT <u>AND</u> SPICY MISO BROTH <u>WITH</u> TOFU

THE JAPANESE EAT MISO BROTH, A SIMPLE BUT HIGHLY NUTRITIOUS SOUP, ALMOST EVERY DAY — IT IS STANDARD BREAKFAST FARE AND IT IS EATEN WITH RICE OR NOODLES LATER IN THE DAY.

SERVES FOUR

INGREDIENTS

    1 bunch of spring onions (scallions)
      or 5 baby leeks
    15g/½oz/⅓ cup fresh
      coriander (cilantro)
    3 thin slices fresh root ginger
    2 star anise
    1 small dried red chilli
    1.2 litres/2 pints/5 cups dashi stock
      or vegetable stock
    225g/8oz pak choi (bok choy) or
      other Asian greens, thickly sliced
    200g/7oz firm tofu, cut into
      2.5cm/1in squares
    45–60ml/3–4 tbsp red miso
    30–45ml/2–3 tbsp Japanese soy
      sauce (shoyu)
    1 fresh red chilli, seeded
      and shredded

1 Cut the coarse green tops off half of the spring onions or leeks and place in a pan with the coriander stalks, ginger, star anise and dried chilli. Pour in the dashi or vegetable stock. Heat gently until boiling, then simmer for 10 minutes. Strain, return to the pan and reheat until simmering.

2 Slice the remaining spring onions or leeks finely on the diagonal and add the green portion to the soup with the pak choi or greens and squares of tofu. Cook for 2 minutes.

3 Mix 45ml/3 tbsp of the miso with a little of the hot soup in a bowl, then stir it into the soup. Taste the soup and add more miso with soy sauce to taste.

4 Coarsely chop the coriander leaves and stir most of them into the soup with the white part of the spring onions or leeks. Cook for 1 minute, then ladle the soup into heated serving bowls. Sprinkle with the remaining chopped coriander and the shredded fresh red chilli and serve immediately.

COOK'S TIPS

• Dashi powder is available in most Asian and Chinese stores. Alternatively, make your own by gently simmering 10–15cm/4–6in kombu seaweed in 1.2 litres/2 pints/5 cups water for 10 minutes. Do not boil the stock vigorously as this would make the dashi bitter. Remove the kombu, then add 15g/½oz dried bonito flakes and bring to the boil. Strain immediately through a fine sieve.

• Kombu seaweed is usually dried, pickled or shaved thinly in dry sheets. Wash dried Kombu before using.

• Red miso is a paste made from fermented beans and grains. Buy it from Asian food stores. It will keep almost indefinitely in an airtight container in the refrigerator.

CHORIZO IN OLIVE OIL

SPANISH CHORIZO SAUSAGE HAS A DELICIOUSLY PUNGENT CHILLI TASTE. FRYING CHORIZO WITH ONIONS AND OLIVE OIL IS ONE OF ITS SIMPLEST AND MOST DELICIOUS USES.

SERVES FOUR

INGREDIENTS
    75ml/5 tbsp extra virgin
      olive oil
    350g/12oz chorizo, sliced
    1 large onion, thinly sliced
    fresh flat leaf parsley, to garnish
    warm crusty bread, to serve

1 Heat the olive oil in a medium frying pan and fry the sliced chorizo sausage over a high heat until beginning to colour around the edges. Remove the sausage from the pan with a slotted spoon and set aside.

COOK'S TIPS
• The robust seasoning of garlic, chilli and paprika used in chorizo flavours the ingredients it is cooked with, so there is no need to add extra flavouring.
• A mezzaluna is a handy alternative to a knife and is used with a seesaw motion.

2 Add the thinly sliced onion to the pan and fry for about 10–15 minutes until softened and golden brown. The longer you cook them, the more mellow their flavour will be.

3 Return the chorizo sausage slices to the frying pan and cook for 1 minute more to heat them through thoroughly.

4 Roughly chop the fresh parsley using a sharp knife or mezzaluna.

5 Tip the mixture into a warmed, shallow serving dish and sprinkle over the chopped flat leaf parsley. Serve at once while they are hot, with warm crusty bread.

VARIATION
Chorizo is usually available in large supermarkets or delicatessens. Other similarly rich, spicy sausages can be used instead.

CHILLI AND GARLIC PRAWNS

FOR THIS SIMPLE SPANISH TAPAS DISH, YOU REALLY NEED FRESH SHELLFISH THAT WILL ABSORB THE FLAVOUR OF THE GARLIC AND CHILLI WHILE BEING FRIED.

SERVES FOUR

INGREDIENTS
    350–450g/12oz–1lb raw king prawns
      (jumbo shrimp)
    2 fresh red fresno or serrano chillies
    75ml/5 tbsp olive oil
    3 garlic cloves, crushed
    salt and ground black pepper
    crusty bread, to serve

1 Remove the heads and shells from the prawns, leaving the tails intact.

COOK'S TIP
Have everything ready for last minute cooking so that it is served still sizzling.

2 Cut each fresno or serrano chilli in half lengthways. Scrape out and discard all the seeds. Heat the olive oil in a flameproof dish, suitable for serving. (Alternatively, use a frying pan and have a warmed serving dish ready in a preheated oven.)

3 Add all the prawns, chillies and crushed garlic to the pan and cook over a high heat for about 3 minutes, stirring until the prawns turn pink. Season lightly with salt and pepper and serve immediately with crusty bread to mop up the juices.

FLASH-FRIED SQUID WITH PAPRIKA AND GARLIC

THESE QUICK-FRIED SQUID ARE GOOD SERVED WITH A DRY SHERRY OR MANZANILLA AS AN APPETIZER OR AS PART OF MIXED TAPAS. FOR A FIRST COURSE, SERVE THEM ON A BED OF SALAD LEAVES.

SERVES FOUR TO SIX

INGREDIENTS
500g/1¼lb very small squid, cleaned
90ml/6 tbsp olive oil
1 fresh red chilli, seeded and
  finely chopped
10ml/2 tsp Spanish mild smoked
  paprika (*pimentón dulce*)
30ml/2 tbsp plain (all-purpose) flour
2 garlic cloves, finely chopped
15ml/1 tbsp sherry vinegar
5ml/1 tsp shredded lemon rind
30–45ml/2–3 tbsp finely chopped
  fresh parsley
salt and ground black pepper
salad leaves, to serve (optional)

1 Choose small squid that are no longer than 10cm/4in. Cut the body sacs into rings and cut the tentacles into bitesize pieces.

2 Place the squid in a bowl and add 30ml/2 tbsp of the oil, half the chilli and the paprika. Season with a little salt and some pepper, cover and marinate for 2–4 hours in the refrigerator.

COOK'S TIPS
• Make sure the wok or pan is very hot, as the squid should cook for only 1–2 minutes: any longer and it will begin to toughen.
• Smoked paprika, known as *pimentón dulce* in Spain, has a wonderful smoky flavour. If you cannot find it, use mild paprika, which should be described as such on the packet.

3 Heat the remaining oil in a preheated wok or fairly deep frying pan over a high heat until very hot. Toss the squid in the flour and divide it into 2 batches. Add the first batch of squid to the wok or frying pan and stir-fry quickly, turning the squid constantly for 1–2 minutes, or until the squid rings become opaque and the tentacles have curled.

4 Sprinkle in half the garlic. Stir to mix then turn out on to a plate and keep warm. Repeat the stir-frying with the second batch of squid and garlic.

5 Sprinkle the sherry vinegar, lemon rind, remaining chilli and parsley over the squid. Taste for seasoning and serve hot or cool, on a bed of salad leaves, if you like.

CARIBBEAN CHILLI CRAB CAKES

CRAB MEAT MAKES WONDERFUL FISH CAKES, AS EVIDENCED WITH THESE GUTSY MORSELS. THE RICH, SPICY TOMATO DIP IS DELICIOUS, BUT YOU COULD ALSO SERVE A FRESH TOMATO AND CHILLI SALSA.

MAKES ABOUT FIFTEEN

INGREDIENTS
    225g/8oz white crab meat (fresh, frozen or canned)
    115g/4oz cooked floury potatoes, mashed
    30ml/2 tbsp fresh herb seasoning
    2.5ml/½ tsp mild mustard
    2.5ml/½ tsp ground black pepper
    ½ fresh hot chilli, seeded and finely chopped
    5ml/1 tsp chopped fresh oregano
    1 egg, beaten
    plain (all-purpose) flour, for dredging
    vegetable oil, for frying
    lime wedges, coriander (cilantro) sprigs and fresh whole chillies, to garnish
For the tomato dip
    15g/½oz/1 tbsp butter
    ½ onion, finely chopped
    2 drained canned plum tomatoes, chopped
    1 garlic clove, crushed
    150ml/¼ pint/⅔ cup water
    5–10ml/1–2 tsp malt vinegar
    15ml/1 tbsp chopped fresh coriander (cilantro)
    ½ fresh chilli, seeded and chopped

1 To make the crab cakes, mix the crab meat, potatoes, herb seasoning, mustard, pepper, chilli, oregano and egg in a large bowl. Chill the mixture in the bowl for at least 30 minutes.

COOK'S TIP
Use French Dijon mustard for this dish as it is not as overpowering as English.

2 Meanwhile, make the tomato dip. Melt the butter in a small pan and sauté the onion, tomatoes and garlic for about 5 minutes until the onion is tender. Add the water, vinegar, coriander and fresh chilli. Bring to the boil, then reduce the heat and simmer for 10 minutes.

3 Pour the mixture into a blender or food processor and blend to a smooth purée. Scrape into a pan or bowl. Keep warm or chill.

4 Preheat the oven. Using a spoon, shape the crab mixture into rounds and dredge with flour, shaking off the excess. Heat a little oil in a frying pan and fry, a few at a time, for 2–3 minutes on each side. Drain the crab cakes on kitchen paper and keep warm in a low oven while cooking the remainder.

5 Garnish with lime wedges, coriander sprigs and whole chillies. Serve with the tomato dip.

PERI-PERI PRAWNS WITH AIOLI

THE NAME PERI-PERI REFERS TO THE SMALL, EXTREMELY HOT ANGOLAN CHILLIES FROM WHICH THIS
PORTUGUESE DISH IS TRADITIONALLY MADE. ANY SMALL HOT CHILLI CAN BE USED INSTEAD.

SERVES FOUR

INGREDIENTS
    1 fresh red chilli (such as bird's eye),
        seeded and finely chopped
    2.5ml/½ tsp paprika
    2.5ml/½ tsp ground coriander
    1 garlic clove, crushed
    juice of ½ lime
    30ml/2 tbsp olive oil
    20 large raw prawns (shrimp) in
        shells, heads removed and deveined
    salt and ground black pepper
    whole chillies, to garnish (optional)
For the aioli (quick method)
    150ml/¼ pint/⅔ cup mayonnaise
    2 garlic cloves, crushed
    5ml/1 tsp Dijon mustard
For the aioli (classic method)
    2 egg yolks
    2 crushed garlic cloves
    5ml/1 tsp granulated sugar
    5ml/1 tsp Dijon mustard
    10ml/2 tsp lemon juice
    250ml/8fl oz/1 cup mixed olive oil
        and sunflower oil

1 To make the aioli by the quick method, mix the mayonnaise, garlic and mustard in a small bowl and set aside. For the classic method, put the egg yolks in a blender or food processor and add the garlic, sugar, mustard and lemon juice. Process until mixed, then, with the motor running, add the oil through the hole in the lid or feeder tube, drip by drip at first, then in a steady stream, until all the oil has been added and the aioli is smooth.
Any dish that contains raw egg should not be served to young children, pregnant women or the elderly.

2 Make a peri-peri marinade by mixing the chilli, paprika, coriander, garlic, lime juice and olive oil in a non-metallic bowl. Add salt and pepper to taste. Pour over the prawns and mix well. Cover and leave in a cool place to marinate for 30 minutes, turning the prawns in the mixture from time to time.

3 Thread the prawns on to metal skewers and cook under the grill (broiler) or on the barbecue, basting and turning frequently, for 6–8 minutes until pink. Serve with the aioli, garnished with extra chillies, if you like.

FIENDISH FRITTERS

THESE DELECTABLE FRITTERS COME FROM THE PHILIPPINES. UNUSUALLY, THEY ARE FIRST SHALLOW FRIED, THEN DEEP-FRIED. EAT THEM FRESH FROM THE PAN, DIPPED IN THE PIQUANT SAUCE.

SERVES TWO TO FOUR

INGREDIENTS

   16 raw prawns (shrimp),
     in the shell
   225g/8oz/2 cups plain
     (all-purpose) flour
   5ml/1 tsp baking powder
   2.5ml/½ tsp salt
   1 egg, beaten
   1 small sweet potato
   1 garlic clove, crushed
   115g/4oz/2 cups beansprouts,
     soaked in cold water for
     10 minutes and well drained
   vegetable oil, for shallow and
     deep-frying
   4 spring onions
     (scallions), chopped
For the dipping sauce
   1 jumbo garlic clove, sliced
   45ml/3 tbsp rice or
     wine vinegar
   15–30ml/1–2 tbsp water
   salt, to taste
   6–8 small fresh red chillies

1 Mix together all the 5 ingredients for the dipping sauce and divide between 2–4 small wide bowls. The garlic slices and whole chillies will float on top.

2 Put the prawns in a pan with cold water to cover. Bring to the boil,reduce the heat and then simmer for about 4–5 minutes or until the prawns are pink and tender when pierced with the tip of a sharp knife. Lift them out with a slotted spoon and drain well. Discard the heads and the body shell, but leave the tails on. Strain and reserve the cooking liquid. Set aside and leave to cool.

VARIATIONS
• Use cooked tiger prawns (jumbo shrimp) if you prefer. In this case, make the batter using ready-made fish stock or chicken stock.
• You could substitute 15ml/1 tbsp very finely sliced fresh ginger for the garlic in the dipping sauce, if you like.

3 Sift the flour, baking powder and salt into a bowl. Add the beaten egg and about 300ml/½ pint/1¼ cups of the reserved prawn stock and beat to make a batter that has the consistency of double (heavy) cream.

4 Peel the sweet potato and grate it coarsely. Add it to the batter, then stir in the crushed garlic. Pat the beansprouts dry in kitchen paper and add to the batter.

5 Pour the oil for shallow frying into a large frying pan. It should be about 5mm/¼in deep. Pour more oil into a wok for deep-frying. Heat the oil in the frying pan. Taking a generous spoonful of the batter, drop it carefully into the frying pan so that it spreads out to a fritter about 10cm/4in across.

6 Add more batter to the pan but do not let the fritters touch. As soon as the fritters have set, top each one with a single prawn and a few pieces of chopped spring onion. Continue to cook over a medium heat for 1 minute, then remove with a spatula.

7 Heat the oil in the wok to 190°C/375°F and deep-fry the fritters in batches until they are crisp and golden brown. Drain on kitchen paper and then arrange on a serving plate or platter. Serve with the dipping sauce.

CEVICHE

FRESH FISH IS "COOKED" BY BEING MARINATED IN A MIXTURE OF MANGO, LIME JUICE AND CHILLIES. THE RESULT IS AN APPETIZER WITH A WONDERFULLY FRESH FLAVOUR.

SERVES SIX

INGREDIENTS
    350g/12oz medium cooked
        prawns (shrimp)
    350g/12oz scallops, removed from
        their shells, with corals intact
    2 tomatoes, about 175g/6oz
    1 red onion, finely chopped
    1 small mango
    350g/12oz salmon fillet
    1 fresh red chilli
    12 limes
    30ml/2 tbsp caster (superfine) sugar
    2 pink grapefruit
    3 oranges
    salt and ground black pepper
    lime slices, to garnish (optional)

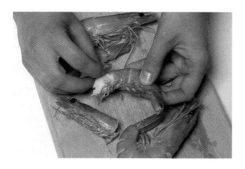

1 Peel the prawns and place them in a large bowl. Cut the scallop meat into 1cm/½in dice. Add it to the bowl.

2 Dice the tomatoes. Peel the mango and cut off a thick slice close to the flat side of the stone (pit). Repeat on the other side. Score the flesh with criss-cross lines, then fold the slices inside out so the dice stand proud of the skin. Slice these off the skin and into a bowl.

3 Skin the salmon, if necessary, then cut it into small pieces.Slit the chilli and scrape out and discard the seeds. Dice the flesh. Add the tomatoes, mango, salmon, chilli and onion to the shellfish in the bowl.

4 Squeeze 8 of the limes and add the juice to the bowl, with the sugar and seasoning. Stir, cover and leave the ceviche to marinate for 3 hours in the refrigerator.

5 Segment the grapefruit, oranges and remaining limes. Drain off as much excess lime juice as possible from the marinated fish and gently fold in the fruit segments. Season to taste and arrange on a platter. Garnish with lime slices, if you like. Serve immediately.

COOK'S TIP
Take very special care in choosing the fish for this dish; it must be very fresh and served on the day it is prepared.

THAI-STYLE MARINATED SALMON

MADE IN A SIMILAR FASHION TO THE SCANDINAVIAN SPECIALITY, GRAVLAX, THIS IS A WONDERFUL WAY OF PREPARING SALMON. START THE PREPARATION TWO TO FIVE DAYS BEFORE YOU INTEND TO EAT IT.

SERVES FOUR TO SIX

INGREDIENTS
tail piece of 1 salmon, about
  675g/1½lb, cleaned and prepared
  (see below)
20ml/4 tsp coarse sea salt
20ml/4 tsp granulated sugar
2.5cm/1in piece fresh root
  ginger, grated (shredded)
2 lemon grass stalks
4 kaffir lime leaves, finely chopped
  or shredded
grated (shredded) rind of
  1 kaffir lime
1 fresh red chilli, seeded and
  finely chopped
5ml/1 tsp black peppercorns,
  coarsely crushed
30ml/2 tbsp chopped fresh coriander
  (cilantro), plus sprigs to garnish
wedges of kaffir lime, to garnish
For the dressing
150ml/¼ pint/⅔ cup mayonnaise
juice of ½ lime
10ml/2 tsp chopped fresh
  coriander (cilantro)

1 Ask your fishmonger to scale the fish and remove the skin, splitting the fish lengthways to remove it from the backbone in 2 matching fillets. Use tweezers to remove all the bones from the salmon.

2 In a bowl, mix together the salt, sugar and ginger. Remove the outer leaves from the lemon grass and slice the inner portion finely. Add to the bowl, with the lime leaves, lime rind, chilli, peppercorns and coriander.

3 Place one-quarter of the spice mixture in a shallow dish. Place one salmon fillet, skin-side down, on top of the spices. Spread two-thirds of the remaining mixture over the flesh then place the remaining fillet on top, flesh-side down. Arrange the rest of the spice mixture over the fish.

COOK'S TIP
Kaffir lime leaves and the rind of the fruit are very aromatic and a distinctive feature of Thai cooking. They should be available from Asian food stores. If not, substitute ordinary limes.

4 Cover the fish with foil, then place a board on top. Add some weights, such as clean cans of food. Chill for 2–5 days, turning the fish each day in the spicy marinade to ensure that the flavour permeates all parts of the fish.

5 Make the dressing by mixing the mayonnaise, lime juice and chopped coriander in a bowl.

6 Scrape the spices off the fish. Slice it as thinly as possible. Serve with the lime dressing, garnished with fresh coriander and wedges of kaffir lime.

PAN-STEAMED CHILLI MUSSELS

IF YOU CAN TAKE THE HEAT, USE BIRD'S EYE CHILLIES FOR THIS SIMPLE DISH, OR SUBSTITUTE ONE RED CAYENNE OR TWO RED FRESNO CHILLIES. THE LEMON GRASS ADDS A REFRESHING TANG.

2 Cut off the lower 5cm/2in of each lemon grass stalk and chop finely. Add to the pan, with the shallots, kaffir lime leaves, chillies, Thai fish sauce and lime juice.

3 Cover the pan with a lid and place it over medium-high heat. Steam for 5–7 minutes, shaking the pan occasionally, until the mussels open. Discard any of the mussels that have not opened.

SERVES FOUR TO SIX

INGREDIENTS
   1kg/2¼lb live mussels
   2 lemon grass stalks
   4 shallots, chopped
   4 kaffir lime leaves, roughly torn
   1–2 fresh red chillies, seeded
     and sliced
   15ml/1 tbsp Thai fish sauce
     (*nam pla*)
   30ml/2 tbsp lime juice
   2 spring onions (scallions), chopped,
     to garnish
   coriander (cilantro) leaves,
     to garnish

1 Scrub the mussels and remove the beards, discarding any mussels that are damaged or that fail to close when tapped with a knife. Place in a large heavy pan.

4 Using a slotted spoon, transfer the cooked mussels to a serving dish, along with any liquid that has been produced. Garnish with chopped spring onions and coriander leaves. Serve immediately.

SPICY SHELLFISH WONTONS

THESE TASTY WONTONS LOOK A BIT LIKE TORTELLINI BUT THE TASTE IS MORE THAI THAN TRIESTE. WATER CHESTNUTS ADD A LIGHT CRUNCH TO THE CRAB AND CHILLI FILLING.

SERVES FOUR

INGREDIENTS
 225g/8oz raw prawns (shrimp),
  peeled and deveined
 115g/4oz white crab meat,
  picked over
 4 drained canned water chestnuts,
  finely diced
 1 spring onion (scallion),
  finely chopped
 1 small fresh green chilli, seeded and
  finely chopped
 1.5ml/¼ tsp grated (shredded) fresh
  root ginger
 1 egg, separated
 20–24 wonton wrappers
 salt and ground black pepper
 coriander (cilantro) leaves, to garnish
For the dressing
 30ml/2 tbsp rice vinegar
 15ml/1 tbsp chopped pickled ginger
 90ml/6 tbsp olive oil
 15ml1/ tbsp soy sauce
 45ml/3 tbsp chopped
  coriander (cilantro)
 30ml/2 tbsp diced red (bell) pepper

1 Finely dice the prawns and place them in a bowl. Stir in the next 5 ingredients and the egg white. Season with salt and pepper and mix well.

2 Place a wonton wrapper on a board. Put about 5ml/1 tsp of the filling just above the centre of the wrapper. With a pastry brush, moisten the edges of the wrapper with a little of the egg yolk. Bring the bottom of the wrapper up over the filling. Press gently to expel any air, then seal neatly in a triangle.

3 For a more elaborate shape, bring the 2 side points up over the filling, overlap the points and pinch the ends firmly together. Space the filled wontons on a large baking sheet lined with greaseproof (waxed) paper, so that they do not stick together.

4 Half-fill a large pan with water. Bring to simmering point. Add the filled wontons, a few at a time, and simmer for 2–3 minutes. The wontons will float to the surface and when they are cooked and ready to remove, the wrappers will be translucent and the filling cooked. Remove the wontons with a large slotted spoon, drain them briefly, then spread them on trays. Keep warm while cooking the remaining wontons.

5 Make the dressing by whisking all the ingredients together in a bowl. Divide the warm wontons among 4 serving dishes, drizzle with the spicy dressing and serve garnished with a handful of coriander leaves.

SPICED SCALLOPS IN THEIR SHELLS

SCALLOPS ARE EXCELLENT STEAMED. WHEN SERVED WITH THIS SPICY GINGER AND CHILLI SAUCE, THEY MAKE A DELICIOUS APPETIZER. EACH PERSON SPOONS SAUCE ON TO THE SCALLOPS BEFORE EATING.

SERVES FOUR

INGREDIENTS
 8 scallops, shelled (ask the
  fishmonger to reserve the cupped
  side of 4 shells)
 2 slices fresh root ginger, shredded
 1 garlic clove, shredded
 2 spring onions (scallions), green
  parts only, shredded
 salt and ground black pepper
For the sauce
 1 garlic clove, crushed
 15ml/1 tbsp grated (shredded) fresh
  root ginger
 2 spring onions (scallions), white
  parts only, chopped
 1–2 fresh green chillies, seeded and
  finely chopped
 15ml/1 tbsp light soy sauce
 15ml/1 tbsp dark soy sauce
 10ml/2 tsp sesame oil

1 Remove the dark beard-like fringe and tough muscle from the scallops. Leave the corals attached.

COOK'S TIPS
• When the fishmonger is preparing the scallops, ask for the gills and mantle to use in soup or stock.
• If you do not have a bamboo steamer, you can use a flat-based stainless steel steamer or flour sifter.

2 Place 2 scallops in each shell. Season lightly with salt and pepper, then sprinkle the ginger, garlic and spring onion green on top. Place the shells in a bamboo steamer and steam for about 6 minutes until the scallops look opaque (you may do this in batches).

3 Meanwhile, make the sauce. Mix the garlic and ginger in a bowl and stir in the white parts of the spring onions. Add the chillies, both soy sauces and the sesame oil. Stir well and set aside.

4 Carefully remove each shell from the steamer, taking care not to spill the juices, and arrange them on a serving plate with the sauce bowl in the centre. Serve immediately.

MUSSELS IN CHILLI AND BLACK BEAN SAUCE

THE LARGE GREEN-SHELLED MUSSELS FROM NEW ZEALAND ARE PERFECT FOR THIS DELICIOUS DISH.
BUY THE COOKED MUSSELS ON THE HALF-SHELL — IT IS AN ELEGANT WAY TO SERVE THEM.

2 Remove the sauce from the heat and stir in the sesame oil and soy sauce. Mix thoroughly.

3 Have ready a bamboo steamer or a pan holding 5cm/2in of simmering water, and fitted with a metal trivet. Place the mussels in a single layer on a heatproof plate that will fit inside the steamer or pan. Spoon over the sauce.

SERVES FOUR

INGREDIENTS
    15ml/1 tbsp vegetable oil
    2.5cm/1in piece of fresh root ginger,
      finely chopped
    2 garlic clove, finely chopped
    1 fresh red chilli, seeded
      and chopped
    15ml/1 tbsp black bean sauce
    15ml/1 tbsp dry sherry
    5ml/1 tsp granulated sugar
    5ml/1 tsp sesame oil
    10ml/2 tsp dark soy sauce
    20 cooked New Zealand green-
      shelled mussels
    2 spring onions (scallions),
      1 shredded and 1 cut into fine rings

1 Heat the vegetable oil in a pan or wok. Fry the ginger, garlic and chilli with the black bean sauce for a few seconds, then add the sherry and sugar and cook for 30 seconds more, stirring with cooking chopsticks or a wooden spoon to ensure the sugar is dissolved.

4 Sprinkle all the spring onions over the mussels. Place in the steamer or cover the plate tightly with foil and place it on the trivet in the pan. It should be just above the level of the water. Cover and steam over a high heat for about 10 minutes or until the mussels have heated through. Serve immediately.

CHILLI CRABS

EAT THESE CRABS SINGAPOREAN STYLE, WITH THE FINGERS. GIVE GUESTS CRAB CRACKERS FOR THE CLAWS AND HAVE SOME FINGER BOWLS OR HOT TOWELS TO HAND AS THE MEAL WILL BE MESSY!

SERVES FOUR

INGREDIENTS
    2 cooked crabs, each about
        675g/1½lb
    90ml/6 tbsp sunflower oil
    2.5cm/1in piece fresh root ginger,
        peeled and chopped
    2–3 garlic cloves, crushed
    1–2 fresh red chillies, seeded and
        pounded to a paste
    175ml/6fl oz/¾ cup tomato ketchup
    30ml/2 tbsp soft light brown sugar
    15ml/1 tbsp light soy sauce
    120ml/4fl oz/½ cup boiling water
    salt
    hot toast and cucumber chunks,
        to serve

1 Prepare each crab in turn. Twist off the large claws, then turn the crab on its back with its mouth and eyes facing away from you. Using both of your thumbs, push the body, with the small legs attached, upwards from beneath the flap, separating the body from the main shell in the process. Discard the stomach sac and grey spongy lungs.

2 Using a teaspoon, scrape the brown creamy meat from the large shell into a small bowl. Twist the legs from the body. Cut the body section in half. Pick out the white meat and add it to the bowl. Pick out the meat from the legs, or leave it for guests to remove at the table.

3 Heat the oil in a wok and gently fry the ginger, garlic and fresh chilli paste for 1–2 minutes without browning. Stir in the ketchup, sugar and soy sauce, with salt to taste and heat gently.

4 Stir in all the crab meat. Pour in the boiling water, stir well and heat through over a high heat. Pile on serving plates. If the crab claws were left intact, add them to the plate, with the cucumber. Serve immediately, with pieces of toast.

NONYA PORK SATAY

THERE ARE FEW DISHES AS DELICIOUS AS SATAY. THE SKEWERS OF SPICED MEAT CAN BE SERVED AS SNACKS, AS PART OF A BARBECUE OR AS A LIGHT MEAL.

SERVES EIGHT TO TWELVE

INGREDIENTS
    450g/1lb pork fillet (tenderloin)
    15ml/1 tbsp soft light brown sugar
    1cm/½in cube shrimp paste
    1–2 lemon grass stalks, trimmed
    30ml/2 tbsp coriander
        seeds, dry-fried
    6 macadamia nuts or blanched almonds
    2 onions, roughly chopped
    3–6 fresh red chillies, seeded and
        roughly chopped
    2.5ml/½ tsp ground turmeric
    300ml/½ pint/1¼ cups canned
        coconut milk
    30ml/2 tbsp groundnut (peanut) oil
        or sunflower oil
    salt

COOK'S TIP
How many chillies you use for the marinade depends on their strength.

1 Soak 8–12 bamboo skewers in water for at least 1 hour to prevent them from scorching when they are placed under the grill (broiler).

2 Cut the pork into small chunks, then spread it out in a single layer in a shallow dish. Sprinkle with the sugar to help release the juices. Wrap the shrimp paste in foil and heat it briefly in a dry frying pan or warm it on a skewer held over a gas flame.

3 Cut off the lower 5cm/2in of the lemon grass stalks and chop finely. Process the dry-fried coriander seeds to a powder in a food processor. Add the nuts and chopped lemon grass, process briefly, then add the onions, chillies, shrimp paste, turmeric and a little salt; process to a fine paste. Pour in the coconut milk and oil. Switch the machine on very briefly to mix.

4 Pour the mixture over the pork, stir well, cover and leave to marinate for 1–2 hours.

5 Preheat the grill or prepare the barbecue. Drain the bamboo skewers and thread 3–4 pieces of marinated pork on each. Cook the skewered meat for 8–10 minutes, turning often until tender and basting frequently with the remaining marinade. Serve as soon as they are cooked.

CHICKEN SATAY

*CONCERTINAS OF TENDER CHICKEN, SERVED WITH A CHILLI-FLAVOURED PEANUT SAUCE, ARE
IRRESISTIBLE. GARNISH WITH SLICED FRESH RED CHILLIES FOR EXTRA FIRE.*

SERVES FOUR

INGREDIENTS
    4 boneless, skinless chicken
      breast portions
    10ml/2 tsp soft light brown sugar
For the marinade
    5ml/1 tsp cumin seeds
    5ml/1 tsp fennel seeds
    7.5ml/1½ tsp coriander seeds
    6 small onions, chopped
    1 garlic clove, crushed
    1 lemon grass stalk, trimmed
    3 macadamia nuts or 6 cashew nuts
    2.5ml/½ tsp ground turmeric
For the peanut sauce
    4 small onions, sliced
    2 garlic cloves, crushed
    1cm/½in cube shrimp paste
    6 cashew nuts or almonds
    2 lemon grass stalks, trimmed, lower
      5cm/2in sliced
    45ml/3 tbsp sunflower oil, plus extra
    5–10ml/1–2 tsp chilli powder
    400ml/14fl oz can coconut milk
    60–75ml/4–5 tbsp tamarind water or
      30ml/2 tbsp tamarind concentrate
      mixed with 45ml/3 tbsp water
    15ml/1 tbsp soft light brown sugar
    175g/6oz/½ cup crunchy peanut butter

1 Cut the chicken into 16 thin strips,
sprinkle with the sugar and set aside.

2 Make the marinade. Dry-fry the
spices, then grind to a powder in a food
processor. Set aside. Add the onions
and garlic to the processor. Chop the
lower 5cm/2in of the lemon grass and
add with the nuts, spices and turmeric.
Grind to a paste; scrape into a bowl.

3 Add the chicken and stir well until
coated. Cover loosely with clear film
(plastic wrap) and leave to marinate for
at least 4 hours. Soak 16 bamboo
skewers for 1 hour in a bowl of warm
water before use to prevent scorching.

4 Prepare the sauce. Pound or process
the onions with the garlic and shrimp
paste. Add the nuts and the lower
parts of the lemon grass stalks. Process
to a fine purée. Heat the oil in a wok
and fry the purée for 2–3 minutes.
Add the chilli powder and cook for
2 minutes more.

5 Stir in the coconut milk and bring
slowly to the boil. Reduce the heat and
stir in the tamarind water and brown
sugar. Add the peanut butter and cook
over a low heat, stirring gently, until
fairly thick. Keep warm. Prepare the
barbecue or preheat the grill (broiler).

6 Thread the chicken on to the bamboo
skewers. Cook on the barbecue or
under the grill for about 5 minutes or
until golden and tender, brushing with
oil occasionally. Serve with the hot
peanut sauce handed around in a
separate bowl.

LITTLE ONONS COOKED WITH CHILLIES

WHOLE DRIED CHILLIES GIVE THIS SIMPLE DISH AN UNDERLYING WARMTH THAT ADDS TO ITS APPEAL.
FOR A SMOKY FLAVOUR, USE CHIPOTLE CHILLIES, OR AN ANAHEIM RED CHILLI.

SERVES SIX

INGREDIENTS
105ml/7 tbsp olive oil
675g/1½lb small onions
150ml/¼ pint/⅔ cup dry white wine
2 bay leaves
2 garlic cloves, bruised
1–2 small dried red chillies
15ml/1 tbsp coriander seeds, toasted
  and lightly crushed
2.5ml/½ tsp granulated sugar
a few fresh thyme sprigs
30ml/2 tbsp currants
10ml/2 tsp chopped fresh oregano
5ml/1 tsp grated (shredded)
  lemon rind
15ml/1 tbsp chopped fresh flat
  leaf parsley
30–45ml/2–3 tbsp pine nuts, toasted
salt and ground black pepper

1 Spoon 30ml/2 tbsp of the olive oil into a wide pan. Add the onions, place the pan over a medium heat and cook gently for about 5 minutes, or until the onions begin to colour. Use a slotted spoon to remove the onions from the pan and set them aside.

2 Add the remaining oil to the pan, with the wine, bay leaves, garlic, chillies, coriander seeds, sugar and thyme. Bring to the boil and cook for 5 minutes.

3 Return the onions to the pan. Add the currants, reduce the heat and cook gently for 15–20 minutes, or until the onions are tender but not falling apart. Use a slotted spoon to transfer the onions to a serving dish.

4 Boil the liquid vigorously until it reduces considerably. Taste and adjust the seasoning, if necessary, then pour it over the onions. Sprinkle the chopped fresh oregano over the cooked onions, cool, cover and then chill them for several hours.

VARIATION
The same method can be used for courgettes (zucchini), celery, small mushrooms, fennel and baby leeks. Cut the larger vegetables in 2.5cm/1in pieces and cook as for small onions.

5 Just before serving, stir in the grated lemon rind, chopped parsley and toasted pine nuts.

COOK'S TIPS
• Serve this dish as part of a mixed hors d'oeuvre – an antipasto – perhaps with a mild mayonnaise-dressed celeriac salad and some thinly sliced prosciutto or other air-dried ham.
• The aim of an hors d'oeuvre is to provide something beautifully fresh-looking that will arouse your appetite. Each dish should have its own taste.

CHILLI SPICED ONION KOFTAS

THESE DELICIOUS DEEP-FRIED INDIAN ONION FRITTERS ARE PEPPED UP WITH GREEN CHILLIES.
SERVE THEM WITH A YOGURT DIP, TO DAMP DOWN THEIR FIRE.

SERVES FOUR TO FIVE

INGREDIENTS
675g/1½lb onions, halved and
  thinly sliced
5ml/1 tsp salt
5ml/1 tsp ground coriander
5ml/1 tsp ground cumin
2.5ml/½ tsp ground turmeric
1–2 fresh green chillies, seeded and
  finely chopped
45ml/3 tbsp chopped fresh
  coriander (cilantro)
90g/3½oz/¾ cup chickpea flour
2.5ml/½ tsp baking powder
vegetable oil, for deep-frying
To serve
  lemon wedges
  fresh coriander (cilantro) sprigs
  yogurt and herb dip (see Cook's Tips)

1 Put the onion slices in a colander, add the salt and toss well. Stand the colander on a plate or bowl and leave for 45 minutes, tossing once or twice with a fork. Rinse the onions, then squeeze out the excess moisture. Tip the onions into a bowl. Add the ground coriander, cumin, turmeric, chillies and fresh coriander. Mix well.

COOK'S TIPS
• Chickpea flour, available from supermarkets and Indian food stores, is sometimes labelled gram flour or *besan*.
• To make a yogurt and herb dip, stir 30ml/2 tbsp each of chopped fresh coriander (cilantro) and mint into 250ml/8fl oz/1 cup thick yogurt. Add salt, ground toasted cumin seeds and a pinch of sugar. Top with a chopped chilli.

2 Add the chickpea flour and baking powder, then use your hand to mix all the ingredients thoroughly.

3 Shape the mixture by hand into 12–15 koftas. They should be about the size of golf balls.

4 Heat the oil for deep-frying to 180–190°C/350–375°F or until a cube of day-old bread browns in about 45 seconds.

5 Fry the koftas, 4–5 at a time, until deep golden brown all over. Drain each batch on kitchen paper and keep warm until all the koftas are cooked. Serve with lemon wedges, coriander sprigs and a yogurt and herb dip.

PEPPERS WITH CHEESE AND CHILLI FILLING

SWEET PEPPERS AND CHILLIES ARE NATURAL COMPANIONS, SO IT ISN'T SURPRISING THAT THEY WORK SO WELL TOGETHER IN THIS TRADITIONAL BULGARIAN APPETIZER OR LIGHT SNACK.

3 Using a sharp knife, carefully peel away the skin from the peppers.

4 Beat together all the ingredients for the filling in a bowl. Divide evenly among the 4 peppers.

5 Reshape the peppers to look whole. Dip them into the seasoned flour, then in the egg and then the flour again.

6 Heat the olive oil for shallow frying in a large pan and fry the peeled peppers gently for 6–8 minutes, turning once with a spatula, until they are golden brown and the filling is set. Drain the peppers thoroughly on kitchen paper before serving with a cucumber and tomato salad.

SERVES TWO TO FOUR

INGREDIENTS
  4 red, yellow or green sweet peppers, either bell peppers or long peppers
  50g/2oz/½ cup plain (all-purpose) flour, seasoned
  1 egg, beaten
  olive oil, for shallow frying
  cucumber and tomato salad, to serve
For the filling
  1 egg
  90g/3½oz/generous ½ cup finely crumbled feta cheese
  30ml/2 tbsp chopped fresh parsley
  1 small fresh red or green chilli, seeded and finely chopped

1 Preheat the grill (broiler). Slit open the peppers lengthways on one side only, enabling you to scoop out the seeds and remove the cores, but leaving them in one piece.

2 Place the peppers in a grill (broiling) pan. Cook under medium heat until the skin is charred and blackened. Place the peppers in a plastic bag, tie the top to keep the steam in and set aside for 20 minutes.

COOK'S TIP
Feta cheese should have a bland, salt-edged taste. If kept in brine for some time it will be saltier and may need to be first soaked in water.

MOLETTES

MEXICAN STREET TRADERS SELL THIS TASTY SNACK WITH A CHUNKY SALSA, SPIKED WITH CHILLIES.

SERVES FOUR

INGREDIENTS

4 crusty finger rolls
50g/2oz/¼ cup butter, softened
225g/8oz/1⅓ cups canned
  refried beans
30ml/2 tbsp chopped bottled pickled
  jalapeño chillies
150g/5oz/1¼ cups grated (shredded)
  medium Cheddar cheese
green salad leaves, to garnish
120ml/4fl oz/½ cup tomato salsa,
  to serve

1 Preheat the grill (broiler). Cut the rolls in half, then take a sliver off the base so that they lie flat. Remove a little of the crumb. Spread them lightly with butter.

2 Arrange the rolls on a baking sheet and grill (broil) for about 5 minutes, or until they are crisp and golden.

3 Meanwhile, heat the refried beans over a low heat in a small pan, stirring occasionally to avoid them sticking. Add the pickled jalapeño chillies.

4 Scoop the beans on to the rolls, then sprinkle the grated cheese on top. Place them back under the grill until the cheese melts. Garnish with salad leaves and serve with the tomato salsa. If the salsa is not very spicy, add a seeded and finely chopped chilli to enhance the flavour.

EGGS MOTULENOS

A TASTY AND FILLING SNACK, TORTILLAS ARE TOPPED WITH BEANS, FRIED EGG AND HOT CHILLI SAUCES.

SERVES FOUR

INGREDIENTS

225g/8oz/generous 1 cup black
  beans, soaked overnight in water
1 small onion, finely chopped
2 garlic cloves, crushed
small bunch of fresh coriander
  (cilantro), chopped
150g/5oz/1 cup frozen peas
4 corn tortillas
30ml/2 tbsp oil
4 eggs
150g/5oz cooked ham, diced
60ml/4 tbsp hot chilli sauce
75g/3oz/generous ½ cup feta
  cheese, crumbled
salt and ground black pepper
tomato salsa, to serve

1 Drain the beans, rinse them under cold water and drain again. Put them in a pan, add the onion and garlic with water to cover. Bring to the boil, then simmer for 40 minutes. Stir in the coriander, season to taste, and keep hot.

2 Cook the peas in a small pan of boiling water until they are just tender. Drain and set aside. Heat the tortillas, following the instructions on the packet.

3 Heat the oil in a frying pan and fry the eggs until the whites are set. Lift them on to a plate and keep them warm while you quickly heat the ham and peas in the oil remaining in the pan.

COOK'S TIP
When frying eggs, crack them into a saucer first, to avoid breaking the yolk. Then slide into the pan.

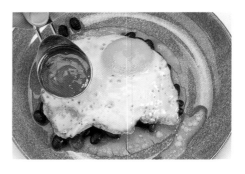

4 Place the tortillas on warmed plates and top each one with some beans. Place an egg on each tortilla, spoon over 15ml/1 tbsp hot chilli sauce, then surround each egg with some peas and ham. Sprinkle feta over the peas and serve at once, with salsa on the side.

VARIATIONS
Tortillas with a foundation of black beans and feta cheese can be covered with a variety of toppings. Try them with a dab of salsa and sliced radishes. Or try courgettes (zucchini), guacamole and spring onions (scallions).

CHICKEN FLAUTAS <u>WITH</u> FRESNO CHILLI SALSA

CRISP FRIED TORTILLAS WITH A CHICKEN AND CHEESE FILLING MAKE A DELICIOUS LIGHT MEAL, ESPECIALLY WHEN SERVED WITH A SPICY TOMATO SALSA.

MAKES TWELVE

INGREDIENTS
    2 skinless, boneless chicken
      breast portions
    15ml/1 tbsp vegetable oil
    1 onion, chopped
    2 garlic cloves, crushed
    90g/3½oz/generous ½ cup crumbled
      feta cheese
    12 corn tortillas
    oil, for frying
    salt and ground black pepper
For the salsa
    3 tomatoes, peeled seeded
      and chopped
    juice of ½ lime
    small bunch of fresh coriander
      (cilantro), chopped
    ½ small onion, finely chopped
    3 fresh green fresno chillies or
      similar fresh green chillies, seeded
      and chopped

1 Start by making the salsa. Mix the chopped tomatoes, lime juice, chopped coriander, onion and chillies in a bowl. Season with salt to taste, cover and chill until needed.

COOK'S TIP
When it comes to cooking the flutes, you might find it easier to keep the cocktail sticks or toothpicks in place until after the flutes have been fried. Remove them before serving.

2 Put the chicken portions in a large pan, add water to cover and bring to the boil. Reduce the heat and simmer for 15–20 minutes or until the chicken is cooked. Remove the chicken from the pan and let it cool a little. Using 2 forks, shred the chicken into small pieces. Set it aside.

3 Heat the oil in a frying pan and fry the onion and garlic over a low heat for about 5 minutes, or until the onion has softened but not coloured. Add the shredded chicken, with salt and pepper to taste. Mix well, remove from the heat and stir in the feta.

4 Before attempting to roll the tortillas, soften 3 or 4 at a time by steaming them on a plate over boiling water. Alternatively, wrap them in microwave-safe clear film (plastic wrap) and then heat them in a microwave oven on full power for about 30 seconds.

5 Place a teaspoonful of the chicken filling on one of the tortillas. Roll the tortilla tightly around the filling to make a neat cylinder. Secure with a cocktail stick or toothpick. Immediately cover the roll with clear film to prevent the tortilla from drying out and splitting. Fill and roll the remaining tortillas in exactly the same way, covering them each time with clear film.

6 Pour oil into a frying pan to a depth of 2.5cm/1in. Heat it until a small cube of day-old bread, added to the oil, rises to the surface and bubbles at the edges before turning golden. Remove the cocktail sticks or toothpicks, then add the flutes to the pan, a few at a time.

7 Fry the flutes for 2–3 minutes until golden, turning frequently. Drain on kitchen paper and serve at once, with the spicy tomato salsa.

QUESADILLAS

FILLED WITH CHEESE AND CHILLIES, THESE TORTILLAS ARE THE MEXICAN EQUIVALENT OF TOASTED SANDWICHES. SERVE THEM AS SOON AS THEY ARE COOKED, OR THEY WILL BECOME CHEWY.

SERVES FOUR

INGREDIENTS
  200g/7oz mozzarella, Monterey Jack
    or mild Cheddar cheese
  1 fresh fresno chilli
  8 wheat flour tortillas, about
    15cm/6in across
  onion relish or classic tomato salsa,
    to serve

VARIATIONS
Try spreading a thin layer of your favourite Mexican salsa on the tortilla before adding the cheese, or adding a few pieces of cooked chicken before folding the tortilla in half.

1 If using mozzarella cheese, place it in the freezer for 30 minutes to make it easier to slice. Drain it thoroughly and pat it dry, then slice it into thin strips. Monterey Jack and Cheddar cheese should both be coarsely grated (shredded), as finely grated cheese will melt and ooze away when cooking. Set the cheese aside in a bowl.

2 Spear the chilli on a long-handled metal skewer and roast it over the flame of a gas burner until the skin blisters and darkens. Do not let the flesh burn. Alternatively, dry-fry it in a griddle pan until the skin is scorched. Place the roasted chilli in a strong plastic bag and tie the top to keep the steam in. Set aside for 20 minutes.

3 Remove the chilli from the bag and peel off the skin. Cut off the stalk, then slit the chilli and scrape out the seeds. Cut the flesh into 8 thin strips.

4 Warm a large frying pan or griddle. Place 1 wheat tortilla on the pan or griddle at a time, sprinkle about one-eighth of the cheese on to 1 half and add a strip of chilli. Fold the tortilla over the cheese and press the edges gently together. Cook the tortilla for 1 minute, then turn over and cook the other side for 1 minute. You can prepare these in advance but cook only when needed.

5 Remove the filled tortilla from the pan or griddle, cut it into 3 triangles or 4 strips and serve at once, with the onion relish or tomato salsa.

TORTAS

FILLED ROLLS WITH A DIFFERENCE, TORTAS ARE LIKE EDIBLE TREASURE CHESTS, WITH MEAT, CHEESE, CHILLIES AND TOMATOES PILED ON TOP OF REFRIED BEANS.

SERVES TWO

INGREDIENTS

2 fresh jalapeño chillies
juice of ½ lime
2 French bread rolls or 2 pieces of
  French bread
115g/4oz/⅔ cup home-made or
  canned refried beans
150g/5oz roast pork
2 small tomatoes, sliced
115g/4oz Cheddar cheese, sliced
small bunch of fresh
  coriander (cilantro)
30ml/2 tbsp crème fraîche

VARIATIONS
The essential ingredients of a *torta* are refried beans and chillies. Everything else is subject to change. Ham, chicken or turkey could all be used instead of pork, or another kind of cheese, and lettuce is often added.

1 Cut the chillies in half, scrape out the seeds, then cut the flesh into thin strips. Put it in a bowl, pour over the lime juice and leave to stand.

2 If using rolls, slice them in half and remove some of the crumb so that they are slightly hollowed. If using French bread, slice each piece in half lengthways and hollow likewise. Set the tops aside and spread the bottom halves with the refried beans.

3 Cut the pork into thin shreds and put these on top of the refried beans. Top with the tomato slices. Drain the jalapeño strips and put them on top of the tomato slices. Add the cheese and sprinkle with coriander leaves.

4 Turn the top halves of the bread or rolls over, so that the cut sides are uppermost, and spread these with crème fraîche. Sandwich back together again and serve.

CHILLIES RELLENOS

STUFFED CHILLIES ARE POPULAR ALL OVER MEXICO. THE TYPE OF CHILLI USED DIFFERS FROM REGION TO REGION, BUT LARGER CHILLIES ARE OBVIOUSLY EASIER TO STUFF THAN SMALLER ONES.

MAKES SIX

INGREDIENTS

6 fresh poblano or Anaheim chillies
2 potatoes, total weight about
  400g/14oz
200g/7oz/scant 1 cup cream cheese
200g/7oz/1¾ cups grated (shredded)
  mature (sharp) Cheddar cheese
5ml/1 tsp salt
2.5ml/½ tsp ground black pepper
2 eggs, separated
115g/4oz/1 cup plain
  (all-purpose) flour
2.5ml/½ tsp white pepper
oil, for frying
dried chilli flakes, to garnish (optional)

1 Make a neat slit down one side of each chilli. Place them in a dry frying pan over a medium heat, turning them frequently until the skins blister.

2 Place the chillies in a strong plastic bag and tie the top to keep the steam in. Set aside for 20 minutes, then carefully peel off the skins and remove the seeds through the slits, keeping the chillies whole. Dry the chillies with kitchen paper and set them aside.

COOK'S TIP
Take care when making the filling; mix gently, in order to avoid breaking up the diced potato.

VARIATION
Whole ancho (dried poblano) chillies can be used instead of fresh chillies, but will need to be reconstituted in water before they can be seeded and stuffed.

3 Scrub or peel the potatoes and cut them into 1cm/½in dice. Bring a large pan of water to the boil, add the potatoes and let the water return to boiling point. Lower the heat and simmer for 5 minutes or until the potatoes are just tender. Do not overcook. Drain them thoroughly.

4 Put the cream cheese in a bowl and stir in the grated Cheddar cheese, with 2.5ml/½ tsp of the salt and all the black pepper. Add the par-cooked potato and mix gently.

5 Spoon some of the potato filling into each chilli. Put them on a plate, cover with clear film (plastic wrap) and chill for 1 hour so the filling becomes firm.

6 Put the egg whites in a clean, grease-free bowl and whisk them to firm, dry peaks. In a separate bowl, beat the yolks until pale, then carefully fold in the whites. Scrape the mixture into a large, shallow dish. Spread out the plain flour in another large shallow dish and season it with the remaining salt and the white pepper.

7 Heat the oil for frying to 190°C/ 375°F. Coat a few chillies first in seasoned flour and then in egg before adding carefully to the hot oil.

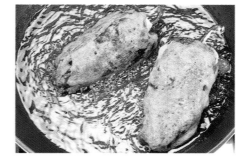

8 Fry the chillies in batches until golden and crisp. Drain on kitchen paper and serve hot, garnished with a sprinkle of chilli flakes, if you like.

SPICY PEANUT BALLS

TASTY RICE BALLS, ROLLED IN CHOPPED PEANUTS AND DEEP-FRIED, MAKE A DELICIOUS SNACK. SERVE THEM AS THEY ARE OR WITH A CHILLI SAUCE FOR DIPPING.

2 Add three-quarters of the cooked rice to the paste in the food processor, and process until smooth and sticky. Scrape into a mixing bowl and stir in the remainder of the rice. Wet your hands and shape the mixture into small balls.

3 Roll the balls, a few at a time, in the chopped peanuts, making sure they are evenly coated.

4 Heat the oil for deep-frying to 180–190°C/350–375°F or until a cube of day-old bread browns in about 45 seconds. Deep-fry the peanut balls until crisp. Drain on kitchen paper, then pile on to a platter. Serve hot with lime wedges and a chilli dipping sauce, if you like.

MAKES SIXTEEN

INGREDIENTS
  1 garlic clove, crushed
  1cm/½in piece of fresh root ginger, peeled and finely chopped
  1 small fresh red chilli, seeded and roughly chopped
  1.5ml/¼ tsp ground turmeric
  5ml/1 tsp granulated sugar
  2.5ml/½ tsp salt
  5ml/1 tsp chilli sauce
  10ml/2 tsp soy sauce
  30ml/2 tbsp chopped fresh coriander (cilantro)
  juice of ½ lime
  225g/8oz/2 cups cooked white long grain rice
  115g/4oz/1 cup peanuts, chopped
  vegetable oil, for deep-frying
  lime wedges and chilli dipping sauce, to serve (optional)

1 Put the crushed garlic, ginger and chilli in a food processor. Add the turmeric and process to a paste. Add the granulated sugar, salt, chilli sauce and soy sauce, with the chopped coriander and lime juice. Process briefly to mix.

COOK'S TIP
Coat the balls in the peanuts and then chill for 30 minutes before deep-frying.

SPRING ROLLS WITH FIERY CHILLI SAUCE

THIS POPULAR SNACK COMES FROM SOUTH-EAST ASIA, AND WOULD MAKE A TASTY FIRST COURSE. THE SAUCE IS TRADITIONALLY MADE WITH HOT CHILLIES, BUT SUBSTITUTE MILDER ONES, IF YOU PREFER.

MAKES FIFTEEN

INGREDIENTS
  25g/1oz cellophane noodles soaked
    for 10 minutes in hot water to cover
  6–8 dried wood ears, soaked for
    30 minutes in warm water to cover
  225g/8oz minced (ground) pork
  225g/8oz fresh or canned crab meat
  4 spring onions (scallions),
    finely chopped
  5ml/1 tsp Thai fish sauce (*nam pla*)
  250g/9oz packet spring roll wrappers
  flour and water paste, to seal
  vegetable oil, for deep-frying
  salt and ground black pepper
For the sauce
  2 fresh red chillies, seeded
  2 garlic cloves, chopped
  15ml/1 tbsp granulated sugar
  45ml/3 tbsp Thai fish sauce
    (*nam pla*)
  juice of 1 lime or ½ lemon

2 Mix the noodles and the wood ears with the pork and set aside. Remove any cartilage from the crab meat and add to the pork mixture with the spring onions and Thai fish sauce. Season to taste, mixing well.

3 Place a spring roll wrapper in front of you, diamond-fashion. Spoon some mixture just below the centre, across the width, fold over the nearest point and roll once.

4 Fold in the sides to enclose the mixture, then brush the edges with flour paste and roll up to seal. Repeat with the remaining spring roll wrappers and filling mixture.

5 Heat the oil in a wok or deep-fryer to 190°C/375°F. Deep-fry the rolls in batches for 8–10 minutes or until they are cooked through. Drain them well on kitchen paper and serve hot. To eat, dip the rolls in the fiery chilli sauce.

1 Make the sauce by pounding the chillies and garlic to a paste. Scrape into a bowl and mix in the sugar and fish sauce, with citrus juice to taste. Drain the noodles and snip them into 2.5cm/1in lengths. Drain the wood ears, trim away any rough stems and slice the caps finely. Mix with the noodles.

COOK'S TIPS
• Wood ears (Chinese black fungus) is a gelatinous species collected and cultivated in China.
• Serve the rolls Vietnamese-style by wrapping each one in a lettuce leaf with a few sprigs of fresh mint and coriander (cilantro) and a stick of cucumber.

POTATO SKINS <u>WITH</u> CAJUN DIP

DIVINELY CRISP AND NAUGHTY, THESE POTATO SKINS TASTE GREAT WITH THE PIQUANT CHILLI DIP.

SERVES TWO

INGREDIENTS
  2 large baking potatoes, about
    275g/10oz each
  vegetable oil, for frying
For the dip
  120ml/4fl oz/½ cup natural
    (plain) yogurt
  1 garlic clove, crushed
  5ml/1 tsp tomato purée (paste)
  2.5ml/½ tsp green chilli purée or
    ½ small fresh green chilli, chopped
  1.5ml/¼ tsp celery salt
  salt and ground black pepper

COOK'S TIP
If you prefer, you can microwave the
potatoes to save time. This will take
about 10 minutes.

1 Preheat the oven to 180°C/350°F/
Gas 4. Bake the potatoes for about 1 hour,
until tender. Cut them in half and scoop
out the flesh, leaving a thin layer on the
skins. Keep the flesh for another meal.

2 To make the piquant chilli dip, mix
all the ingredients in a bowl. Chill until
ready to serve.

3 Heat a 1cm/½in layer of oil in a large,
shallow pan. Cut each potato skin in
half again, then fry them until crisp and
golden on both sides. Drain on kitchen
paper, sprinkle with salt and black
pepper and spoon a dollop of piquant
chilli dip into each skin. Serve the
remaining dip separately so that people
can help themselves.

SPICY POTATO WEDGES WITH CHILLI DIP

THESE DRY-ROASTED POTATO WEDGES WITH CRISP SPICY CRUSTS ARE DELICIOUS WITH THE CHILLI DIP.

SERVES TWO

INGREDIENTS
  2 baking potatoes, about 225g/
    8oz each
  30ml/2 tbsp olive oil
  2 garlic cloves, crushed
  5ml/1 tsp ground allspice
  5ml/1 tsp ground coriander
  15ml/1 tbsp paprika
  salt and ground black pepper
For the dip
  15ml/1 tbsp olive oil
  1 small onion, finely chopped
  1 garlic clove, crushed
  200g/7oz can chopped tomatoes
  1 fresh red chilli, seeded and
    finely chopped
  15ml/1 tbsp balsamic vinegar
  15ml/1 tbsp chopped fresh coriander
    (cilantro), plus extra to garnish

1 Preheat the oven to 200°C/400°F/
Gas 6. Cut the potatoes in half, then
into 8 wedges.

2 Add the wedges to a pan of cold
water. Bring to the boil, then reduce the
heat and simmer gently for 10 minutes
or until the wedges have softened
slightly but the flesh has not started to
disintegrate. Drain well and pat dry on
kitchen paper.

COOK'S TIP
To save time, par-boil the potatoes and
toss them with the spices in advance,
but make sure that the potato wedges
are perfectly dry and completely covered
in the spice mixture before roasting.

3 Mix the olive oil, garlic, allspice,
coriander and paprika in a roasting pan.
Add salt and pepper to taste. Add the
potatoes to the pan and shake to coat
them thoroughly. Roast for 20 minutes,
until the wedges are browned, crisp and
fully cooked. Turn the potato wedges
occasionally during the roasting time.

4 Meanwhile, make the chilli dip. Heat
the oil in a small pan, add the onion
and garlic, and cook for 5–10 minutes
until soft.

5 Tip in the chopped tomatoes, with any
juice. Stir in the chilli and vinegar. Cook
gently for 10 minutes until the mixture
has reduced and thickened, then taste
and check the seasoning. Stir in the
chopped fresh coriander.

6 Pile the spicy potato wedges on a
plate, garnish with the extra coriander
and serve with the chilli dip.

VARIATION
Instead of balsamic vinegar, try brown
rice vinegar, which has a mellow flavour.

Courgette Fritters <u>with</u> Chilli Jam

Chilli jam is hot, sweet and sticky — rather like a thick chutney. It adds a piquancy to these fritters but is also delicious with pies or a chunk of cheese.

MAKES TWELVE

INGREDIENTS
  450g/1lb/3½ cups coarsely grated
    (shredded) courgettes (zucchini)
  50g/2oz/⅔ cup freshly grated
    Parmesan cheese
  2 eggs, beaten
  60ml/4 tbsp unbleached plain (all-
    purpose) flour
  vegetable oil, for frying
  salt and ground black pepper
For the chilli jam
  75ml/5 tbsp olive oil
  4 large onions, diced
  4 garlic cloves, chopped
  1–2 fresh Thai chillies, seeded
    and sliced
  25g/1oz/2 tbsp soft dark
    brown sugar

1 First make the chilli jam. Heat the oil in a frying pan until hot, then add the onions and garlic. Reduce the heat to low, then cook for 20 minutes, stirring frequently, until the onions are very soft.

VARIATION
Substitute Pecorino Romano for Parmesan cheese. It is good for grating.

2 Leave the onion mixture to cool, then scrape into a food processor or blender. Add the chillies and sugar, and blend until smooth, then return the mixture to the pan. Cook for 10 minutes, stirring frequently, until the liquid evaporates and the mixture has the consistency of jam. Cool slightly.

3 To make the fritters, squeeze the courgettes in a dishtowel to remove any excess water, then tip them into a bowl. Add the Parmesan, eggs and flour. Mix well, then season with salt and pepper.

4 Heat enough oil to cover the base of a large frying pan. Add 30ml/2 tbsp of the mixture for each fritter and cook 3 fritters at a time. Cook them for 2–3 minutes on each side until golden, then remove from the pan and keep hot while you cook the remaining fritters. Drain on kitchen paper and serve warm with a large spoonful of the chilli jam.

COOK'S TIP
Any leftover chilli jam can be kept in an airtight jar in the refrigerator for up to 1 week.

THAI TEMPEH CAKES WITH CHILLI SAUCE

MADE FROM SOYA BEANS, TEMPEH IS SIMILAR TO TOFU BUT HAS A NUTTIER TASTE. HERE, IT IS COMBINED WITH CHILLIES, LEMON GRASS AND GINGER AND FORMED INTO SMALL PATTIES.

MAKES EIGHT

INGREDIENTS
 2 chillies, seeded and finely chopped
 1 lemon grass stalk, trimmed
 2 garlic cloves, chopped
 2 spring onions (scallions),
   finely chopped
 2 shallots, finely chopped
 2.5cm/1in piece fresh root ginger,
   finely chopped
 60ml/4 tbsp chopped fresh coriander
   (cilantro), plus extra to garnish
 250g/9oz tempeh, thawed if
   frozen, sliced
 15ml/1 tbsp lime juice
 5ml/1 tsp granulated sugar
 45ml/3 tbsp plain (all-purpose) flour
 1 large (US extra large) egg,
   lightly beaten
 vegetable oil, for frying
 salt and ground black pepper
For the dipping sauce
 45ml/3 tbsp mirin or dry sherry
 45ml/3 tbsp white wine vinegar
 2 spring onions (scallions),
   thinly sliced
 15ml/1 tbsp granulated sugar
 2 fresh red chillies, finely chopped
 30ml/2 tbsp chopped fresh
   coriander (cilantro)

1 To make the dipping sauce, mix the mirin, vinegar, spring onions, sugar, chillies, coriander and a large pinch of salt in a small bowl and set aside.

COOK'S TIP
Chill the tempeh cakes for 30 minutes in the refrigerator before frying. It will prevent them from breaking.

2 Place the chopped chillies in a food processor or blender. Cut off the lower 5cm/2in piece of the lemon grass stalk and chop it roughly. Add it to the processor or blender, with the garlic, spring onions, shallots, ginger and coriander. Process to a coarse paste; the mixture should not be too smooth at this stage.

3 Add the tempeh, lime juice and sugar, then process again until combined. Add the flour and egg, with salt and pepper to taste, and process again until the mixture forms a coarse, sticky paste.

4 Wet your hands, then take a generous spoonful of the tempeh mixture and form it into a round between your palms. Repeat with the remaining mixture, wetting your hands slightly each time.

5 Heat enough oil to cover the base of a large frying pan. Fry the tempeh cakes, in batches if necessary, for 5–6 minutes, turning once, until golden. Drain on kitchen paper. Pile on to plates and garnish with the extra coriander. Serve warm, with the dipping sauce.

PARTY PIZZETTES WITH A HINT OF CHILLI

BRUSHING PIZZA DOUGH WITH CHILLI OIL BEFORE ADDING A FLAVOURSOME TOPPING GIVES A TANTALIZING SUGGESTION OF WARMTH WHEN YOU BITE INTO THESE DELICIOUS SNACKS.

SERVES FOUR

INGREDIENTS

    150g/5oz packet pizza dough mix
    5ml/1 tsp salt
    120ml/4fl oz/½ cup lukewarm water
    30ml/2 tbsp chilli oil
    75g/3oz mozzarella cheese, grated
    1 garlic clove, chopped
    ½ small red onion, thinly sliced
    4–6 pieces sun-dried tomatoes in oil,
      drained and thinly sliced
    115g/4oz cooked, peeled
      prawns (shrimp)
    30ml/2 tbsp chopped fresh basil
    salt and ground black pepper
    shredded basil leaves, to garnish

4 Prick each of the pizza bases all over with a fork and brush lightly with 15ml/1 tbsp of the chilli oil. Top with the grated mozzarella cheese, being careful to leave a 1cm/½in border all round.

5 Divide the garlic, onion, sun-dried tomatoes, prawns and basil among the pizza bases. Season and drizzle over the remaining chilli oil. Bake for 8–10 minutes until crisp and golden. Garnish with basil leaves and serve immediately.

1 Preheat the oven to 220ºC/425ºF/ Gas 7. Tip the pizza dough mix into a mixing bowl and stir in the salt. Pour in the water and mix to a soft dough.

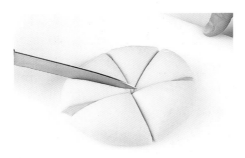

2 Knead the dough on a lightly floured surface for 5 minutes until smooth and elastic. Divide it into 8 equal pieces.

3 Roll out each piece to a small oval 5mm/¼in thick. Place well apart on 2 greased baking sheets.

CHILLI YOGURT CHEESE IN OLIVE OIL

YOGURT, HUNG IN MUSLIN TO DRAIN OFF THE WHEY, MAKES A SUPERB SOFT CHEESE. HERE IT IS
BOTTLED IN OLIVE OIL WITH CHILLI AND HERBS, READY FOR SERVING ON TOAST AS A SUMMER SNACK.

FILLS TWO 450G/1LB JARS

INGREDIENTS
800g/1¾lb/about 4 cups Greek
  (US strained, plain) yogurt
2.5ml/½ tsp salt
10ml/2 tsp crushed dried chillies or
  chilli powder
15ml/1 tbsp chopped fresh rosemary
15ml/1 tbsp chopped fresh thyme
  or oregano
about 300ml/½ pint/1¼ cups olive
  oil, preferably garlic-flavoured
lightly toasted country bread, to serve

1 Sterilize a 30cm/12in square of muslin or cheesecloth by steeping it in boiling water. Drain and lay over a large plate. Mix the yogurt with the salt and tip on to the centre of the cloth. Bring up the sides of the cloth and tie firmly.

2 Hang the bag from a kitchen cabinet handle or in any convenient, cool position that allows a bowl to be placed underneath to catch the whey. Leave for 2–3 days until the yogurt stops dripping.

3 Sterilize two 450g/1lb clean glass preserving or jam jars by heating them in the oven at 150°C/300°F/Gas 2 for 15 minutes.

4 Mix the dried chillies and herbs in a bowl. Take teaspoonfuls of the cheese and roll into balls between the palms of your hands. Lower into jars, sprinkling each layer with the herb mixture.

5 Pour the oil over the cheese until the balls are completely covered. Close the jars tightly and store in the refrigerator for up to 3 weeks.

6 To serve the cheese, spoon out of the jars with a little of the flavoured olive oil and spread on to lightly toasted bread.

SPICED FETA WITH CHILLI SEEDS AND OLIVES

HERE CHILLI SEEDS FLAVOUR MARINATED CUBES OF FETA CHEESE SPIKED WITH SPICES AND OLIVES.
SPOON THE CHEESE CUBES OVER GREEN LEAVES AND SERVE WITH WARM BREAD AS AN APPETIZER.

MAKES FOUR TO FIVE SMALL JARS

INGREDIENTS
500g/1¼lb feta cheese
50g/2oz/½ cup stuffed olives
10ml/2 tsp coriander seeds
10ml/2 tsp whole peppercorns
5ml/1 tsp chilli seeds
few sprigs fresh rosemary or thyme
750ml/1¼ pint/3 cups virgin olive oil

1 Drain the feta cheese, dice it and put it in a bowl. Slice the olives. Using a pestle, crush the coriander seeds and peppercorns in a mortar and add them to the cheese, with the olives, chilli seeds and rosemary or thyme leaves. Toss lightly.

2 Sterilize 4–5 small, clean, glass jars by heating them in the oven at 150°C/300°F/Gas 2 for 15 minutes.

3 Spoon the cheese into the warm, dry sterilized jars and top up with olive oil, making sure that the cheese is well covered by the oil. Close the jars tightly and store them in the refrigerator for up to 3 weeks.

COOK'S TIP
Seal the jars with screw-topped or clip-down lids. The jars need to be totally airtight to keep the cheese fresh.

Although chillies have a reputation for robust flavour, they can also be surprisingly subtle, a fact that creative cooks have capitalized on for centuries. If it's fiery fish you're after, try Cajun Blackened Fish or Balinese Fish Curry. Step into calmer waters to savour Salmon with Tequila Cream Sauce or Fish and Shellfish Laksa, which adds soothing noodles to a hot fish broth brimming with vegetables. Rice performs a similar function in the dramatic Aromatic Mussel Risotto and the delectable Louisiana Shellfish Gumbo.

Fiery Fish
and Shellfish

THREE-COLOUR FISH KEBABS

FOR FOOD TO BE APPETIZING, IT NEEDS TO LOOK AS WELL AS TASTE GOOD, AND THIS DISH, WITH ITS SWEET TOMATO AND CHILLI SALSA, SCORES ON BOTH COUNTS.

SERVES FOUR

INGREDIENTS
    120ml/4fl oz/½ cup olive oil
    finely grated (shredded) rind and
        juice of 1 large lemon
    5ml/1 tsp crushed chilli flakes
    350g/12oz monkfish fillet, cubed
    350g/12oz swordfish fillet, cubed
    350g/12oz thick salmon fillet or
        steak, cubed
    2 red, yellow or orange (bell)
        peppers, cored, seeded and cut
        into squares
    30ml/2 tbsp finely chopped fresh flat
        leaf parsley
    salt and ground black pepper
For the salsa
    2 ripe tomatoes, finely chopped
    1 garlic clove, crushed
    1 fresh red chilli, seeded
        and chopped
    45ml/3 tbsp extra virgin olive oil
    15ml/1 tbsp lemon juice
    15ml/1 tbsp finely chopped fresh flat
        leaf parsley
    pinch of granulated sugar

1 Put the oil in a shallow glass or china bowl and add the lemon rind and juice, the chilli flakes and pepper to taste. Whisk to combine, then add the fish chunks. Turn to coat evenly.

2 Add the pepper squares, stir, then cover and marinate in a cool place for 1 hour, turning occasionally. Preheat the grill (broiler) or prepare the barbecue.

COOK'S TIP
Don't let the fish marinate for more than an hour. The lemon juice will start to break down the fibres of the fish after this time and it will be quickly overcooked.

3 Drain the fish and peppers, reserving the marinade, then thread them on to 8 oiled metal skewers. Barbecue or grill (broil) the skewered fish for 5–8 minutes, turning once to ensure even cooking.

4 Meanwhile, make the salsa by mixing all the ingredients in a bowl, seasoning to taste with salt and pepper. Heat the reserved marinade in a small pan, remove from the heat and stir in the parsley, with salt and pepper to taste. Serve the fish kebabs hot, with the marinade spooned over, accompanied by the tomato and chilli salsa.

SEARED TUNA <u>WITH</u> RED ONION SALSA

A FRUITY CHILLI SUCH AS ITALIA WOULD BE GOOD IN THIS SALSA, AS WOULD A PEACHY POBLANO CHILLI. THE SALSA MAKES A FINE ACCOMPANIMENT FOR THE TUNA.

SERVES FOUR

INGREDIENTS
  4 tuna loin steaks, each weighing
    about 175–200g/6–7oz
  5ml/1 tsp cumin seeds, toasted
    and crushed
  pinch of dried red chilli flakes
  grated (shredded) rind and juice
    of 1 lime
  45–60ml/3–4 tbsp extra virgin
    olive oil
  salt and ground black pepper
  lime wedges and coriander (cilantro)
    sprigs, to garnish
For the salsa
  1 small red onion, finely chopped
  6 red or yellow cherry tomatoes,
    roughly chopped
  1 avocado, peeled, stoned (pitted)
    and chopped
  2 kiwi fruit, peeled and chopped
  1 fresh red or green chilli, seeded
    and finely chopped
  60ml/4 tbsp chopped fresh
    coriander (cilantro)
  leaves from 6 fresh mint sprigs,
    finely chopped
  5–10ml/1–2 tsp Thai fish sauce
  (*nam pla*)
    about 5ml/1 tsp muscovado
    (molasses) sugar

1 Wash the tuna steaks and pat them dry with kitchen paper. Sprinkle with half the crushed cumin seeds, the dried chilli flakes, a little salt and freshly ground black pepper and half the lime rind and juice. Rub in 30ml/ 2 tbsp of the olive oil and set aside in a glass or china dish for 30 minutes.

2 Meanwhile, make the salsa: mix the onion, tomatoes, avocado, kiwi fruit, fresh chilli, chopped coriander and mint in a bowl. Add the remaining crushed cumin, the rest of the lime rind and half the remaining lime juice. Add Thai fish sauce and sugar to taste. Set aside for 15–20 minutes for the flavours to develop, then add a further seasoning of Thai fish sauce, lime juice and olive oil to taste.

3 Heat a ridged, cast-iron grill (broiling) pan for at least 5 minutes. Cook the tuna, allowing about 3 minutes on each side if you like it rare or a little longer for a medium result.

4 Serve the tuna steaks immediately, garnished with lime wedges and coriander sprigs. Serve the salsa separately or spoon some or all of it on the plates with the tuna.

SWORDFISH TACOS

COOKED CORRECTLY, SWORDFISH IS MOIST AND MEATY, AND SUFFICIENTLY ROBUST TO MORE THAN HOLD ITS OWN WHEN MIXED WITH CHILLIES. IT MAKES A VERY TASTY FILLING FOR TACOS.

SERVES SIX

INGREDIENTS
  3 swordfish steaks
  30ml/2 tbsp vegetable oil
  2 garlic cloves, crushed
  1 small onion, chopped
  3 fresh green chillies, seeded
    and chopped
  3 tomatoes
  small bunch of fresh coriander
    (cilantro), chopped
  6 fresh corn tortillas
  ½ Iceberg lettuce, shredded
  salt and ground black pepper
  lemon wedges, to serve (optional)

1 Preheat the grill (broiler). Put the swordfish on an oiled rack over a grill (broiling) pan and grill (broil) for no longer than 2–3 minutes on each side. When cool, remove the skin and flake the fish into a bowl.

2 Heat the oil in a pan and gently fry the crushed garlic, and chopped onion and chillies for 5 minutes or until the onion is soft.

3 Cut a cross in the base of each tomato. Put them in a heatproof bowl and pour over boiling water. After 30 seconds, plunge into cold water. Drain and remove the skins. Cut them in half and squeeze out the seeds and dice the flesh.

4 Add the tomatoes and swordfish to the onion mixture. Cook for 5 minutes over a low heat. Add the coriander and cook for 1–2 minutes. Season to taste with salt and pepper.

5 Wrap the tortillas in foil and steam on a plate over boiling water until pliable. Place some shredded lettuce and fish mixture on each tortilla. Fold in half and serve immediately, with lemon wedges if you like.

SWORDFISH WITH CHILLI AND LIME SAUCE

SWORDFISH IS A PRIME CANDIDATE FOR THE BARBECUE, AS LONG AS IT IS NOT OVERCOOKED. IT TASTES WONDERFUL WITH A SPICY SAUCE WHOSE FIRE IS TEMPERED WITH CRÈME FRAÎCHE.

SERVES FOUR

INGREDIENTS
  2 fresh serrano chillies
  4 tomatoes
  45ml/3 tbsp olive oil
  grated (shredded) rind and juice
    of 1 lime
  4 swordfish steaks
  2.5ml/½ tsp salt
  2.5ml/½ tsp ground black pepper
  175ml/6fl oz/¾ cup crème fraîche
  fresh flat leaf parsley, to garnish

1 Roast the chillies in a dry griddle pan until the skins are blistered. Put in a plastic bag and tie the top. Set aside for 20 minutes, then peel off the skins. Cut off the stalks, then slit the chillies, scrape out the seeds and slice the flesh.

2 Cut a cross in the base of each tomato. Place them in a heatproof bowl and pour over boiling water to cover. After 30 seconds, lift the tomatoes out on a slotted spoon and plunge them into a bowl of cold water. Drain. The skins will have begun to peel back from the crosses. Remove the skin from the tomatoes, then cut them in half and squeeze out the seeds. Chop the flesh into 1cm/½in pieces.

3 Heat 15ml/1 tbsp of the oil in a small pan and add the strips of chilli, with the lime rind and juice. Cook for 2–3 minutes, then stir in the tomatoes. Cook for 10 minutes, stirring the mixture occasionally, until the tomato is pulpy. Preheat the grill (broiler) or prepare the barbecue.

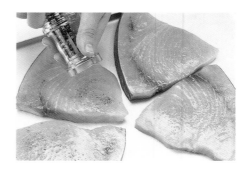

4 Brush the swordfish steaks with olive oil and season. Barbecue or grill (broil) for 3–4 minutes or until just cooked, turning once. Meanwhile, stir the crème fraîche into the sauce and heat it through gently. Pour over the swordfish steaks. Serve garnished with fresh parsley. This is delicious served with chargrilled vegetables.

SALMON <u>WITH</u> TEQUILA CREAM SAUCE

ROASTED JALAPEÑO CHILLIES AND LIGHTLY AGED REPOSADA TEQUILA ARE A WINNING COMBINATION. THIS EXCITING AND UNUSUAL FISH DISH IS PERFECT FOR A DINNER PARTY.

SERVES FOUR

INGREDIENTS
3 fresh green jalapeño chillies
45ml/3 tbsp olive oil
1 small onion, finely chopped
150ml/¼ pint/⅔ cup fish stock
grated (shredded) rind and juice
  of 1 lime
120ml/4fl oz/½ cup single
  (light) cream
30ml/2 tbsp reposada tequila
1 firm avocado
4 salmon fillets
salt and ground white pepper
strips of green (bell) pepper and
  fresh flat leaf parsley, to garnish

1 Roast the chillies in a frying pan until the skins are blistered but not burnt. Put them in a strong plastic bag and tie the top to keep the steam in. Set aside.

2 Heat 15ml/1 tbsp of the oil in a pan. Add the onion and fry for 3–4 minutes, then pour in the stock with the lime rind and juice. Cook for 10 minutes, until the stock starts to reduce. Remove the chillies from the bag. Peel them, then slit and scrape out the seeds.

3 Stir the cream into the onion and stock mixture. Slice the chilli flesh into strips and add to the pan. Cook over a gentle heat, stirring constantly, for 2–3 minutes. Season to taste with salt and white pepper.

4 Stir the tequila into the onion and chilli mixture. Leave the pan over a very low heat. Peel the avocado, remove the stone (pit) and slice the flesh. Brush the salmon fillets on one side with a little of the remaining oil.

5 Heat a frying pan or ridged griddle pan until very hot and add the salmon, oiled side down. Cook for 2–3 minutes, until the underside is golden, then brush the top with oil, turn each fillet over and cook the other side until the fish is cooked and flakes easily when tested with the tip of a sharp knife.

6 Serve on a pool of sauce, with the avocado slices. Garnish with strips of green pepper and fresh parsley. This dish is good with fried potatoes.

SALMON EN PAPILLOTE WITH SPICED LEEKS

COOKING THE FISH "EN PAPILLOTE" MAKES A LOT OF SENSE, ENSURING THAT IT RETAINS ITS FLAVOUR WHILE IT COOKS IN ITS STEAMY PARCEL WITH LEEKS, YELLOW PEPPERS AND CHILLI.

SERVES SIX

INGREDIENTS

25ml/5 tsp groundnut
  (peanut) oil
2 yellow (bell) peppers, seeded
  and thinly sliced
4cm/1½in fresh root ginger, peeled
  and finely shredded
1 large fennel bulb, finely sliced,
  feathery tops chopped
  and reserved
1 fresh green chilli, seeded and
  finely shredded
2 large leeks, cut into 10cm/4in
  lengths and shredded lengthways
30ml/2 tbsp chopped chives
10ml/2 tsp light soy sauce
6 portions salmon fillet, each
  weighing 150–175g/5–6oz, skinned
10ml/2 tsp toasted sesame oil
salt and ground black pepper

1 Heat the oil in a large non-stick frying pan and cook the peppers, ginger and fennel for 5–6 minutes, until they have softened but not browned. Add the chilli and leeks, and cook for 2–3 minutes. Stir in half the chives and the soy sauce with seasoning to taste. Set aside.

2 Preheat the oven to 190°C/375°F/ Gas 5. Cut six 35cm/14in circles of baking parchment or foil. Divide the vegetable mixture among the circles of paper or foil and place a portion of salmon on each pile of vegetables. Drizzle with sesame oil and sprinkle with the remaining chives and the chopped fennel tops. Season with salt and pepper to taste.

3 Fold the baking parchment or foil over to enclose the fish and vegetable mixture, rolling and twisting the edges together to seal the parcels.

4 Place the parcels on a baking sheet and bake for 15–20 minutes, until the parcels are puffed up and, if made with paper, lightly browned. Transfer the parcels to warmed individual plates and serve immediately.

COOK'S TIPS
• This dish is excellent when you are entertaining, as the parcels can be prepared ahead of cooking.
• Toasted sesame oil is used as an ingredient for seasoning, flavouring or marinating, rather than for cooking. It burns at a low temperature.

RED SNAPPER WITH CHILLI, GIN AND GINGER SAUCE

CHILLIES, GINGER AND GIN ADD SPICE AND PIQUANCY TO A COLOURFUL FISH DISH THAT TASTES EVERY BIT AS GOOD AS IT LOOKS. BAKED IN THE OVEN, IT IS IDEAL FOR ENTERTAINING.

SERVES FOUR

INGREDIENTS

1 red snapper, about
  1.6kg/3½lb, cleaned
30ml/2 tbsp sunflower oil
1 onion, chopped
2 garlic cloves, crushed
50g/2oz/½ cup sliced button
  (white) mushrooms
5ml/1 tsp ground coriander
15ml/1 tbsp chopped fresh parsley
30ml/2 tbsp grated (shredded) fresh
  root ginger
2 fresh red chillies, seeded
  and sliced
15ml/1 tbsp cornflour (cornstarch)
45ml/3 tbsp gin
300ml/½ pint/1¼ cups chicken or
  vegetable stock
salt and ground black pepper
For the garnish
  15ml/1 tbsp sunflower oil
  6 garlic cloves, sliced
  1 lettuce heart, finely shredded
  1 bunch fresh coriander (cilantro),
   tied with red raffia

1 Preheat the oven to 190°C/375°F/ Gas 5. Grease a flameproof dish that is large enough to hold the fish. Make several diagonal cuts on one side of the fish.

2 Heat the oil in a frying pan and gently fry the onion, garlic and sliced mushrooms for 2–3 minutes. Stir in the ground coriander and the chopped parsley. Season with salt and pepper to taste.

3 Spoon the filling into the cavity of the fish, then lift the snapper into the dish. Pour in enough cold water to cover the base of the dish. Sprinkle the ginger and chillies over, then cover and bake for 30–40 minutes, basting from time to time. Remove the cover for the last 10 minutes.

4 Carefully lift the snapper on to a serving dish, cover with foil and keep hot. Tip the cooking juices from the dish into a pan.

5 Mix the cornflour and gin in a cup and stir into the cooking juices. Pour in the stock. Bring to the boil and cook gently for 3–4 minutes or until thickened, stirring. Taste for seasoning, then pour into a bowl.

6 Make the garnish. Heat the oil in a small pan and stir-fry the garlic and lettuce over a high heat until crisp. Spoon alongside the snapper. Place the coriander bouquet on the other side. Serve with the sauce.

SPICED FISH WITH CHILLIES, LEMON AND RED ONIONS

SOMETIMES IT'S THE SIMPLEST DISHES THAT MAKE THE MOST IMPACT. THIS DISH NOT ONLY LOOKS PRETTY, IT ALSO TASTES GOOD, WITH PAPRIKA AND FRESH RED CHILLIES GIVING IT CHARACTER.

SERVES FOUR

INGREDIENTS

4 halibut or cod steaks or cutlets, about 175g/6oz each
juice of 1 lemon
5ml/1 tsp crushed garlic
5ml/1 tsp paprika
5ml/1 tsp ground cumin
4ml/¾ tsp dried tarragon
about 60ml/4 tbsp olive oil, plus extra for frying the onion
flour, for dusting
300ml/½ pint/1¼ cups fish stock
2 fresh red chillies, seeded and finely chopped
30ml/2 tbsp chopped fresh coriander (cilantro)
1 red onion, cut into rings
salt and ground black pepper

1 Place the fish in a single layer in a shallow dish. Mix together the lemon juice, garlic, paprika, cumin, tarragon and a little salt and pepper. Spoon over the fish, cover loosely with clear film (plastic wrap) and marinate for a few hours or overnight in the refrigerator. The longer the fish is left to marinate, the stronger the flavour will be.

2 Gently heat the olive oil in a large non-stick frying pan. Drain the fish, dust the pieces with flour, then fry for a few minutes on each side, until golden brown all over.

3 Pour the fish stock around the fish, and simmer, covered, for about 5 minutes until the fish is thoroughly cooked through.

4 Add the chopped red chillies and 15ml/1 tbsp of the coriander to the pan. Simmer for 5 minutes.

5 Transfer the fish and sauce to a serving plate and keep warm.

6 Wipe the pan, heat some extra olive oil and stir-fry the onion rings until speckled brown. Arrange them over the fish, with the remaining chopped coriander and serve at once.

CAJUN BLACKENED FISH WITH PAPAYA SALSA

THIS IS AN EXCELLENT WAY OF COOKING FILLETS OF SNAPPER OR COD, LEAVING IT MOIST IN THE MIDDLE AND CRISP AND SPICY ON THE OUTSIDE.

SERVES FOUR

INGREDIENTS
    5ml/1 tsp black peppercorns
    5ml/1 tsp cumin seeds
    5ml/1 tsp white mustard seeds
    10ml/2 tsp paprika
    5ml/1 tsp chilli powder
    5ml/1 tsp dried oregano
    10ml/2 tsp dried thyme
    4 skinned fish fillets, 225g/8oz each
    50g/2oz/¼ cup butter, melted
    salt
    lime wedges and coriander (cilantro)
      sprigs, to garnish
For the papaya salsa
    1 papaya
    1 fresh red chilli
    ½ small red onion, diced
    45ml/3 tbsp chopped fresh
      coriander (cilantro)
    grated rind and juice of 1 lime

1 Start by making the salsa. Cut the papaya in half and scoop out the seeds. Remove the skin, cut the flesh into small dice and place it in a bowl. Slit the chilli, remove and discard the seeds and finely chop the flesh.

2 Add the onion, chilli, coriander, lime rind and juice to the papaya. Season with salt to taste. Mix well and set aside.

3 Dry-fry the peppercorns, cumin and mustard seeds in a pan, then grind them to a fine powder. Add the paprika, chilli powder, oregano, thyme and 5ml/ 1 tsp salt. Grind again and spread on a plate.

4 Preheat a heavy frying pan over a medium heat for about 10 minutes. Brush the fish fillets with the melted butter then dip them in the spices until well coated.

5 Place the fish in the hot pan and cook for 1–2 minutes on each side until blackened. Garnish with lime and coriander, and serve with the salsa.

COOK'S TIP
Cooking fish in this way can be a smoky affair, so make sure the kitchen is well ventilated or use an extractor fan.

CARIBBEAN FISH STEAKS

THIS QUICK AND EASY RECIPE IS A GOOD EXAMPLE OF HOW CHILLIES, CAYENNE AND ALLSPICE CAN ADD AN EXOTIC ACCENT TO A TOMATO SAUCE FOR FISH.

SERVES FOUR

INGREDIENTS
    4 cod steaks
    5ml/1 tsp muscovado
      (molasses) sugar
    10ml/2 tsp angostura bitters
    salt
    steamed okra or green beans,
    to serve
For the tomato sauce
    45ml/3 tbsp oil
    6 shallots, finely chopped
    1 garlic clove, crushed
    1 fresh green chilli, seeded and
      finely chopped
    400g/14oz can chopped tomatoes
    2 bay leaves
    1.5ml/¼ tsp cayenne pepper
    5ml/1 tsp crushed allspice
    juice of 2 limes

1 First make the tomato sauce. Heat the oil in a frying pan and fry the shallots, until soft. Add the garlic and chilli, and cook for 2 minutes. Stir in tomatoes, bay, cayenne, allspice and lime juice, with salt to taste.

VARIATION
Almost any robust fish steaks or fillets can be cooked in this way.

2 Cook gently for 15 minutes, then add the cod steaks and baste with the tomato sauce. Cover and cook for 10 minutes or until the cod steaks are cooked. Keep hot in a warmed dish.

3 Stir the sugar and angostura bitters into the sauce, simmer for 2 minutes, then pour it over the fish. Serve with steamed okra or green beans.

ESCABECHE

CHILLIES ARE OFTEN USED IN PICKLES, AND HERE THEY PLAY A ROLE IN THIS TRADITIONAL RECIPE FOR PICKLED FISH. ESCABECHE ORIGINATED IN SPAIN, BUT IS NOW POPULAR THE WORLD OVER.

SERVES SIX

INGREDIENTS
    675–900g/1½–2lb white fish fillets,
      such as sole, plaice or flounder
    45–60ml/3–4 tbsp seasoned flour
    vegetable oil, for shallow frying
    spring onions (scallions), finely
      shredded, to garnish (optional)
    boiled long grain rice, to serve
For the sauce
    30ml/2 tbsp vegetable oil
    2.5cm/1in piece fresh root ginger,
      peeled and thinly sliced
    2–3 garlic cloves, crushed
    1 onion, cut into thin rings
    ½ large green (bell) pepper, seeded
      and cut in small neat squares
    ½ large red (bell) pepper, seeded and
      cut in small neat squares
    2 small fresh chillies, seeded and
      finely sliced
    1 carrot, cut into matchsticks
    25ml/1½ tbsp cornflour (cornstarch)
    450ml/¾ pint/scant 2 cups water
    45–60ml/3–4 tbsp cider vinegar
    15ml/1 tbsp light soft brown sugar
    5–10ml/1–2 tsp Thai fish sauce
      (*nam pla*)
    salt and ground black pepper

1 Wipe the fish fillets. Leave them whole, or cut them into serving portions, if you prefer. Pat dry on kitchen paper then dust lightly with seasoned flour.

2 Heat the oil for shallow frying in a frying pan and fry the fish fillets or portions in batches until golden and almost cooked. Transfer to an ovenproof dish and keep warm.

3 Make the sauce in a wok. Heat the oil and fry the ginger, garlic and onion until the onion rings have softened.

4 Add the pepper squares with half the chilli slices and all the carrot. Stir-fry for 1 minute. Put the cornflour in a bowl and stir in a little of the water to make a paste. Stir in the remaining water, the vinegar and the sugar.

5 Pour the cornflour mixture over the vegetables in the wok and stir until the sauce boils and thickens a little. Season with fish sauce, and salt and pepper if needed.

6 Add the fried fish to the sauce and reheat briefly without stirring. Transfer to a warmed oval serving platter. Garnish with the remaining finely sliced fresh chilli and some shredded spring onions, if using. Serve with boiled long grain rice.

COOK'S TIPS
• Red snapper could be used for this recipe, in which case ask your fishmonger to cut it into fillets.
• If you like, you can substitute a flavoured white wine vinegar, such as garlic or chilli, for the cider vinegar.

COCONUT SALMON

CHILLIES AND COCONUT MILK HAVE A SPECIAL AFFINITY, THE FORMER FURNISHING FIRE WHILE THE LATTER IS COOL AND CREAMY. THIS DELECTABLE DISH CAN BE MADE IN NEXT TO NO TIME.

SERVES FOUR

INGREDIENTS
  10ml/2 tsp ground cumin
  10ml/2 tsp chilli powder
  2.5ml/½ tsp ground turmeric
  30ml/2 tbsp white wine vinegar
  1.5ml/¼ tsp salt
  4 salmon steaks, about
    175g/6oz each
  45ml/3 tbsp oil
  1 onion, chopped
  2 fresh green chillies, seeded
    and chopped
  2 garlic cloves, crushed
  2.5cm/1in piece root ginger,
    grated (shredded)
  5ml/1 tsp ground coriander
  175ml/6fl oz/¾ cup coconut milk
  spring onion (scallion) rice, to serve
  fresh coriander (cilantro) sprigs,
    to garnish

1 In a small bowl, mix half the cumin with the chilli powder, turmeric, vinegar and salt. Place the salmon in a single layer in a non-metallic dish and rub all over with the paste. Cover and leave to marinate for 15 minutes.

COOK'S TIP
Make coconut milk by dissolving grated (shredded) creamed coconut (coconut cream) in boiling water, then strain.

2 Heat the oil in a wide, deep-sided frying pan and fry the onion, chillies, garlic and ginger for 5–6 minutes. Scrape the mixture into a food processor or blender and process to a paste. Use a hand-held blender if you prefer.

3 Return the paste to the pan. Add the coriander and remaining cumin, then pour in the coconut milk, stirring constantly. Bring to the boil, then simmer for 5 minutes.

4 Add the salmon steaks and spoon the sauce over them. Cover and cook for 15 minutes until the fish is tender. Serve with spring onion rice and garnish with coriander sprigs.

CREOLE FISH STEW

HERE'S YOUR CHANCE TO EXPERIMENT WITH A HABANERO CHILLI — IF YOU DARE. HABANEROS HAVE A WONDERFUL FLAVOUR, SO IF YOU FEAR THEIR FIRE, START WITH HALF OF ONE.

SERVES FOUR TO SIX

INGREDIENTS
  2 whole red bream or large snapper,
    prepared and cut into 2.5cm/1in
    thick slices
  30ml/2 tbsp Creole or Cajun
    spice seasoning
  30ml/2 tbsp malt vinegar
  flour, for dusting
  oil, for frying
  fresh herb sprigs, to garnish
For the sauce
  30ml/2 tbsp vegetable oil
  15g/½oz/1 tbsp butter
  1 onion, finely chopped
  3 fresh tomatoes, peeled and
    finely chopped
  2 garlic cloves, crushed
  2 fresh thyme sprigs
  600ml/1 pint/2½ cups fish stock
    or water
  2.5ml/½ tsp ground cinnamon
  1 fresh hot chilli, chopped
  1 red (bell) pepper, seeded and
    finely chopped
  1 green (bell) pepper, seeded and
    finely chopped
  salt

1 Spread out the fish slices in a large non-metallic dish and sprinkle with the spice seasoning and vinegar, turning to coat. Cover and set aside to marinate for 2 hours or overnight in the refrigerator.

COOK'S TIP
Handle all chillies with care, especially habaneros. Wear gloves and wash all utensils in hot soapy water when preparation is complete.

2 Make the sauce. Heat the oil and butter in a large frying pan and sauté the onion for 5 minutes. Add the tomatoes, garlic and thyme, stir well and simmer for 5 minutes more. Stir in the stock or water, cinnamon and chilli. Leave over a low heat while you cook the fish.

3 When ready to cook, place a little flour on a large plate. Coat the fish pieces, shaking off any excess flour.

4 Heat a little oil in a large frying pan and fry the fish pieces, in batches if necessary, for about 5 minutes until golden brown.

5 Add the fish pieces and the chopped red and green peppers to the sauce and simmer until the fish is cooked through, and the sauce is thick and flavoursome. Adjust the seasoning with salt to taste. Garnish with fresh herb sprigs and serve hot.

FIERY FISH STEW

CHILLI POWDER AND FRESH CHILLIES ARE USED IN THIS SPICY DISH, SO THERE'S DOUBLE DELIGHT FOR ANYONE WHO LIKES THEIR FOOD GOOD AND HOT.

2 Stir in the salt, ground cumin, ground coriander and chilli powder, and cook for 3–4 minutes.

3 Add the tomatoes and potatoes, then stir in the fish stock. Bring to the boil, then reduce the heat and simmer for 10 minutes.

SERVES FOUR

INGREDIENTS
  30ml/2 tbsp oil
  5ml/1 tsp cumin seeds
  1 onion, chopped
  1 red (bell) pepper, thinly sliced
  1 garlic clove, crushed
  2 fresh red chillies, finely chopped
  2 bay leaves
  2.5ml/½ tsp salt
  5ml/1 tsp ground cumin
  5ml/1 tsp ground coriander
  5ml/1 tsp chilli powder
  400g/14oz can chopped tomatoes
  2 large potatoes, cut into 2.5cm/
   1in chunks
  300ml/½ pint/1¼ cups fish stock
  4 cod fillets
  chapatis, to serve

1 Heat the oil in a large, deep-sided frying pan and fry the cumin seeds for 2 minutes until they begin to splutter. (You may need to cover the pan at this stage to prevent the seeds from leaping out, but do not let them burn.) Add the onion, pepper, garlic, chillies and bay leaves, and fry for 5–7 minutes until the onions have browned.

4 Add the fish, then cover and simmer for 10 minutes, or until the fish is tender. Serve with the chapatis.

COOK'S TIP
The potatoes will help to moderate the heat of this curry, but if you prefer a milder flavour, use half the amount of fresh chillies and a mild chilli powder.

STEAMED FISH WITH CHILLI SAUCE

CHILLIES CAN BE USED IN MANY DIFFERENT WAYS. HERE THEY FLAVOUR A WHOLE FISH SIMPLY BY BEING STREWN OVER DURING STEAMING. AN EXTRA KICK COMES FROM THE HOT SAUCE.

SERVES FOUR

INGREDIENTS
  1 large, firm fish such as bass or
    grouper, scaled and cleaned
  1 fresh banana leaf or piece of foil
  2 lemon grass stalks, trimmed
  30ml/2 tbsp rice wine
  3 fresh red chillies, seeded and
    finely sliced
  2 garlic cloves, finely chopped
  2cm/¾in piece fresh root ginger,
    finely shredded
  2 spring onions (scallions), chopped
  30ml/2 tbsp Thai fish sauce (*nam pla*)
  juice of 1 lime
For the hot chilli sauce
  10 fresh red chillies, seeded and
    roughly chopped
  4 garlic cloves, halved
  60ml/4 tbsp Thai fish sauce
    (*nam pla*)
  15ml/1 tbsp granulated sugar
  75ml/5 tbsp lime juice

1 Rinse the fish under cold running water. Pat dry with kitchen paper. With a sharp knife, slash the skin of the fish a few times on both sides.

2 Place the fish on a banana leaf or a piece of foil. Cut off the lower 5cm/2in of the lemon grass and chop it finely. Put it in a bowl, stir in all the remaining ingredients and spoon the mixture over the fish.

COOK'S TIP
Ten chillies may seem a lot for the sauce, but bear in mind that the mixture is meant to be used sparingly.

3 Place a rack or a small upturned plate in the base of a wok and pour in boiling water to a depth of 5cm/2in.
Lift the banana leaf or piece of foil holding the fish, and place on the rack or plate (the water should not come into contact with the fish). Cover with a lid and steam for about 10–15 minutes or until the fish is cooked.

4 Place all the chilli sauce ingredients in a food processor and process until smooth. You may need to add a little cold water. Scrape into a bowl.

5 Serve the fish hot, on the banana leaf if you like, with the chilli sauce to spoon sparingly over the top. This dish goes very well with boiled rice or potatoes.

BALINESE FISH CURRY

A SIMPLE FISH CURRY IS THE IDEAL DISH TO PREPARE WHEN YOU DON'T HAVE A GREAT DEAL OF TIME.
THE CURRY SAUCE CAN BE MADE IN ADVANCE, AND THE FISH TAKES ONLY MINUTES TO COOK.

SERVES FOUR TO SIX

INGREDIENTS
  675g/1½lb cod or haddock fillet
  celery leaves or chopped fresh chilli,
    to garnish
  boiled rice, to serve
For the sauce
  1cm/½in cube shrimp paste
  2 red or white onions
  2.5cm/1in fresh root ginger, peeled
    and sliced
  1cm/½in fresh galangal, peeled
    and sliced
  2 garlic cloves
  1–2 fresh red chillies, seeded
    and sliced
  90ml/6 tbsp sunflower oil
  15ml/1 tbsp dark soy sauce
  5ml/1 tsp tamarind pulp, soaked in
    30ml/2 tbsp warm water
    then strained
  250ml/8fl oz/1 cup water

1 Skin the fish, remove any bones with a pair of tweezers, and then cut the flesh into bitesize pieces. Pat dry with kitchen paper and set aside.

2 Grind the shrimp paste, onions, ginger, galangal, garlic and fresh chillies to a paste in a food processor or with a mortar and pestle.

VARIATIONS
• Use 450g/1lb cooked tiger prawns (jumbo shrimp) instead of fish. Add them 3 minutes before the end of the cooking time.
• If you don't have any fresh chillies, use 5–10ml/1–2 tsp chilli powder.

3 Heat 30ml/2 tbsp of the oil in a pan and fry the spices, stirring, for about 2 minutes. Add the soy sauce and the tamarind liquid, with the water. Cook for 2–3 minutes, stirring.

4 Heat the remaining oil in a separate pan and fry the fish for 2–3 minutes. Turn once only so that the pieces stay whole. Lift out with a slotted spoon and put into the sauce.

5 Cook the fish in the sauce for 3 minutes, until cooked through. Spoon on to a serving dish, garnish with feathery celery leaves or a little chopped fresh chilli and serve with the rice.

COOK'S TIPS
• Save time by asking the fishmonger to skin the fish for you.
• Tamarind has a refreshing acid taste.

FISH MOOLIE

THIS IS A VERY POPULAR SOUTH-EAST ASIAN FISH CURRY IN A COCONUT SAUCE. CHOOSE A FIRM-TEXTURED FISH SO THAT THE PIECES STAY INTACT DURING THE BRIEF COOKING PROCESS.

SERVES FOUR

INGREDIENTS

500g/1¼lb firm-textured fish fillets, skinned and cut into 2.5cm/1in cubes
2.5ml/½ tsp salt
50g/2oz/⅔ cup desiccated (dry unsweetened shredded) coconut
6 shallots or small onions, roughly chopped
6 blanched almonds
2–3 garlic cloves, roughly chopped
2.5cm/1in piece fresh root ginger, peeled and sliced
2 lemon grass stalks, trimmed
10ml/2 tsp ground turmeric
45ml/3 tbsp vegetable oil
2 × 400ml/14fl oz cans coconut milk
1–3 fresh red or green chillies, seeded and sliced
salt and ground black pepper
fresh chives, to garnish
boiled long grain rice, to serve

1 Spread out the pieces of fish in a shallow dish and sprinkle them with the salt. Dry-fry the coconut in a wok over medium to low heat, turning all the time until it is crisp and golden (see Cook's Tip below).

2 Tip the dry-fried coconut into a food processor and process until you have an oily paste. Scrape into a bowl and reserve.

3 Add the shallots or onions, almonds, garlic and ginger to the food processor. Cut off the lower 5cm/2in of the lemon grass stalks, chop them roughly and add to the other ingredients in the processor. Process the mixture to a paste. Bruise the remaining lemon grass and set the stalks aside.

4 Add the ground turmeric to the mixture in the processor and process briefly to mix.

5 Heat the oil in the clean wok. Add the onion mixture and cook for a few minutes without browning. Stir in the coconut milk and bring to the boil, stirring constantly to prevent the mixture from curdling.

6 Add the cubes of fish, most of the sliced chillies and the bruised lemon grass stalks. Cook for 3–4 minutes. Stir in the coconut paste (moistened with some of the sauce if necessary) and cook for a further 2–3 minutes only. Do not overcook the fish. Taste and adjust the seasoning.

7 Remove the lemon grass stalks. Spoon the moolie on to a hot serving dish and sprinkle with the remaining slices of chilli. Garnish with chopped and whole chives and serve with boiled long grain rice.

COOK'S TIP
Dry-frying is a feature of Malay cooking that demands the cook's close attention. The coconut must be constantly on the move so that it becomes crisp and uniformly golden in colour.

FISH AND SHELLFISH LAKSA

A LAKSA IS A SOUPY MALAYSIAN STEW OF FISH, POULTRY, MEAT OR VEGETABLES WITH NOODLES. LAKSAS ARE OFTEN VERY HOT AND ARE COOLED BY ADDING COCONUT MILK.

SERVES FOUR TO FIVE

INGREDIENTS

- 3 fresh medium-hot red chillies, seeded and roughly chopped
- 4–5 garlic cloves
- 5ml/1 tsp mild paprika
- 10ml/2 tsp shrimp paste
- 25ml/1½ tbsp chopped fresh root ginger
- 7 small red shallots
- 25g/1oz fresh coriander (cilantro), preferably with roots
- 45ml/3 tbsp groundnut (peanut) oil
- 5ml/1 tsp fennel seeds, crushed
- 2 fennel bulbs, cut into thin wedges
- 600ml/1 pint/2½ cups fish stock
- 300g/11oz thin vermicelli rice noodles
- 450ml/¾ pint/scant 2 cups coconut milk
- juice of 1–2 limes
- 30–45ml/2–3 tbsp Thai fish sauce (*nam pla*)
- 450g/1lb firm white fish fillet, cut into chunks
- 20 large raw prawns (jumbo shrimp), peeled and deveined
- small bunch of fresh holy basil or regular basil
- 2 spring onions (scallions), sliced

1 Process the chillies, garlic, paprika, shrimp paste, ginger and two of the shallots to a paste in a food processor, blender or spice grinder. Remove the roots and stems from the coriander, wash thoroughly and pat dry with kitchen paper. Add them to the paste; chop and reserve the coriander leaves. Add 15ml/1 tbsp of the oil to the paste and process again until fairly smooth. Scrape into a bowl.

2 Heat the remaining oil in a large pan. Add the remaining shallots, with the fennel seeds and fennel wedges. Cook until lightly browned, then add 45ml/ 3 tbsp of the paste and stir-fry for 1–2 minutes. Pour in the fish stock and bring to the boil. Reduce the heat and simmer for 8–10 minutes.

3 Meanwhile, cook the vermicelli rice noodles according to the instructions on the packet. Drain thoroughly and set aside.

4 Pour the coconut milk into the pan of shallots, stirring constantly to prevent sticking, then add the juice of 1 lime, with 30ml/2 tbsp of the fish sauce. Stir well to combine. Bring to a gentle simmer and taste, adding more of the coconut paste, lime juice or fish sauce as necessary.

5 Add the fish to the pan. Cook for 2–3 minutes, then add the raw prawns and cook for a further 3–4 minutes or until they just turn pink.

6 Chop most of the basil and add it to the pan with the reserved chopped coriander leaves.

7 Divide the noodles among 4–5 deep bowls, then ladle in the stew. Sprinkle with spring onions and the remaining whole basil leaves. Serve immediately.

VERMICELLI <u>WITH</u> SPICY CLAM SAUCE

THERE'S A SUBTLE CHILLI FLAVOUR IN THIS ITALIAN DISH. THE TRICK IS TO USE ENOUGH TO MAKE IT LIVELY, AS HERE, BUT NOT SO MUCH THAT YOU CAN'T TASTE THE CLAMS.

SERVES FOUR

INGREDIENTS

1kg/2¼lb fresh clams, well scrubbed
250ml/8fl oz/1 cup dry white wine
2 garlic cloves, bruised
1 large handful fresh flat leaf parsley
30ml/2 tbsp olive oil
1 small onion, finely chopped
8 ripe Italian plum tomatoes, peeled,
  seeded and finely chopped
½–1 fresh red chilli, seeded and
  finely chopped
350g/12oz dried vermicelli
salt and ground black pepper

1 Discard any clams that are open or that do not close when sharply tapped against the work surface.

2 Put the wine, garlic and half the parsley into a pan, then the clams. Cover and bring to the boil. Cook for 5 minutes, shaking the pan.

3 Tip the clams into a large colander set over a bowl and let the liquid drain through. Leave the clams until cool enough to handle, then remove about two-thirds of them from their shells, tipping the clam liquor into the bowl of cooking liquid. Discard any clams that have failed to open. Set both shelled and unshelled clams aside, keeping the unshelled clams warm in a bowl covered with a lid.

4 Heat the olive oil in a pan, add the onion and stir over the heat for about 5 minutes until softened and lightly coloured. Add the tomatoes, then strain in the clam cooking liquid. Stir in the chilli and salt and pepper to taste.

5 Bring to the boil, half-cover the pan and simmer gently for 15–20 minutes. Meanwhile, cook the pasta according to the instructions on the packet. Chop the remaining parsley finely.

6 Add the shelled clams to the tomato sauce, stir well and heat through very gently for 2–3 minutes.

7 Drain the cooked pasta well and tip it into a warmed bowl. Taste the sauce for seasoning, then pour the sauce over the pasta and toss everything together well. Garnish with the reserved unshelled clams, arranging them attractively on top of the pasta. Sprinkle the chopped parsley over the pasta and serve immediately.

BLACK PASTA WITH SQUID SAUCE

ANOTHER SHELLFISH DISH WITH A SUBTLE, RATHER THAN A STRIDENT, CHILLI FLAVOUR. DON'T BE TEMPTED TO OMIT THE CHILLI FLAKES — THE DISH WOULD BE THE POORER FOR THEIR ABSENCE.

SERVES FOUR

INGREDIENTS

105ml/7 tbsp olive oil
2 shallots, finely chopped
3 garlic cloves, crushed
45ml/3 tbsp chopped fresh parsley
675g/1½lb cleaned squid, cut into rings and rinsed
150ml/¼ pint/⅔ cup dry white wine
400g/14oz can chopped tomatoes
2.5ml/½ tsp dried chilli flakes or powder
450g/1lb squid ink tagliatelle
salt and ground black pepper

1 Heat the oil in a pan and cook the shallots until pale golden, then add the garlic. When the garlic colours a little, add 30ml/2 tbsp of the parsley, stir, then add the squid and stir again. Cook for 3–4 minutes, then pour in the dry white wine.

2 Simmer for a few seconds, then add the tomatoes and chilli flakes. Season with salt and pepper. Cover and simmer gently for about 1 hour, until the squid is tender. Add more water during the cooking time if necessary.

3 Bring a large pan of lightly salted water to the boil and cook the squid ink tagliatelle, following the instructions on the packet, or until it is *al dente*. Drain and return the pasta to the pan. Add the squid sauce and mix well to coat the tagliatelle evenly. Serve in warmed dishes, sprinkling each portion with the remaining chopped parsley.

COOK'S TIPS

• Tagliatelle flavoured with squid ink looks amazing and tastes deliciously of the sea. Look for it in good Italian delicatessens and better supermarkets.
• If you make your own pasta, you can buy sachets of squid ink from delicatessens.
• If you prepare the squid yourself, you will find the ink sac in the innards.

CHILLI RAVIOLI <u>WITH</u> CRAB

CHILLI PASTA LOOKS AND TASTES SENSATIONAL. ADD A CREAMY CRAB FILLING AND YOU'VE GOT A GREAT TALKING POINT FOR A DINNER PARTY.

SERVES FOUR

INGREDIENTS
 300g/11oz/2¾ cups strong white
   (bread) flour
 5ml/1 tsp salt
 5–10ml/1–2 tsp crushed dried
   red chillies
 3 eggs
 75g/3oz/6 tbsp butter
 juice of 1 lemon
For the filling
 175g/6oz/¾ cup mascarpone cheese
 175g/6oz crab meat
 30ml/2 tbsp finely chopped fresh flat
   leaf parsley
 finely grated (shredded) rind
   of 1 lemon
 pinch of crushed dried chillies
 salt and ground black pepper

1 Put the flour, salt and dried chillies in a food processor. Add 1 egg and pulse until the ingredients are mixed. Switch the processor to maximum speed and add the remaining eggs through the feeder tube. As soon as the mixture forms a dough, transfer it to a clean work surface and knead for 5 minutes, until smooth and elastic. Wrap in clear film (plastic wrap) and leave to rest for 15 minutes.

COOK'S TIPS
• Mascarpone is a very rich Italian cream cheese that can be used for savoury and sweet dishes.
• You can use a mixture of light and dark crab meat for this dish.
• This dish is best served with a crisp green or herb salad.

2 Make the filling. Put the mascarpone in a bowl and mash it with a fork. Add the crab meat, parsley, lemon rind and crushed dried chillies, with salt and pepper to taste. Stir well.

3 Using a pasta machine, roll out one-quarter of the pasta dough into a 90cm–1 metre/36–39in strip. Cut into two 45–50cm/18–20in lengths. With a 6cm/2½in fluted cutter, firmly cut out 8 squares from each strip.

4 Using a teaspoon, put a mound of filling in the centre of half the squares. Brush a little water around the edge of the filled squares, then top with the plain squares and press the edges to seal. For a decorative finish, press the edges with the tines of a fork.

5 Put the ravioli on floured dishtowels, sprinkle lightly with flour and leave to dry while repeating the process with the remaining dough to make 32 ravioli altogether.

6 Bring a large pan of lightly salted water to the boil and cook the ravioli for 4–5 minutes. Meanwhile, melt the butter and lemon juice in a small pan until sizzling.

7 Drain the ravioli and divide them among 4 warmed bowls. Drizzle the lemon butter over the ravioli and serve.

CHARGRILLED SQUID WITH CHILLIES

IF YOU LIKE YOUR FOOD HOT, USE THE CHILLI SEEDS WITH THE FLESH. IF NOT, SLIT THE CHILLIES IN HALF LENGTHWAYS, SCRAPE OUT THE SEEDS AND DISCARD THEM BEFORE CHOPPING THE FLESH.

SERVES TWO

INGREDIENTS

2 whole prepared squid,
  with tentacles
75ml/5 tbsp olive oil
30ml/2 tbsp balsamic vinegar
250g/9 oz/1¼ cups hot cooked rice
2 fresh red chillies, finely chopped
60ml/4 tbsp dry white wine
salt and ground black pepper
sprigs of fresh parsley, to garnish

1 Rinse the squid and pull away the outer skin. Dry on kitchen paper. Make a lengthways cut down the body of each squid, and open out flat. Score the flesh on both sides of the bodies in a criss-cross pattern. Chop the tentacles. Place all the squid in a china or glass dish. Whisk the oil and vinegar in a small bowl, season to taste and pour over the squid. Cover and marinate for about 1 hour.

2 Heat a ridged cast-iron pan. When hot, add 1 squid body. Cook over a medium heat for 2–3 minutes, pressing with a spatula to keep it flat. Repeat on the other side. Cook the other squid body in the same way.

3 Cut the squid bodies into diagonal strips. Pile the rice into the centre of 2 heated soup plates and top with the squid, arranging them criss-cross fashion. Keep hot either in the oven or over pans of simmering water while you cook the tentacles and chillies.

4 Heat a pan. Add the marinated chopped tentacles and the finely chopped chillies to the pan and toss over a medium heat for 2 minutes. Stir in the marinade and wine, then drizzle the mixture over the squid and rice. Garnish with the parsley and serve.

SQUID AND CHILLI RISOTTO

SQUID NEEDS TO BE COOKED VERY QUICKLY OR VERY SLOWLY. HERE THE SQUID IS MARINATED IN LIME AND KIWI FRUIT — A POPULAR METHOD IN NEW ZEALAND FOR TENDERIZING SQUID.

SERVES THREE TO FOUR

INGREDIENTS
    about 450g/1lb squid
    about 45ml/3 tbsp olive oil
    15g/½oz/1 tbsp butter
    1 onion, finely chopped
    2 garlic cloves, crushed
    1 fresh red chilli, seeded and
        finely sliced
    275g/10oz/1½ cups risotto rice
    175ml/6fl oz/¾ cup dry white wine
    1 litre/1¾ pints/4 cups simmering
        fish stock
    30ml/2 tbsp chopped fresh
        coriander (cilantro)
    salt and ground black pepper
For the marinade
    2 ripe kiwi fruit, chopped
        and mashed
    1 fresh red chilli, seeded and
        thinly sliced
    30ml/2 tbsp lime juice

1 If not already cleaned, prepare the squid by cutting off the tentacles at the base and pulling to remove the quill. Discard the quill and intestines, if necessary, and pull away the thin outer skin. Rinse the body and cut into thin strips: cut the tentacles into short pieces, discarding both the beak and the eyes.

2 Put the kiwi fruit for the marinade in a bowl, then stir in the chilli and lime juice. Add the squid, stirring to coat all the strips in the mixture. Season with salt and pepper, cover with clear film (plastic wrap) and set aside in the refrigerator for 4 hours or overnight.

3 Drain the squid. Heat 15ml/1 tbsp of the olive oil in a frying pan and cook the strips, in batches if necessary, for about 30–60 seconds over a high heat. It is important that the squid cooks very quickly to keep it tender.

4 Transfer the cooked squid to a plate and set aside. Don't worry if some of the marinade clings to the squid, but if too much juice accumulates in the pan, pour this into a jug and add more olive oil when cooking the next batch, so that the squid fries rather than simmers. Reserve the accumulated juices in a jug.

5 Heat the remaining oil with the butter in a large pan and gently fry the onion and garlic for 5–6 minutes until soft. Add the sliced chilli to the pan and fry for 1 minute more.

COOK'S TIPS
• You can only make a true risotto with Italian risotto rice. Names to look for are Arborio, Carnaroli, Roma and Baldo. These are the rices that give the right kind of creamy texture.
• As in this recipe, always use a well-flavoured stock.

6 Add the rice. Cook for a few minutes, stirring, until the rice is coated with oil and is slightly translucent, then stir in the wine until it has been absorbed.

7 Gradually add the hot stock and the reserved cooking liquid from the squid, a ladleful at a time, stirring the rice constantly and waiting until each quantity of stock has been absorbed before adding the next.

8 When the rice is about three-quarters cooked, stir in the squid and continue cooking the risotto until all the stock has been absorbed and the rice is tender, but retains a bit of "bite". Stir in the chopped coriander, cover with the lid or a dishtowel, and leave to rest for a few minutes before serving.

VARIATIONS
• Use a long hot chilli, such as cayenne, for this dish, or try a milder variety, such as a red fresno.
• You can use a habanero if you like, but one-quarter or half will probably be sufficient, and remember to wear gloves when you handle it.

AROMATIC MUSSEL RISOTTO

FRESH ROOT GINGER ADDS A DISTINCTIVE FLAVOUR TO THIS DISH, WHILE THE GREEN CHILLIES GIVE IT A LITTLE HEAT. USE JALAPEÑOS OR SERRANOS.

SERVES THREE TO FOUR

INGREDIENTS
   900g/2lb live mussels
   about 250ml/8fl oz/1 cup dry
     white wine
   30ml/2 tbsp olive oil
   1 onion, chopped
   2 garlic cloves, crushed
   1–2 fresh green chillies, seeded and
     finely sliced
   2.5cm/1in piece of fresh root
     ginger, grated (shredded)
   275g/10oz/1½ cups risotto rice
   900ml/1½ pints/3¾ cups simmering
     fish stock
   30ml/2 tbsp chopped fresh
     coriander (cilantro)
   30ml/2 tbsp double (heavy) cream
   salt and ground black pepper

1 Scrub the mussels, discarding any that do not close when sharply tapped. Place in a large pan. Add half the wine and bring to the boil. Cover the pan and cook the mussels for 4–5 minutes until they have opened, shaking the pan occasionally. Drain, reserving the liquid and discarding any mussels that have failed to open. Remove most of the mussels from their shells, reserving a few in their shells for decoration. Strain the mussel liquid.

2 Heat the oil and fry the onion and garlic for 3–4 minutes until beginning to soften. Stir in the chillies. Continue to cook over a low heat for 1–2 minutes, stirring frequently, then stir in the grated ginger and fry very gently for 1 minute more.

3 Add the rice and cook over a medium heat for 2 minutes, stirring, until the rice is coated in oil and the grains become translucent.

4 Stir in the reserved cooking liquid from the mussels. When this has been absorbed, add the remaining wine and cook, stirring, until this has been absorbed. Now add the hot fish stock, a little at a time, making sure that each addition has been absorbed before adding the next.

5 When the rice is about three-quarters cooked, stir in the shelled mussels. Add the coriander and season. Continue adding stock to the risotto until it is creamy and the rice is tender but slightly firm in the centre.

6 Remove the risotto from the heat, stir in the cream, cover and leave to rest for a few minutes. Warm a serving dish and spoon in the risotto, garnish with the reserved mussels in their shells, and serve immediately.

CRAB WITH GREEN RICE

THIS IS A POPULAR DISH IN THE WESTERN COASTAL AREAS OF MEXICO. OTHER TYPES OF SHELLFISH CAN BE USED IF YOU PREFER, AND THE DISH ALSO WORKS WELL WITH WARM CORN TORTILLAS.

SERVES FOUR

INGREDIENTS

225g/8oz/generous 1 cup long grain white rice
500g/1¼lb/3⅓ cups drained canned tomatillos
large bunch of fresh coriander (cilantro)
1 onion, roughly chopped
3 poblano or other fresh green chillies, seeded and chopped
3 garlic cloves
45ml/3 tbsp olive oil
500g/1¼lb crab meat
300ml/½ pint/1¼ cups fish stock
60ml/4 tbsp dry white wine
salt
sliced spring onions (scallions), to garnish

1 Put the rice in a heatproof bowl, pour over boiling water to cover and leave to stand for 20 minutes. Drain thoroughly.

2 Put the tomatillos in a food processor or blender and process until smooth. Chop half the coriander and add to the tomatillo purée, with the onion, chillies and garlic. Process again until the mixture is smooth.

3 Heat the oil in a large pan. Add the rice and fry over a medium heat for 5 minutes, stirring from time to time, until all the oil has been absorbed. Stir occasionally to prevent the rice from sticking.

4 Stir in the tomatillo mixture, with the crab meat, stock and wine. Cover and cook over a low heat for about 20 minutes or until all the liquid has been absorbed. Stir occasionally and add a little more liquid if the rice starts to stick to the pan. Add salt as required, then spoon into a dish and garnish with coriander and the sliced spring onions.

COOK'S TIP
Tomatillos are the edible purplish fruit of a ground cherry.

LOUISIANA SHELLFISH GUMBO

GUMBO IS A SOUP, BUT IS SERVED OVER RICE AS A MAIN COURSE. IN THIS VERSION, CHILLI IS ADDED TO THE "HOLY TRINITY" OF ONION, CELERY AND SWEET PEPPER.

SERVES SIX

INGREDIENTS
  450g/1lb fresh mussels
  450g/1lb raw prawns (shrimp),
    in the shell
  1 cooked crab, about 1kg/2¼lb
  small bunch of parsley, leaves
    chopped and stalks reserved
  150ml/¼ pint/⅔ cup vegetable oil
  115g/4oz/1 cup plain
    (all-purpose) flour
  1 green (bell) pepper, seeded
    and chopped
  1 large onion, chopped
  2 celery sticks, sliced
  1 fresh green chilli, seeded
    and chopped
  3 garlic cloves, finely chopped
  75g/3oz smoked spiced sausage,
    skinned and sliced
  275g/10oz/1½ cups white long
    grain rice
  6 spring onions (scallions), sliced
  Tabasco sauce, to taste
  salt

1 Wash the mussels in several changes of cold water, pulling away the black "beards". Discard broken mussels or any that do not close when tapped firmly.

2 Bring 250ml/8fl oz/1 cup water to the boil in a deep pan. Add the prepared mussels, cover the pan tightly and cook over a high heat, shaking frequently, for 3 minutes. As the mussels open, lift them out with tongs into a sieve set over a bowl. Discard any that fail to open. Shell the mussels, discarding most of the shells but reserving a few.

3 Peel the prawns and set them aside, reserving a few for the garnish. Put the shells and heads into the pan.

4 Remove all the meat from the crab, separating the brown and white meat. Add all the pieces of shell to the pan and stir in 5ml/1 tsp salt.

5 Return the mussel liquid from the bowl to the pan and make it up to 2 litres/ 3½ pints/8 cups with water. Bring the shellfish stock to the boil, skimming it regularly. When there is no more froth on the surface, add the parsley stalks and simmer for 15 minutes. Cool the reduced stock, then strain into a liquid measure and make it up to 2 litres/ 3½ pints/8 cups with water.

6 Heat the oil in a heavy pan and stir in the flour. Stir constantly over a medium heat with a wooden spoon or whisk until the roux reaches a golden-brown colour. Immediately add the pepper, onion, celery, chilli and garlic. Continue cooking for about 3 minutes until the onion is soft. Stir in the sausage. Reheat the stock.

7 Stir the brown crab meat into the roux, then ladle in the hot stock a little at a time, stirring constantly until it has all been smoothly incorporated. Bring to a low boil, partially cover the pan, then simmer for 30 minutes.

8 Meanwhile, cook the rice in plenty of lightly salted boiling water until the grains are tender.

9 Add the prawns, mussels, white crab meat and spring onions to the gumbo. Return to the boil and season with salt if necessary. Taste and add a dash or two of Tabasco sauce to heighten the heat generated by the chilli. Simmer for a further minute, then add the chopped parsley leaves. Serve immediately, ladling the soup over the hot rice in soup plates.

COOK'S TIP
It is vital to stir constantly to darken the roux without burning. Should black specks occur at any stage of cooking, discard the roux and start again. Have the pepper, onion, celery, chilli and garlic ready to add to the roux the minute it reaches the correct golden-brown stage, as this stops it from becoming too dark.

SALT AND PEPPER PRAWNS

THIS SPICY DISH FLAVOURED WITH CHILLIES, GINGER AND FRIED SALT AND PEPPERCORNS MAKES A DELICIOUS SUPPERTIME TREAT. SERVE WITH CRUSTY WARM BREAD.

2 Carefully remove and discard the heads and legs from the raw prawns. Leave the body shells and the tails in place. Pat the prepared prawns dry with kitchen paper.

3 Heat the oil for deep-frying to 190°C/375°F or until a cube of day-old bread, added to the oil, browns in 30–45 seconds. Fry the prawns for 1 minute, then lift them out and drain thoroughly on kitchen paper. Spoon 30ml/2 tbsp of the hot oil into a large frying pan, leaving the rest of the oil to one side to cool.

4 Heat the oil in the frying pan. Add the fried salt, with the finely chopped onion, garlic, ginger, chillies and sugar. Toss together for 1 minute, then add the prawns and toss them over the heat for 1 minute more until they are coated and the shells are impregnated with the seasonings. Serve at once, garnished with the spring onions.

SERVES THREE TO FOUR

INGREDIENTS
    15–18 large raw prawns (shrimp),
      in the shell, about 450g/1lb
    vegetable oil, for deep-frying
    1 small onion, finely chopped
    2 garlic cloves, crushed
    1cm/½in piece fresh root ginger,
      peeled and very finely grated
    1–2 fresh red chillies, seeded and
      finely sliced
    2.5ml/½ tsp granulated sugar
    3–4 spring onions (scallions), sliced,
      to garnish
For the fried salt
    10ml/2 tsp salt
    5ml/1 tsp Sichuan peppercorns

1 Make the fried salt by dry-frying the salt and peppercorns in a heavy frying pan over a medium heat until the peppercorns begin to release their aroma. Cool the mixture, then tip into a mortar and crush with a pestle or process in a blender.

COOK'S TIPS
• These succulent prawns beg to be eaten with the fingers, so provide finger bowls or hot cloths for your guests.
• "Fried salt" is also known as "Cantonese salt" or simply "salt and pepper mix". It is widely used as a table condiment or as a dip for deep-fried or roasted food, but can also be an ingredient, as here. It is best when freshly prepared.
• Black or white peppercorns can be substituted for the Sichuan peppercorns.

FIVE-SPICE SQUID WITH CHILLI AND BLACK BEAN SAUCE

SQUID IS PERFECT FOR STIR-FRYING AS IT BENEFITS FROM BEING COOKED QUICKLY. THE SPICY SAUCE MAKES THE IDEAL ACCOMPANIMENT AND CAN BE MADE VERY QUICKLY.

SERVES SIX

INGREDIENTS

450g/1lb small prepared squid
45ml/3 tbsp oil
2.5cm/1in piece fresh root
   ginger, grated (shredded)
1 garlic clove, crushed
8 spring onions (scallions), cut
   diagonally into 2.5cm/1in lengths
1 red (bell) pepper, seeded and cut
   into strips
1 fresh green chilli, seeded and
   thinly sliced
6 mushrooms, sliced
5ml/1 tsp five-spice powder
30ml/2 tbsp black bean sauce
30ml/2 tbsp soy sauce
5ml/1 tsp granulated sugar
15ml/1 tbsp rice wine or dry sherry

2 Heat a wok briefly and add the oil. When it is hot, stir-fry the squid quickly. Remove the squid strips from the wok with a slotted spoon and set aside. Add the ginger, garlic, spring onions, red pepper, chilli and mushrooms to the oil in the wok and stir-fry for 2 minutes.

3 Return the partially cooked squid to the wok and stir in the five-spice powder. Stir in the black bean sauce, soy sauce, sugar and rice wine or sherry. Bring to the boil and cook, stirring, for 1 minute. Serve immediately in warmed bowls.

1 Rinse the squid and pull away the outer skin. Dry on kitchen paper. Make a lengthways slit down the body of each squid, then open out the body flat. Score the outside of the bodies in a criss-cross pattern with the tip of a sharp knife. Cut the squid into strips.

COOK'S TIPS
• Use a dried chilli, if you prefer. The pasilla has a special affinity for shellfish. Slit the chilli and shake out most of the seeds, then soak it in hot water for 20 minutes before cooking it.
• Five-spice powder is made up of 5–6 spices including star anise, cinnamon, fennel, cloves and Sichuan peppercorns.
• You can use either thick or thin soy sauces, but the thin version is more salty.

STIR-FRIED PRAWNS ON CRISP NOODLE CAKE

THE CONTRAST BETWEEN THE CRISP NOODLE CAKE AND THE SUCCULENT VEGETABLES AND SHELLFISH WORKS EXTREMELY WELL, AND THE CHILLI RINGS ADD COLOUR AND A FINAL BURST OF HEAT.

SERVES FOUR

INGREDIENTS
  300g/11oz thin dried egg noodles
  60ml/4 tbsp vegetable oil
  500g/1¼lb medium raw king
    prawns (jumbo shrimp), peeled
    and deveined
  2.5ml/½ tsp ground coriander
  15ml/1 tbsp ground turmeric
  2 garlic cloves, finely chopped
  2 slices fresh root ginger,
    finely chopped
  tender parts of 2 lemon grass stalks,
    finely chopped
  2 shallots, finely chopped
  15ml/1 tbsp tomato purée (paste)
  250ml/8fl oz/1 cup coconut milk
  15–30ml/1–2 tbsp lime juice
  15–30ml/1–2 tbsp Thai fish sauce
    (*nam pla*)
  1 cucumber, peeled, seeded and cut
    into 5cm/2in batons
  4–6 fresh kaffir lime leaves (optional)
  1 tomato, seeded and cut into strips
  2 fresh red chillies, seeded and
    finely sliced in rings
  salt and ground black pepper
  2 spring onions (scallions), finely
    sliced, and a few coriander
    (cilantro) sprigs, to garnish

1 Bring a pan of lightly salted water to the boil, add the egg noodles and remove the pan from the heat. Cover and set aside for about 10 minutes, until just tender. Drain, rinse under cold running water and drain again well.

COOK'S TIPS
• Any red chillies can be used here, but you would be wise to avoid incendiary varieties like habanero or Scotch bonnet. Red fresno chillies, red serranos or even a mild red wax chilli would be suitable.
• You can, of course, use fresh noodles for this dish. It is always worth buying them if you can, because they can be frozen and then used as needed. They defrost quickly when dropped in boiling water.

2 Heat 15ml/1 tbsp of the oil in a large frying pan. Add the noodles in an even layer and fry for 4–5 minutes until they form a crisp, golden cake. Turn the noodle cake over and fry the other side. Alternatively, make 4 individual cakes. Keep hot.

3 In a bowl, toss the prawns with the ground coriander, turmeric, garlic, ginger and lemon grass. Add salt and pepper to taste.

4 Heat the remaining oil in a large frying pan. Fry the shallots for 1 minute, then add the prawns and fry for 2 minutes more. Using a slotted spoon, remove the prawns.

5 Stir the tomato purée and coconut milk into the mixture remaining in the pan. Stir in lime juice to taste and season with the fish sauce. Bring the sauce to a simmer, gently stir in the prawns, then add the cucumber and the kaffir lime leaves, if using. Simmer gently until the prawns are cooked and the sauce has reduced to a nice coating consistency.

6 Add the tomato, stir until just warmed through, then add the chillies. Serve the prawns in the sauce on top of the crisp noodle cake(s), and garnish with the sliced spring onions and coriander sprigs.

THAI FRIED NOODLES

THE CHILLI FLAVOUR SIMPLY TEASES THE TASTE BUDS IN THIS CLASSIC THAI RECIPE. IT IS MADE WITH RICE NOODLES AND IS CONSIDERED ONE OF THE NATIONAL DISHES OF THAILAND.

SERVES FOUR TO SIX

INGREDIENTS

350g/12oz rice noodles
45ml/3 tbsp vegetable oil
15ml/1 tbsp chopped garlic
16 raw king prawns (jumbo shrimp),
  shelled, tails left intact
  and deveined
2 eggs, lightly beaten
15ml/1 tbsp dried shrimps, rinsed
30ml/2 tbsp pickled white radish
50g/2oz fried beancurd (tofu), cut
  into small slivers
2.5ml/½ tsp dried chilli flakes
115g/4oz chives, preferably garlic
  chives, cut into 5cm/2in lengths
225g/8oz/3–4 cups beansprouts
50g/2oz/½ cup roasted peanuts,
  coarsely ground
5ml/1 tsp granulated sugar
15ml/1 tbsp dark soy sauce
30ml/2 tbsp Thai fish sauce
  (*nam pla*)
30ml/2 tbsp tamarind or lime juice
30ml/2 tbsp coriander (cilantro)
  leaves, to garnish
1 kaffir lime, to garnish

1 Soak the noodles in warm water for 20–30 minutes, then drain.

2 Heat 15ml/1 tbsp of the oil in a wok. Add the garlic and fry until golden. Stir in the prawns and cook for about 1–2 minutes until pink, tossing from time to time. Remove and set aside.

VARIATION
If you are unable to find kaffir limes use the juciest variety available.

3 Heat another 15ml/1 tbsp of oil in the wok. Add the eggs and tilt the wok to spread them into a thin sheet. Stir to scramble and break the egg into small pieces. Remove from the wok and set aside with the prawns.

4 Heat the remaining oil in the same wok. Add the dried shrimps, pickled radish, beancurd and chilli flakes. Stir briefly. Add the soaked noodles and stir-fry for 5 minutes.

5 Add the chives, half the beansprouts and half the peanuts. Season with the sugar, soy sauce, fish sauce and tamarind or lime juice. Mix well and cook until the noodles are heated through.

6 Return the prawn and egg mixture to the wok and mix with the noodles. Serve immediately, garnished with the rest of the beansprouts, peanuts, the coriander leaves and lime wedges.

Chillies crop up across the globe, featuring in delectable dishes from places as far apart as Thailand and Tobago. This chapter chooses some of the best, from a classic Mexican mole to a sweet and spicy Moroccan tagine. Peanuts are partnered with chillies in a Caribbean chicken dish, while China's choice is the famous Sichuan Chicken with Kung Po Sauce. The collection includes dishes that would do you proud at dinner parties, but also features family favourites such as Chilli Beef Pizza, Tandoori Chicken and Spaghetti with Meatballs.

Sizzling Poultry and Meat Dishes

HOT AND SPICY PAN-FRIED CHICKEN

THIS TASTY MEAL CAN BE MILD OR HOT, DEPENDING ON THE TYPE OF CHILLI CHOSEN. THE CHICKEN NEEDS TO BE FRIED OVER A FIERCE HEAT, SO CUT IT INTO SMALL PIECES.

SERVES TWO

INGREDIENTS

    2 skinless, boneless chicken
      breast portions
    1 small fresh red or green chilli,
      seeded and thinly sliced
    2 garlic cloves, thinly sliced
    3 spring onions (scallions), sliced
    4–5 thin slices fresh root ginger
    2.5ml/½ tsp ground coriander
    2.5ml/½ tsp ground cumin
    30ml/2 tbsp olive oil
    25ml/1½ tbsp lemon juice
    30ml/2 tbsp pine nuts
    15ml/1 tbsp raisins (optional)
    oil, for frying
    15ml/1 tbsp chopped fresh
      coriander (cilantro)
    15ml/1 tbsp chopped fresh mint
    salt and ground black pepper
    fresh mint sprigs and lemon wedges,
      to garnish
    bread, rice or couscous, to serve

2 In a bowl, mix the chilli, garlic, spring onions, ginger, spices, olive oil, lemon juice, pine nuts and raisins, if using. Season, then spoon the mixture over the chicken pieces, stirring so that each piece is coated. Cover with clear film (plastic wrap) and leave in a cool place for 1–2 hours.

3 Brush a wok or shallow pan with oil and heat. Lift the chicken slices out and reserve the marinade. Stir-fry them over a fairly high heat for 3–4 minutes until browned on both sides.

4 Add the reserved marinade and continue to cook over a high heat for 6–8 minutes until the chicken has browned and is cooked through. (The timing will depend on the thickness of the chicken.)

5 Reduce the heat and stir in the chopped fresh coriander and mint. Cook for 1 minute, then transfer to a heated platter and serve immediately, garnished with mint sprigs and lemon wedges. Serve with bread or with rice or couscous.

1 Cut the chicken breast portions horizontally into 3–4 thin slices: this will speed up cooking. Place the slices in a shallow bowl.

COOK'S TIPS
• It is important to cut the meat thinly. Larger portions would have less contact with the pan, tending to braise rather than fry them.
• This will be sufficient for 2 as a main course or 4 as a starter. Serve the chicken with bread, rather than rice or couscous, if it is to be a starter.

CARIBBEAN PEANUT CHICKEN

LIKE COCONUT, PEANUTS AND PEANUT BUTTER GO PARTICULARLY WELL WITH CHILLIES. PEANUT BUTTER MAKES THIS SAUCE GLORIOUSLY RICH AND CREAMY. USE A MEDIUM-HOT CHILLI.

SERVES FOUR

INGREDIENTS
  4 skinless, boneless chicken breast
    portions, cut into thin strips
  225g/8oz/generous 1 cup white long
    grain rice
  15g/½oz/1 tbsp butter, plus extra
    for greasing
  30ml/2 tbsp groundnut (peanut) oil
  1 onion, finely chopped
  2 tomatoes, peeled, seeded
    and chopped
  1 fresh green chilli, seeded
    and sliced
  60ml/4 tbsp smooth peanut butter
  450ml/¾ pint/scant 2 cups
    chicken stock
  lemon juice, to taste
  salt and ground black pepper
  lime wedges and fresh flat leaf
    parsley sprigs, to garnish
For the marinade
  15ml/1 tbsp sunflower oil
  1–2 garlic cloves, crushed
  5ml/1 tsp chopped fresh thyme
  25ml/1½ tbsp medium curry powder
  juice of ½ lemon

1 Mix all the marinade ingredients in a large bowl and stir in the chicken. Cover loosely with clear film (plastic wrap) and set aside in a cool place for 2–3 hours.

COOK'S TIP
If the casserole is not large enough to allow you to toss the rice with the chicken mixture before serving, invert a large, deep plate over the casserole, turn both over and toss the mixture on the plate before serving.

2 Meanwhile, cook the rice in a large pan of lightly salted boiling water until tender. Drain well and turn into a generously buttered casserole.

3 Preheat the oven to 180°C/350°F/ Gas 4. Heat 15ml/1 tbsp of oil with the butter in a flameproof casserole and fry the chicken pieces for 4–5 minutes until evenly brown. Add more oil if necessary.

4 Lift out the chicken and put it on a plate. Add the finely chopped onion to the flameproof casserole and fry for 5–6 minutes until lightly browned, adding more oil if necessary. Stir in the chopped tomatoes and chilli. Cook over a gentle heat for 3–4 minutes, stirring occasionally. Switch off the heat.

5 Mix the peanut butter with the chicken stock. Stir into the tomato and onion mixture, then add the chicken. Stir in the lemon juice, season to taste, then spoon the mixture over the rice in the casserole.

6 Cover the casserole. Cook in the oven for 15–20 minutes or until piping hot. Use a large spoon to toss the rice with the chicken mixture. Serve at once, garnished with the lime and parsley.

CHICKEN WITH CHIPOTLE SAUCE

THIS IS A VERY EASY RECIPE FOR ENTERTAINING, WITH JUST A FEW KEY INGREDIENTS, INCLUDING DRIED CHILLIES. IT IS COOKED IN THE OVEN AND NEEDS NO LAST-MINUTE ATTENTION.

SERVES SIX

INGREDIENTS

6 chipotle chillies
chicken stock (see method
  for quantity)
3 onions
45ml/3 tbsp vegetable oil
6 skinless, boneless chicken
  breast portions
salt and ground black pepper
fresh oregano, to garnish
boiled rice, to serve

1 Put the dried chillies in a bowl and pour over hot water to cover. Leave to stand for at least 20 minutes, until very soft. Drain, reserving the soaking water in a liquid measure. Cut off the stalk from each chilli, then slit them lengthways and scrape out the seeds with a small sharp knife.

2 Preheat the oven to 180°C/350°F/ Gas 4. Chop the flesh of the chillies roughly and put it in a food processor or blender. Add enough chicken stock to the soaking water to make it up to 400ml/14fl oz/1⅔ cups. Pour it into the processor and process until smooth.

3 Peel the onions. Using a sharp knife, cut them in half, then slice them thinly. Separate the slices.

4 Heat the oil in a large frying pan, add the onions and cook over a low to moderate heat for about 5 minutes, or until they have softened but not coloured, stirring occasionally.

5 Using a slotted spoon, transfer the onion slices to a casserole that is large enough to hold all the chicken breast portions in a single layer. Sprinkle the onion slices with a little salt and ground black pepper.

COOK'S TIPS
• It is important to seek out chipotle chillies, as they impart a wonderfully rich and smoky flavour to the chicken.
• Dried chillies of various types can be bought by mail order, as well as from specialist food stores.
• The chilli purée can be prepared ahead of time.
• If tears come to your eyes when peeling onions, peel them under water. Then pat dry with kitchen paper before slicing.

6 Arrange the chicken on top of the onion slices. Sprinkle with a little salt and several grindings of pepper.

7 Pour the chipotle purée over the chicken, making sure that each piece is evenly coated.

8 Bake in the oven for 45–60 minutes or until the chicken is cooked through, but is still moist and tender. Garnish with fresh oregano and serve with boiled white rice.

VARIATION
Prepare the chipotles as in the main method. Put them in a stainless steel pan along with the soaking water; 2 peeled tomatoes, cut in wedges; ½ a sweet onion, chopped; 4 garlic cloves and 75ml/5 tbsp chopped fresh coriander (cilantro). Add water if needed to just cover. Simmer for 30 minutes. Dry-fry 15ml/1 tbsp cumin seeds, grind in a mortar or process in a blender and add to the chilli mixture. Cook for 5 minutes, season with salt, and purée. Refrigerated, it will keep for 1 week.

TURKEY MOLE

A MOLE IS A RICH STEW, SERVED ON FESTIVE OCCASIONS IN MEXICO. TOASTED NUTS, FRUIT AND CHOCOLATE ARE AMONG THE CLASSIC INGREDIENTS; THIS VERSION INCLUDES COCOA POWDER.

SERVES FOUR

INGREDIENTS
1 ancho chilli, seeded
1 guajillo chilli, seeded
115g/4oz/¾ cup sesame seeds
50g/2oz/½ cup whole
  blanched almonds
50g/2oz/½ cup shelled unsalted
  peanuts, skinned
50g/2oz/¼ cup lard (shortening) or
  60ml/4 tbsp vegetable oil
1 small onion, finely chopped
2 garlic cloves, crushed
50g/2oz/⅓ cup canned tomatoes in
  tomato juice
1 ripe plaintain
50g/2oz/⅓ cup raisins
75g/3oz/½ cup ready-to-eat
  pitted prunes
5ml/1 tsp dried oregano
2.5ml/½ tsp ground cloves
2.5ml/½ tsp crushed allspice berries
5ml/1 tsp ground cinnamon
25g/1oz/¼ cup cocoa powder
4 turkey breast steaks
chopped fresh oregano, to garnish

1 Soak both types of dried chilli in a bowl of hot water for 20–30 minutes, then lift them out and chop them roughly. Reserve 250ml/8fl oz/1 cup of the soaking liquid.

COOK'S TIPS

• It is important to use good-quality cocoa powder, which is unsweetened.
• Mexican-style cocoa powder is available from specialist food stores and by mail order.

2 Spread out the sesame seeds in a heavy frying pan. Toast them over a moderate heat, shaking the pan lightly so that they turn golden all over. Do not let them burn, or the sauce will taste bitter. Set aside 45ml/3 tbsp of the toasted seeds for the garnish and tip the rest into a bowl. Toast the blanched almonds and skinned peanuts in the same way and add them to the bowl with the sesame seeds.

3 Heat half the lard or oil in a frying pan, sauté the chopped onion and garlic for 2–3 minutes, then add the chillies and tomatoes. Cook gently for 10 minutes.

4 Peel the plantain and slice it into short diagonal slices. Add it to the onion mixture with the raisins, prunes, dried oregano, spices and cocoa. Stir in the 250ml/8fl oz/1 cup of the reserved water in which the chillies were soaked. Bring to the boil, stirring, then add the toasted sesame seeds, almonds and peanuts. Cook gently for 10 minutes, stirring frequently; do not let the sauce stick to the pan and burn. Remove from the heat and leave to cool slightly.

5 Blend the sauce in batches in a food processor or blender until smooth. The sauce should be fairly thick, but a little water can be added if you think it is necessary.

6 Heat the remaining lard or oil in a flameproof casserole. Add the turkey and brown over a medium heat.

7 Pour the sauce over the steaks and cover the casserole with foil and a tight-fitting lid. Simmer over a gentle heat for 20–25 minutes or until the turkey is cooked, and the sauce has thickened. Sprinkle with the reserved sesame seeds and the chopped fresh oregano. Turkey *Mole* is traditionally served with a rice dish and warm tortillas.

SCORCHING CHILLI CHICKEN

NOT FOR THE FAINT-HEARTED, THIS FIERY, HOT CURRY IS MADE WITH A SPICY CHILLI MASALA PASTE, WHICH IS BLENDED INTO A FRAGRANT SAUCE.

SERVES FOUR

INGREDIENTS

    8 chicken thighs, skinned
    5ml/1 tsp garam masala
    sliced green chillies, to garnish
    chapatis and natural (plain) yogurt,
      to serve
For the paste
    30ml/2 tbsp tomato purée (paste)
    2 garlic cloves, roughly chopped
    2 fresh green chillies, roughly chopped
    5 dried red chillies
    2.5ml/½ tsp salt
    1.5ml/¼ tsp granulated sugar
    5ml/1 tsp chilli powder
    2.5ml/½ tsp paprika
    15ml/1 tbsp curry paste
For the sauce
    30ml/2 tbsp oil
    2.5ml/½ tsp cumin seeds
    1 onion, finely chopped
    2 bay leaves
    5ml/1 tsp ground coriander
    5ml/1 tsp ground cumin
    1.5ml/¼ tsp ground turmeric
    400g/14oz can chopped tomatoes
    150ml/¼ pint/⅔ cup water

1 Put the tomato purée, garlic, fresh green and dried red chillies, salt, sugar, chilli powder, paprika and curry paste into a blender and process until smooth.

2 Heat the oil in a large pan and fry the cumin seeds for 2 minutes. Add the onion and bay, and fry for 5 minutes.

COOK'S TIP
For a milder, fruitier finish, use large red chillies.

3 Stir in the chilli paste and fry for 2–3 minutes, then add the spices. Cook for 2 minutes. Add the tomatoes and water. Bring to the boil. Simmer for 5 minutes until the sauce thickens.

4 Add the chicken and garam masala. Cover and simmer for 25–30 minutes until the chicken is tender. Serve with chapatis and yogurt, garnished with sliced green chillies.

TANDOORI CHICKEN

THIS CLASSIC INDIAN DISH HAS A UNIQUE FLAVOUR. THE CHILLI DOESN'T DOMINATE THE OTHER SPICES, BUT IS NONETHELESS AN ESSENTIAL INGREDIENT.

SERVES FOUR

INGREDIENTS
    8 chicken pieces, such as
      thighs, drumsticks or halved breast
      portions, skinned
    60ml/4 tbsp lemon juice
    10ml/2 tsp salt
    175ml/6fl oz/¾ cup natural
      (plain) yogurt
    5ml/1 tsp chilli powder
    5ml/1 tsp garam masala
    5ml/1 tsp ground cumin
    5ml/1 tsp ground coriander
    2 garlic cloves,
      roughly chopped
    2.5cm/1in piece fresh root ginger,
      roughly chopped
    2 fresh green chillies,
      roughly chopped
    red food colouring (optional)
    25g/1oz/2 tbsp butter, melted
    lemon wedges, salad and cucumber
      raita (see Cook's Tip), to serve
    chopped fresh green chilli or chilli
      powder and a sprig of fresh mint,
      to garnish the raita

1 Cut deep slashes in the chicken pieces. Mix together the lemon juice and half the salt and rub over the chicken. Set aside for 10 minutes.

2 Mix the natural yogurt, the remaining salt, chilli powder, garam masala, ground cumin and ground coriander in a bowl. Put the garlic, ginger and chillies into a food processor or blender and process until smooth. Scrape out of the processor bowl and stir the mixture into the spiced yogurt.

3 Brush the chicken pieces with food colouring, if using, and put them into a dish that is large enough to hold them in a single layer. Spoon over the marinade, turn the pieces until evenly coated, then cover and chill overnight.

4 Preheat the oven to 220°C/425°F/ Gas 7. Put the chicken in a roasting pan and bake for 40 minutes, basting with the melted butter. Serve on a bed of salad, with lemon wedges for squeezing. Offer the raita separately.

COOK'S TIP
Cucumber raita is a wonderfully refreshing dish to serve with anything spicy. To make it, dice 1 cucumber and place it in a bowl. Stir in 300ml/½ pint/ 1¼ cups natural (plain) yogurt, 1.5ml/ ¼ tsp salt and 1.5ml/¼ tsp ground cumin. A chopped fresh green chilli can be added if you like, or top the raita with a dusting of chilli powder and a fresh mint sprig.

SICHUAN CHICKEN WITH KUNG PO SAUCE

THIS RECIPE COMES FROM THE SICHUAN REGION OF WESTERN CHINA, WHERE CHILLIES ARE WIDELY USED. CASHEW NUTS HAVE BECOME A POPULAR INGREDIENT IN CHINESE COOKING.

SERVES THREE

INGREDIENTS

  2 skinless, boneless chicken
    breast portions, total weight
    about 350g/12oz
  1 egg white
  10ml/2 tsp cornflour (cornstarch)
  2.5ml/½ tsp salt
  30ml/2 tbsp yellow salted beans
  15ml/1 tbsp hoisin sauce
  5ml/1 tsp soft light brown sugar
  15ml/1 tbsp rice wine or
    medium-dry sherry
  15ml/1 tbsp wine vinegar
  4 garlic cloves, crushed
  150ml/¼ pint/⅔ cup chicken stock
  45ml/3 tbsp sunflower oil
  2–3 dried red chillies, chopped
  115g/4oz/1 cup roasted cashew nuts
  fresh coriander (cilantro), to garnish

1 Cut the chicken into neat pieces. Lightly whisk the egg white in a dish, whisk in the cornflour and salt, then add the chicken and stir until coated.

2 In a bowl, mash the beans. Stir in the hoisin sauce, brown sugar, rice wine or sherry, vinegar, garlic and stock.

3 Heat a wok, add the oil and stir-fry the chicken for 2 minutes until tender. Lift out the chicken and set aside.

COOK'S TIP
The yellow beans may be too salty for your taste, so if you like, rinse them in water and drain before using them.

4 Heat the oil remaining in the wok and fry the chilli pieces for 1 minute. Return the chicken to the wok and pour in the bean sauce mixture. Bring to the boil, stir in the cashew nuts and heat through. Spoon into a heated serving dish, garnish with the coriander leaves and serve immediately.

STIR-FRIED CHICKEN WITH CHILLI AND BASIL

THIS QUICK AND EASY CHICKEN DISH IS AN EXCELLENT INTRODUCTION TO THAI CUISINE. FIERY CHILLIES PARTNER THE HOLY BASIL, WHICH HAS A PUNGENT FLAVOUR THAT IS SPICY AND SHARP.

2 Add the pieces of chicken to the wok and stir-fry until they change colour. Stir in the fish sauce, soy sauce and sugar. Stir-fry the mixture for 3–4 minutes or until the chicken is fully cooked.

3 Stir in the fresh basil leaves. Spoon the mixture on to a warm serving platter, or individual serving dishes, garnish with the chopped chillies and deep-fried basil, and serve.

SERVES FOUR TO SIX

INGREDIENTS
  450g/1lb skinless, boneless
    chicken breast portions
  45ml/3 tbsp vegetable oil
  4 garlic cloves, thinly sliced
  2–4 fresh red chillies, seeded and
    finely chopped
  45ml/3 tbsp Thai fish sauce
    (*nam pla*)
  10ml/2 tsp dark soy sauce
  5ml/1 tsp granulated sugar
  10–12 holy basil leaves
  2 fresh red chillies, seeded and
    finely chopped, to garnish
  about 20 deep-fried holy basil leaves,
    to garnish

1 Using a sharp knife, cut the chicken breasts into bitesize pieces. Heat the oil in a wok. Add the garlic and chillies and stir-fry over a medium heat for 1–2 minutes until the garlic is golden. Do not let the garlic burn or it will taste bitter.

COOK'S TIPS
• Holy basil is native to Asia and it differs from other basils in that heat develops the flavour. The leaves have the typical basil fragrance with the addition of pepper and mint. A substitute is a mix of ordinary basil and spearmint.
• To deep-fry holy basil leaves, first make sure that the leaves are completely dry or they will splutter when added to the oil. Deep-fry the leaves briefly in hot oil until they are crisp and translucent – this will only take about 30–40 seconds. Lift out the leaves using a slotted spoon or wire basket and leave them to drain on kitchen paper.

RED CHICKEN CURRY WITH BAMBOO SHOOTS

THE CHILLI PASTE THAT IS THE BASIS OF THIS DISH HAS A SUPERB FLAVOUR AND WILL COME IN USEFUL IN ALL SORTS OF SPICY DISHES, SO IT IS WORTH MAKING IT IN QUANTITY.

SERVES FOUR TO SIX

INGREDIENTS

1 litre/1¾ pints/4 cups coconut milk
450g/1lb skinless, boneless chicken
  breast portions, diced
30ml/2 tbsp Thai fish sauce (*nam pla*)
15ml/1 tbsp granulated sugar
225g/8oz canned bamboo shoots,
  rinsed and sliced
5 kaffir lime leaves, torn
salt and ground black pepper

For the red curry paste

12–15 fresh red chillies, seeded
4 shallots, thinly sliced
2 garlic cloves, chopped
15ml/1 tbsp chopped fresh galangal
2 lemon grass stalks, tender
  portions chopped
3 kaffir lime leaves, chopped
4 coriander (cilantro) roots
10 black peppercorns
5ml/1 tsp coriander seeds
2.5ml/½ tsp cumin seeds
good pinch of ground cinnamon
5ml/1 tsp ground turmeric
2.5ml/½ tsp shrimp paste
30ml/2 tbsp oil

To garnish

2 fresh red chillies, chopped
10–12 fresh basil leaves
10–12 fresh mint leaves

1 Make the red curry paste. Combine all the ingredients except for the oil in a mortar. Add 5ml/1 tsp salt. Pound with a pestle, or process in a food processor, until smooth. If you are using a pestle and mortar, you might need to pound the ingredients in batches and then combine them.

2 Add the oil to the paste a little at a time and blend in well. If you are using a food processor or blender, add it slowly through the feeder tube. Scrape the paste into a jar and store in the refrigerator until ready to use.

3 Pour half the coconut milk into a large heavy pan. Gently bring to the boil, stirring all the time until the milk separates, then reduce the heat.

4 Add 30ml/2 tbsp of the red curry paste, stir to mix, and cook for a few minutes to alow the flavours to develop. The sauce should begin to thicken and may need to be stirred frequently to pevent it from sticking to the pan. Add a little more coconut milk if necessary.

5 Add the chicken, fish sauce and sugar. Fry for 3–5 minutes until the chicken changes colour, stirring constantly to prevent it from sticking.

6 Add the rest of the coconut milk, with the bamboo shoots and kaffir lime leaves. Bring back to the boil. Stir in salt and pepper to taste. Serve garnished with the chillies, basil and mint leaves.

COOK'S TIPS

• The surplus curry paste can be stored in a sealed jar in the refrigerator for 3–4 weeks. Alternatively, freeze it in small tubs, each containing about 30ml/ 2 tbsp.

• Young bamboo shoots are cultivated in China for the table. The preparation is laborious, so the canned shoots are used in the West. They provide a crunchy texture, and are a useful contrast to other ingredients.

• The roots of coriander have a deep earthy fragrance and are used widely in Thai cooking. They can be frozen for storage until you need them. Simply cut the roots off and wrap in clear film (plastic wrap).

THAI FRIED RICE WITH CHILLIES

THIS SUBSTANTIAL DISH IS BASED ON THAI FRAGRANT RICE, WHICH IS SOMETIMES KNOWN AS JASMINE RICE. CHICKEN, RED PEPPER AND CHILLIES ADD COLOUR AND EXTRA FLAVOUR.

SERVES FOUR

INGREDIENTS

475ml/16fl oz/2 cups water
50g/2oz/½ cup coconut milk powder
350g/12oz/1¾ cups Thai fragrant
   rice, rinsed and well drained
30ml/2 tbsp groundnut (peanut) oil
2 garlic cloves, chopped
1 small onion, finely chopped
2.5cm/1in piece fresh root
   ginger, grated (shredded)
225g/8oz skinless, boneless chicken
   breast portions, cut into
   1cm/½in dice
1 red (bell) pepper, seeded
   and sliced
1 fresh red chilli, seeded
   and chopped
115g/4oz/⅔ cup drained canned
   sweetcorn kernels
5ml/1 tsp chilli oil
5ml/1 tsp curry powder
2 eggs, beaten
salt
spring onion (scallion) shreds,
   to garnish

2 Heat the oil in a wok, add the garlic, onion and ginger, and stir-fry over a medium heat for 2 minutes.

3 Push the vegetables to the sides of the wok, add the chicken to the centre and stir-fry for 2 minutes. Add the rice. Stir-fry over a high heat for 3 minutes.

4 Stir in the sliced red pepper, chilli, sweetcorn, chilli oil and curry powder, with salt to taste. Toss over the heat for 1 minute. Stir in the beaten eggs and cook for 1 minute more. Everything should be piping hot before serving. Transfer to a heated serving dish, garnish with spring onion shreds and serve.

1 Pour the water into a pan and whisk in the coconut milk powder. Add the rice and bring to the boil. Reduce the heat, cover and cook for 12 minutes or until the rice is tender and the liquid has been absorbed. Remove from the heat at once and spread the rice on a baking sheet and leave until cold.

COOK'S TIP
It is important that the rice is completely cold before being fried. The oil should be very hot when the rice is added.

CHILLI RIBS

CHOOSE REALLY MEATY RIBS FOR THIS DISH AND TRIM OFF ANY EXCESS FAT BEFORE COOKING, AS THE JUICES ARE TURNED INTO A DELICIOUS SAUCE. SERVE ON A BED OF SAUERKRAUT WITH CRUSTY BREAD.

2 Heat the oil in a large pan and cook the ribs, turning until well browned. Put in a roasting pan, adding the onion.

3 Mix the braising liquid ingredients and pour over the ribs. Cover with foil then roast for 1½ hours, or until tender. Remove the foil for the last 30 minutes.

4 Tip the juices from the roasting pan into a small pan. Mix the cornflour with a little cold water in a cup, then stir the mixture into the sauce. Bring to the boil, stirring, then simmer for 2–3 minutes until thickened.

5 Serve the ribs on the sauerkraut, with a little sauce. Garnish with parsley. Serve the remaining sauce separately.

SERVES SIX

INGREDIENTS
    25g/1oz/¼ cup plain
      (all-purpose) flour
    5ml/1 tsp salt
    5ml/1 tsp ground black pepper
    1.6kg/3½lb pork spare ribs, cut into
      individual pieces
    30ml/2 tbsp sunflower oil
    1 onion, finely chopped
    15ml/1 tbsp cornflour (cornstarch)
    flat leaf parsley, to garnish
    sauerkraut, to serve
For the braising liquid
    1 garlic clove, crushed
    1 fresh red chilli, seeded and chopped
    45ml/3 tbsp tomato purée (paste)
    30ml/2 tbsp chilli sauce
    30ml/2 tbsp red wine vinegar
    pinch of ground cloves
    600ml/1 pint/2½ cups beef stock

1 Preheat the oven to 180°C/350°F/ Gas 4. Combine the flour, salt and black pepper in a shallow dish. Add the ribs and toss until evenly coated.

COOK'S TIP
Use mild or hot chilli sauce for this dish. If you can track some down, try using 45–60ml/3–4 tbsp ancho chilli and morello cherry glaze instead of the tomato purée and chilli sauce.

PENNE WITH TOMATO AND CHILLI SAUCE

IN ITS NATIVE ITALY, THIS PASTA DISH GOES UNDER THE NAME "PENNE ALL'ARRABBIATA".

3 Add the chopped mushrooms to the pan and cook in the same way. Remove and set aside with the pancetta or bacon. Crumble 1 dried chilli into the pan, add the garlic and cook gently, stirring, for a few minutes until the garlic turns golden.

4 Add the tomatoes and basil and season with salt. Cook gently, stirring occasionally, for 10–15 minutes. Meanwhile, bring a large pan of salted water to the boil and cook the penne, following the instructions on the packet.

5 Add the pancetta or bacon and the mushrooms to the tomato sauce. Taste for seasoning, adding another chilli if you prefer a hotter flavour. If the sauce is too dry, stir in a tablespoon or so of the pasta water.

6 Drain the pasta and tip it into a warmed bowl. Dice the remaining butter, add it to the pasta with the cheeses, then toss until well coated. Pour the tomato sauce over the pasta, toss well and serve immediately on warmed plates, with a few basil leaves sprinkled on top.

SERVES FOUR

INGREDIENTS
  25g/1oz/½ cup dried
    porcini mushrooms
  90g/3½oz/7 tbsp butter
  150g/5oz pancetta or rindless
    smoked streaky (fatty) bacon, diced
  1–2 dried red chillies
  2 garlic cloves, crushed
  8 ripe Italian plum tomatoes, peeled
    and chopped
  a few fresh basil leaves, torn, plus
    extra to garnish
  350g/12oz/3 cups fresh or
    dried penne
  50g/2oz/⅔ cup freshly grated
    (shredded) Parmesan cheese
  25g/1oz/⅓ cup freshly grated
    (shredded) Pecorino cheese
  salt

1 Soak the dried mushrooms in warm water to cover for 15–20 minutes. Drain, squeeze dry with your hands, then chop finely.

2 Melt 50g/2oz/4 tbsp of the butter in a medium pan. Add the pancetta or bacon and stir-fry until golden and slightly crisp. Remove the pancetta with a slotted spoon and set it aside.

HOT PEPPERONI AND CHILLI PIZZA

THERE ARE FEW TREATS MORE TASTY THAN A HOME-MADE FRESHLY BAKED PIZZA.

SERVES FOUR

INGREDIENTS
  225g/8oz/2 cups strong white
    (bread) flour
  10ml/2 tsp easy-blend (rapid rise)
    dried yeast
  5ml/1 tsp granulated sugar
  2.5ml/½ tsp salt
  15ml/1 tbsp olive oil
  175ml/6fl oz/¾ cup mixed hand-hot
    milk and water
  fresh oregano leaves, to garnish
For the topping
  400g/14oz can chopped tomatoes,
    well drained
  2 garlic cloves, crushed
  5ml/1 tsp dried oregano
  225g/8oz mozzarella cheese,
    coarsely grated
  2 dried red chillies
  225g/8oz pepperoni, sliced
  30ml/2 tbsp drained capers

1 Sift the flour into a bowl. Stir in the yeast, sugar and salt. Make a well in the centre. Stir the olive oil into the milk and water, then stir the mixture into the flour. Mix to a soft dough.

2 Knead the dough on a lightly floured surface for 5–10 minutes until it is smooth and elastic. Return it to the clean, lightly oiled, bowl and cover with clear film (plastic wrap). Leave in a warm place for about 30 minutes or until the dough has doubled in bulk.

3 Preheat the oven to 220°C/425°F/ Gas 7. Knead the dough on a lightly floured surface for 1 minute. Divide it in half and roll each piece out to a 25cm/10in circle. Place on lightly oiled pizza trays or baking sheets.

4 Make the topping. Tip the drained tomatoes into a bowl and stir in the crushed garlic and dried oregano.

5 Spread half the mixture over each round, leaving a clear margin around the edge. Set half the mozzarella aside. Divide the rest between the pizzas. Bake for 7–10 minutes until the dough rim on each pizza is pale golden.

6 Crumble the chillies over the pizzas, then arrange the pepperoni slices and capers on top. Sprinkle with the reserved mozzarella. Return the pizzas to the oven and bake for 7–10 minutes more. Sprinkle over the fresh oregano and serve immediately.

VARIATION
Use bacon instead of sliced pepperoni. Grill (broil) about 6 slices and crumble them over the pizza with the chillies. Omit the capers.

PORK CASSEROLE <u>WITH</u> CHILLIES <u>AND</u> DRIED FRUIT

USING A TECHNIQUE TAKEN FROM SOUTH AMERICAN COOKING, THIS CASSEROLE IS BASED ON A RICH PASTE OF CHILLIES, SHALLOTS AND NUTS. SERVE IT WITH PLAIN BOILED RICE.

SERVES SIX

INGREDIENTS
  25ml/5 tsp plain (all-purpose) flour
  1kg/2¼lb shoulder or leg of pork, cut
    into 5cm/2in cubes
  45–60ml/3–4 tbsp olive oil
  2 large onions, chopped
  2 garlic cloves, finely chopped
  600ml/1 pint/2½ cups fruity
    white wine
  105ml/7 tbsp water
  115g/4oz/⅔ cup ready-to-eat prunes
  115g/4oz/⅔ cup ready-to-eat
    dried apricots
  grated (shredded) rind and juice of
    1 small orange
  pinch of soft light brown
    sugar (optional)
  30ml/2 tbsp chopped fresh parsley
  ½–1 fresh red chilli, seeded and
    finely chopped
  salt and ground black pepper
For the paste
  3 ancho chillies
  2 pasilla chillies
  30ml/2 tbsp olive oil
  2 shallots, chopped
  2 garlic cloves, chopped
  1 fresh green chilli, seeded
    and chopped
  10ml/2 tsp ground coriander
  5ml/1 tsp mild Spanish paprika
    or *pimentón dulce*
  50g/2oz/½ cup blanched
    almonds, toasted
  15ml/1 tbsp chopped fresh oregano
    or 7.5ml/1½ tsp dried oregano
  plain boiled rice, to serve

1 Make the paste first. Toast the dried chillies in a dry frying pan over a low heat for 1–2 minutes, until they are aromatic, then soak them in a bowl of warm water for 20–30 minutes.

2 Drain the chillies, reserving the soaking water, and discard their stalks and seeds. Preheat the oven to 160°C/ 325°F/Gas 3.

3 Heat the oil in a small frying pan. Add the shallots, garlic, fresh chilli and ground coriander, and fry over a very low heat for 5 minutes.

4 Transfer the mixture to a food processor or blender and add the drained chillies, paprika or *pimentón dulce*, almonds and oregano. Process the mixture, adding 45–60ml/3–4 tbsp of the chilli soaking liquid to make a smooth workable paste.

5 Season the flour generously with salt and black pepper, then use to coat the pork. Heat 45ml/3 tbsp of the olive oil in a large, heavy pan and fry the pork, stirring frequently, until sealed on all sides. Transfer the pork cubes to a flameproof casserole.

6 If necessary, add the remaining oil to the pan. When it is hot, fry the onions and garlic gently for 8–10 minutes.

COOK'S TIP
A Californian Chardonnay would be a suitably fruity wine to use.

7 Add the wine and water to the pan. Bring up to the boil, reduce the heat and cook for 2 minutes. Stir in half the paste, bring back to the boil and bubble for a few seconds before pouring over the pork.

8 Season lightly with salt and pepper, stir to mix, then cover and cook in the oven for 1½ hours. Increase the oven temperature to 180°C/350°F/Gas 4.

9 Add the prunes, apricots and orange juice to the casserole. Taste the sauce and add more salt and pepper if needed and a pinch of brown sugar if the orange juice has made the sauce a bit tart. Stir, cover, return to the oven and cook for a further 30–45 minutes.

10 Place the casserole over a direct heat and stir in the remaining paste. Simmer, stirring once or twice, for 5 minutes. Sprinkle with the orange rind, chopped parsley and fresh chilli. Serve with boiled rice.

STUFFED CHILLIES ^{IN A} WALNUT SAUCE

THE POTATO AND MEAT FILLING IN THESE CHILLIES IS A GOOD PARTNER FOR THE RICH, CREAMY SAUCE THAT COVERS THEM. A GREEN SALAD GOES WELL WITH THIS DISH.

SERVES FOUR

INGREDIENTS
    8 ancho chillies
    1 large waxy potato, about 200g/7oz
    45ml/3 tbsp vegetable oil
    115g/4oz lean minced (ground) pork
    50g/2oz/½ cup plain
      (all-purpose) flour
    2.5ml/½ tsp ground white pepper
    2 eggs, separated
    oil, for deep-frying
    salt
    chopped fresh herbs, to garnish
For the sauce
    1 onion, chopped
    5ml/1 tsp ground cinnamon
    115g/4oz/1 cup walnuts or pecan
      nuts, roughly chopped
    50g/2oz/½ cup chopped almonds
    150g/5oz/⅔ cup cream cheese
    50g/2oz/½ cup soft goat's cheese
    120ml/4fl oz/½ cup single
      (light) cream
    120ml/4fl oz/½ cup dry sherry

1 Soak the dried chillies in a bowl of hot water for 20–30 minutes until softened. Drain, then slit them down one side. Scrape out the seeds, taking care to keep the chillies intact.

2 Peel the potato and cut it into 1cm/½in cubes. Heat 15ml/1 tbsp of the oil in a large frying pan, add the pork and cook, stirring, until it has browned evenly.

COOK'S TIP
The potatoes must not break or become too floury. Do not overcook.

3 Add the potato cubes and mix well. Cover and cook over a low heat for 25–30 minutes, stirring occasionally. Season with salt, then remove the filling from the heat and set it aside.

4 Make the sauce. Heat the remaining oil in a separate pan and fry the onion with the cinnamon for 3–4 minutes or until softened. Stir in the nuts and fry for 3–4 minutes more.

5 Add both types of cheese to the pan, with the single cream and dry sherry. Mix well for the flavours to blend. Reduce the heat to the lowest setting and cook until the cheese melts and the sauce starts to thicken. Taste the sauce and season it if necessary.

6 Spread out the flour on a plate or in a shallow dish. Season with the white pepper. Beat the egg yolks in a bowl until they are pale and thick.

7 In a separate, grease-free bowl, whisk the whites until they form soft peaks. Add a generous pinch of salt, then fold in the yolks, a little at a time.

8 Spoon some of the filling into each chilli. Pat the outside dry with kitchen paper. Heat the oil for deep-frying to a temperature of 180°C/350°F.

9 Coat a chilli in flour, then dip it in the egg batter, covering it completely. Drain for a few seconds, then add to the hot oil. Add several more battered chillies, but do not overcrowd the pan. Fry the chillies until golden, then lift out and drain on kitchen paper. Keep hot while cooking successive batches.

10 Reheat the walnut and cheese sauce over a low heat, if necessary. Arrange the chillies on individual plates, spoon a little sauce over each and serve immediately, sprinkled with chopped fresh herbs.

LIVELY LAMB BURGERS WITH CHILLI RELISH

A RED ONION RELISH SPIKED WITH CHILLI WORKS WELL WITH BURGERS. BASED ON MIDDLE-EASTERN-STYLE LAMB THESE CAN BE SERVED WITH PITTA BREAD AND TABBOULEH OR WITH FRIES AND A SALAD.

SERVES FOUR

INGREDIENTS

25g/1oz/3 tbsp bulgur wheat
150ml/¼ pint/⅔ cup hot water
500g/1¼lb lean minced
  (ground) lamb
1 small red onion, finely chopped
2 garlic cloves, finely chopped
1 fresh green chilli, seeded and
  finely chopped
5ml/1 tsp ground toasted
  cumin seeds
5ml/1 tsp grated lemon rind
60ml/4 tbsp chopped fresh flat
  leaf parsley
30ml/2 tbsp chopped fresh mint
olive oil, for frying
salt and ground black pepper

For the relish
2 red (bell) peppers, halved
  and seeded
2 red onions, sliced into wedges
75–90ml/5–6 tbsp extra virgin olive
  oil
350g/12oz cherry tomatoes, chopped
1 fresh red or green chilli, seeded
  and finely chopped
30ml/2 tbsp chopped fresh mint
30ml/2 tbsp chopped fresh parsley
15ml/1 tbsp chopped fresh oregano
  or marjoram
2.5–5ml/½–1 tsp ground toasted
  cumin seeds
5ml/1 tsp grated (shredded)
  lemon rind
juice of ½ lemon
granulated sugar

1 Put the bulgur wheat in a bowl and pour over the hot water. Leave to stand for 15 minutes. Tip into a colander lined with a clean dishtowel. Drain well, then gather up the sides of the towel and squeeze out the excess moisture.

2 Place the bulgur in a bowl and add the lamb, onion, garlic, chilli, cumin, lemon rind, parsley and mint. Mix well, season, then form the mixture into 8 small burgers. Set aside while you make the relish.

3 Grill (broil) the peppers, skin-side up, until the skin chars and blisters. Place in a strong plastic bag and tie the top to keep the steam in. Set aside for about 20 minutes, then remove the peppers from the bag, peel off the skins and dice the flesh finely. Put the diced pepper in a bowl.

4 Meanwhile, brush the onions with 15ml/1 tbsp of the oil and grill for about 5 minutes on each side, until browned. Cool, then chop. Add to the peppers.

5 Add tomatoes, chilli, mint, parsley, oregano or marjoram and the cumin. Stir in 60ml/4 tbsp of the remaining oil, with the lemon rind and juice. Season with salt, pepper and sugar and allow to stand for 20–30 minutes for the flavours to mature.

6 Heat a heavy frying pan or a ridged cast-iron griddle pan over a high heat and grease lightly with oil. Cook the burgers for about 5–6 minutes on each side, or until just cooked at the centre.

7 While the burgers are cooking, taste the relish and adjust the seasoning. Serve the burgers immediately they are cooked, with the relish.

COOK'S TIP
Oregano (*Origanum vulgare*) is also known as wild marjoram. It has a spicier flavour than marjoram (which is also known as sweet marjoram).

LAMB STEW WITH CHILLI SAUCE

THE DRIED CHILLIES IN THIS STEW ADD DEPTH AND RICHNESS TO THE SAUCE, WHILE THE POTATO SLICES ENSURE THAT IT IS SUBSTANTIAL ENOUGH TO SERVE ON ITS OWN.

SERVES SIX

INGREDIENTS
  6 guajillo chillies, seeded
  2 pasilla chillies, seeded
  250ml/8fl oz/1 cup hot water
  3 garlic cloves, peeled
  5ml/1 tsp ground cinnamon
  2.5ml/½ tsp ground cloves
  2.5ml/½ tsp ground black pepper
  15ml/1 tbsp vegetable oil
  1kg/2¼lb lean boneless lamb
    shoulder, cut into 2cm/¾in cubes
  2 large potatoes, scrubbed and cut
    into 1cm/½in thick slices
  salt
  strips of red (bell) pepper and fresh
    oregano, to garnish

COOK'S TIP
When frying the lamb, don't be tempted to cook too many cubes at one time, or the meat will steam rather than fry.

1 Snap or tear the dried chillies into large pieces, put them in a bowl and pour over the hot water. Leave to soak for 20–30 minutes, then tip the contents of the bowl into a food processor or blender. Add the garlic and spices. Process until smooth.

2 Heat the oil in a large pan. Add the lamb cubes, in batches, and stir-fry over a high heat until the cubes are browned on all sides.

3 Return all the lamb cubes to the pan, spread them out, then cover them with a layer of potato slices. Add salt to taste. Put a lid on the pan and cook over a medium heat for 10 minutes.

4 Pour over the chilli mixture and mix well. Replace the lid and simmer over a low heat for about 1 hour or until the meat and the potato are tender. Serve with a rice dish, and garnish with strips of red pepper and fresh oregano.

FIRE FRY

HERE'S ONE FOR LOVERS OF HOT, SPICY FOOD. TENDER STRIPS OF LAMB, MARINATED IN SPICES AND STIR-FRIED WITH A TOP-DRESSING OF CHILLIES, REALLY HITS THE HOT SPOT.

SERVES FOUR

INGREDIENTS

225g/8oz lean lamb fillet (tenderloin)
120ml/4fl oz/½ cup natural
  (plain) yogurt
1.5ml/¼ tsp ground cardamom
5ml/1 tsp grated (shredded) fresh
  root ginger
5ml/1 tsp crushed garlic
5ml/1 tsp hot chilli powder
5ml/1 tsp garam masala
5ml/1 tsp salt
15ml/1 tbsp corn oil
2 onions, chopped
1 bay leaf
300ml/½ pint/1¼ cups water
2 fresh red chillies, seeded and
  sliced in strips
2 fresh green chillies, seeded and
  sliced in strips
30ml/2 tbsp fresh coriander
  (cilantro) leaves

1 Using a sharp knife, cut the lamb into 7.5–10cm/3–4in pieces, then into strips.

2 In a bowl, whisk the yogurt with the cardamom, ginger, garlic, chilli powder, garam masala and salt. Add the lamb strips and stir to coat them in the mixture. Cover and marinate in a cool place for about 1 hour.

COOK'S TIP
This is a useful recipe for a family divided into those who love chillies and those who don't. Serve the doubters before adding the chillies, or perhaps top their portions with strips of a sweet mild chilli or even a peeled red or green (bell) pepper.

3 Heat the oil in a wok or frying pan and fry the onions for 3–5 minutes, or until they are tender and golden brown.

4 Add the bay leaf and then add the marinated lamb with the yogurt and spices, and toss over a medium heat for about 2–3 minutes.

5 Pour over the water, stir well, then cover and cook for 15–20 minutes over a low heat, stirring occasionally. Once the water has evaporated, stir-fry the mixture for 1 minute.

6 Strew the red and green chillies over the stir-fry, with the fresh coriander. Serve hot. Offer a cooling yogurt dip, if you like.

CHILLI BEEF PIZZA

A GREAT PARTY DISH, THIS CAN BE SERVED FOR SUPPER WITH SALADS, PACKED FOR A PICNIC, MADE AS PART OF A BUFFET OR CUT INTO FINGERS FOR OFFERING WITH DRINKS.

SERVES FOUR

INGREDIENTS
  15ml/1 tbsp olive oil, plus extra
    for greasing
  1 red onion, finely chopped
  1 garlic clove, crushed
  ½ red (bell) pepper, seeded and
    finely chopped
  175g/6oz lean minced
    (ground) beef
  2.5ml/½ tsp ground cumin
  2 fresh red chillies, seeded
    and chopped
  115g/4oz/½ cup drained canned
    red kidney beans
  300ml/½ pint/1¼ cups bottled
    or home-made tomato sauce
    for pasta
  15ml/1 tbsp chopped fresh oregano
  50g/2oz/½ cup grated (shredded)
    mozzarella cheese
  75g/3oz/¾ cup grated (shredded)
    Cheddar cheese
  salt and ground black pepper
For the dough
  175g/6oz/1½ cups strong white
    (bread) flour
  25g/1oz/¼ cup corn meal
  1.5ml/¼ tsp salt
  5ml/1 tsp easy-blend (rapid-rise)
    dried yeast
  15ml/1 tbsp olive oil
  about 150ml/¼ pint/⅔ cup
    hand-hot water

1 Make the dough. Sift the strong white flour into a large bowl and add the corn meal, salt and easy-blend yeast. Add the olive oil, then stir in enough of the water to make a soft dough. Knead for 10 minutes, until the dough is smooth and elastic, then place in a greased bowl, cover with clear film (plastic wrap) or a dishtowel and leave in a warm place until doubled in bulk.

2 Heat 15ml/1 tbsp of the oil in a frying pan, add the onion, garlic and pepper and gently fry until soft. Increase the heat, add the beef and brown well, stirring constantly.

3 Add the ground cumin and chopped chillies, and continue to cook, stirring, for about 5 minutes. Stir in the beans with seasoning to taste. Cook for about 10 minutes. Set aside while you make the pizza base. Preheat the oven to 220°C/425°F/Gas 7.

4 Knock back (punch down) the dough, knead briefly, then roll out and line a 30 × 18cm/12 × 7in greased Swiss (jelly) roll tin (pan). Push up the dough edges to make a rim.

5 Spread the tomato sauce over the dough to reach the edge. Spoon over the beef mixture then sprinkle the oregano evenly over the top.

6 Sprinkle over the grated mozzarella and Cheddar cheeses and bake the pizza for 15–20 minutes until crisp and golden. Serve immediately while hot, cut into squares.

SPAGHETTI WITH MEATBALLS

FOR A GREAT INTRODUCTION TO THE CHARM OF CHILLIES, THIS SIMPLE PASTA DISH IS HARD TO BEAT.
CHILDREN LOVE THE GENTLE HEAT OF THE SWEET AND SPICY TOMATO SAUCE.

SERVES SIX TO EIGHT

INGREDIENTS
 350g/12oz minced (ground) beef
 1 egg
 60ml/4 tbsp roughly chopped fresh
  flat leaf parsley
 2.5ml/½ tsp crushed dried
  red chillies
 1 thick slice white bread,
  crusts removed
 30ml/2 tbsp milk
 about 30ml/2 tbsp olive oil
 300ml/½ pint/1¼ cups passata
  (bottled strained tomatoes)
 400ml/14fl oz/1⅔ cups
  vegetable stock
 5ml/1 tsp granulated sugar
 350–450g/12oz–1lb fresh or
  dried spaghetti
 salt and ground black pepper
 shavings of Parmesan cheese,
  to serve

1 Put the beef in a large bowl. Add the egg, with half the parsley and half the crushed chillies. Season with plenty of salt and pepper.

2 Tear the bread into small pieces and place these in a small bowl. Moisten with the milk. Leave to soak for a few minutes, then squeeze out the excess milk and crumble the bread over the meat mixture. Mix everything together with a wooden spoon, then use your hands to squeeze and knead the mixture so that it becomes smooth and quite sticky.

3 Wash your hands, rinse them under the cold tap, then pick up small pieces of the mixture and roll them between your palms to make about 40–60 small balls. Place the meatballs on a tray and chill for 30 minutes.

4 Heat the oil in a large non-stick frying pan. Cook the meatballs in batches until browned on all sides. Pour the passata and stock into a large pan. Heat gently, then add the remaining chillies and the sugar, and season. Add the meatballs and bring to the boil. Reduce the heat, and simmer for 20 minutes.

5 Bring a large pan of lightly salted water to the boil and cook the pasta until it is just tender, following the instructions on the packet. Drain and tip it into a large heated bowl. Pour over the sauce and toss gently. Sprinkle with the remaining parsley and shavings of Parmesan cheese. Serve immediately.

BEEF TAGINE <u>WITH</u> SWEET POTATOES

*THIS WARMING DISH IS EATEN DURING THE WINTER IN MOROCCO WHERE, ESPECIALLY IN THE
MOUNTAINS, THE WEATHER CAN BE SURPRISINGLY COLD.*

SERVES FOUR

INGREDIENTS
  900g/2lb braising or
    stewing beef
  30ml/2 tbsp sunflower oil
  good pinch of ground turmeric
  1 large onion, chopped
  1 fresh red or green chilli, seeded
    and chopped
  7.5ml/1½ tsp paprika
  good pinch of cayenne pepper
  2.5ml/½ tsp ground cumin
  450g/1lb sweet potatoes
  15ml/1 tbsp chopped fresh parsley,
    plus extra to garnish
  15ml/1 tbsp chopped fresh
    coriander (cilantro)
  15g/½oz/1 tbsp butter
  salt and ground black pepper

1 Trim the meat and cut into cubes.
Heat the oil in a flameproof casserole
and add the meat. Sprinkle with the
turmeric and fry for 3–4 minutes until
evenly brown, stirring frequently. Cover
the pan tightly and cook for 15 minutes
over a fairly gentle heat, without lifting
the lid. Preheat the oven to 180°C/
350°F/Gas 4.

2 Add the onion, chilli, paprika,
cayenne pepper and cumin to the
casserole and season. Pour in enough
water to cover the meat. Cover tightly
and cook in the oven for 1–1½ hours
until the meat is very tender, checking
occasionally and adding a little extra
water to keep the stew fairly moist.

3 Meanwhile, peel the sweet potatoes
and slice them straight into a pan of
salted water (sweet potatoes discolour
very quickly if exposed to the air).
Bring to the boil, then simmer for
2–3 minutes until just tender. Drain.

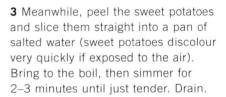

4 Stir the herbs into the meat, adding
a little extra water if the stew appears
dry. Arrange the sweet potato slices
over the meat and dot with the butter.
Cover and cook in the oven, covered,
for a further 10 minutes or until the
potatoes feel very tender when tested
with a skewer. Increase the oven
temperature to 200°C/400°F/Gas 6.

5 Remove the lid of the casserole
and cook in the oven for a further
10 minutes until the potatoes are
golden. Garnish and serve immediately.

CHILLI CON CARNE

THIS FAMOUS TEX-MEX STEW HAS BECOME AN INTERNATIONAL FAVOURITE. SERVE IT WITH RICE OR BAKED POTATOES AND A HEARTY GREEN SALAD.

SERVES EIGHT

INGREDIENTS
1.2kg/2½lb lean braising steak
30ml/2 tbsp sunflower oil
1 large onion, chopped
2 garlic cloves, finely chopped
15ml/1 tbsp plain (all-purpose) flour
300ml/½ pint/1¼ cups red wine
300ml/½ pint/1¼ cups beef stock
30ml/2 tbsp tomato purée (paste)
salt and ground black pepper

For the beans
30ml/2 tbsp olive oil
1 onion, chopped
1 fresh red chilli, seeded
  and chopped
2 × 400g/14oz cans red kidney
  beans, drained and rinsed
400g/14oz can chopped tomatoes

For the topping
6 tomatoes, peeled and chopped
1 fresh green chilli, seeded
  and chopped
30ml/2 tbsp chopped fresh chives
30ml/2 tbsp chopped fresh coriander
  (cilantro), plus sprigs to garnish
150ml/¼ pint/⅔ cup sour cream

2 Use a slotted spoon to remove the onion from the pan, then add the floured beef and cook over a high heat until browned on all sides. Remove from the pan and set aside, then flour and brown another batch of meat.

3 When the last batch of meat has been browned, return the reserved meat and the onion to the pan. Stir in the wine, stock and tomato purée. Bring to the boil, reduce the heat and simmer for 45 minutes, or until the beef is tender.

4 Meanwhile, for the beans, heat the olive oil in a frying pan and cook the onion and chilli until softened. Stir in the kidney beans and tomatoes, and simmer gently for 20–25 minutes, or until thickened and reduced.

5 Mix the tomatoes, chilli, chives and coriander for the topping. Ladle the meat mixture on to warmed plates. Add a layer of bean mixture and tomato topping. Finish with sour cream and garnish with coriander leaves.

1 Cut the meat into thick strips, then cut it crossways into small cubes. Heat the oil in a large, flameproof casserole. Add the chopped onion and garlic, and cook until softened but not coloured. Season the flour and place it on a plate, then toss a batch of meat in it.

VARIATION
This stew is also delicious served with tortillas. Wrap the tortillas in foil and warm through in the oven.

CHILLI BEEF WITH SPICY ONION RINGS

FRUITY, SMOKY AND MILD MEXICAN CHILLIES COMBINE WELL WITH GARLIC IN THIS MARINADE FOR BEEF. ONCE YOU HAVE TASTED THE SPICY ONION RINGS, YOU WILL FIND THEM HARD TO RESIST.

SERVES FOUR

INGREDIENTS

   4 rump (round) or rib-eye beef
     steaks, about 225g/8oz each
For the chilli paste
   3 large pasilla chillies
   2 garlic cloves, finely chopped
   5ml/1 tsp ground toasted
     cumin seeds
   5ml/1 tsp dried oregano
   60ml/4 tbsp olive oil
   salt and ground black pepper
For the spicy onion rings
   2 onions, sliced and separated
     into rings
   250ml/8fl oz/1 cup milk
   75g/3oz/½ cup coarse corn
     meal polenta
   2.5ml/½ tsp dried red chilli flakes
   5ml/1 tsp ground toasted
     cumin seeds
   5ml/1 tsp dried oregano
   vegetable oil, for deep-frying

1 To make the chilli paste, cut the stalks from the chillies, then slit them and shake out most of the seeds. Toast the chillies in a dry frying pan for 2–4 minutes, until they give off their aroma. Place the chillies in a bowl, cover with warm water and leave to soak for 20–30 minutes.

2 Drain the chillies, reserving the soaking water. Put them in a food processor or blender. Add the garlic, cumin, oregano and oil. Process to a smooth paste, adding a little soaking water, if necessary. It should not be too stiff. Season with pepper.

3 Pour the chilli paste all over the meat. Put the steaks in a dish, cover and leave to marinate in the refrigerator for up to 12 hours.

COOK'S TIP
It is always best to allow a few minutes resting time for the steaks after cooking. It relaxes the meat, making it more tender.

4 Make the onion rings. Soak the onions in the milk for 30 minutes. Mix the corn meal, chilli, cumin and oregano in a shallow bowl and season with salt and pepper. Heat the oil for deep-frying to 160–180°C/325–350°F or until a cube of day-old bread browns in about 45 seconds. Drain the onion rings and dip into the corn meal mixture. Fry in batches for 2–4 minutes, until browned and crisp. Do not overcrowd the pan. Drain on kitchen paper.

5 Prepare the barbecue or heat a cast-iron griddle pan. Season the steaks with salt and cook for about 5 minutes on each side for a medium result; adjust the timing for rare or well-done steak. Serve the steaks while hot with the onion rings.

BEEF ENCHILADAS WITH RED SAUCE

DRIED CHILLIES ARE WONDERFUL PANTRY STAPLES. IT IS WORTH HAVING A SUPPLY OF SEVERAL DIFFERENT TYPES, SO YOU'LL ALWAYS HAVE THE MEANS TO MAKE SPICY DISHES LIKE THIS ONE.

SERVES TWO TO THREE

INGREDIENTS

    500g/1¼lb rump (round) steak, cut
      into 5cm/2in cubes
    2 ancho chillies, seeded
    2 pasilla chillies, seeded
    30ml/2 tbsp vegetable oil
    2 garlic cloves, crushed
    10ml/2 tsp dried oregano
    2.5ml/½ tsp ground cumin
    7 fresh corn tortillas
    shredded onion and fresh flat leaf
      parsley, to garnish
    mango and chilli salsa,
      to serve

1 Put the cubed rump steak in a pan and cover with water. Bring to the boil, then lower the heat and simmer for 1–1½ hours, or until very tender.

2 Meanwhile, put the dried chillies in a bowl and pour over hot water to cover. Leave to soak for 20–30 minutes, then tip the contents of the bowl into a blender and whizz to a smooth paste.

3 Drain the steak and let it cool, reserving 250ml/8fl oz/1 cup of the cooking liquid. Meanwhile, heat the oil in a large frying pan and fry the garlic, oregano and cumin for 2 minutes.

4 Stir in the chilli paste and the reserved cooking liquid from the beef. Tear 1 of the tortillas into small pieces and add it to the mixture. Bring to the boil, then lower the heat. Simmer for 10 minutes, stirring occasionally, until the sauce has thickened. Shred the steak, using 2 forks, and stir it into the sauce. Heat through for a few minutes.

5 Spoon some of the meat mixture on to each tortilla and roll it up to make an enchilada. Keep the enchiladas in a warmed dish until you have rolled them all. Garnish the enchiladas with shreds of onion and fresh flat leaf parsley, and serve immediately with mango and chilli salsa.

VARIATIONS
• For a richer version, place the rolled enchiladas side by side in a gratin dish. Pour over 300ml/½ pint/1¼ cups sour cream and 75g/3oz/¾ cup grated (shredded) Cheddar cheese. Grill (broil) for 5 minutes or until the cheese melts and the sauce begins to bubble. Serve immediately, with the salsa.
• For a sharper tasting cheese topping, substitute Parmesan cheese for half the quantity of Cheddar.

MEXICAN SPICY BEEF TORTILLA

THIS DISH IS NOT UNLIKE A LASAGNE, EXCEPT THAT THE SPICY MEAT IS MIXED WITH RICE AND IS LAYERED BETWEEN MEXICAN TORTILLAS, WITH A HOT SALSA SAUCE FOR AN EXTRA KICK.

SERVES FOUR

INGREDIENTS
  1 onion, chopped
  2 garlic cloves, crushed
  1 fresh red chilli, seeded and sliced
  350g/12oz rump (round) steak, cut
    into small cubes
  15ml/1 tbsp oil
  225g/8oz/2 cups cooked long
    grain rice
  beef stock, to moisten
  salt and ground black pepper
  3 large wheat tortillas
For the salsa picante
  2 × 400g/14oz cans
    chopped tomatoes
  2 garlic cloves, halved
  1 onion, quartered
  1–2 fresh red chillies, seeded and
    roughly chopped
  5ml/1 tsp ground cumin
  2.5–5ml/½–1 tsp cayenne pepper
  5ml/1 tsp chopped fresh oregano
  tomato juice or water, if required
For the cheese sauce
  50g/2oz/¼ cup butter
  50g/2oz/½ cup plain
    (all-purpose) flour
  600ml/1 pint/2½ cups milk
  115g/4oz/1 cup grated (shredded)
    Cheddar cheese

1 Make the salsa picante. Place the first 4 ingredients in a blender or food processor and process until smooth.

2 Pour into a pan, add the spices and oregano, and season with salt. Bring to the boil, stirring occasionally. Boil for 1–2 minutes, then lower the heat, cover and simmer for 15 minutes. The sauce should be thick, but of a pouring consistency. If it is too thick, dilute it with a little tomato juice or water. Preheat the oven to 180°C/350°F/Gas 4.

COOK'S TIP
You can use any type of beef for this dish. If stewing steak is used, it should be very finely chopped and the cooking time increased by 10–15 minutes.

3 Make the cheese sauce. Melt the butter in a pan and stir in the flour. Cook for 1 minute. Add the milk, stirring all the time until the sauce boils and thickens. Stir in all but 30ml/2 tbsp of the cheese and season. Set aside.

4 Put the onion, garlic and chilli in a large bowl. Mix in the meat. Heat the oil in a pan and stir-fry the meat for 10 minutes or until it has browned. Stir in the rice and stock to moisten. Season to taste.

5 Pour about one-quarter of the cheese sauce into the base of a round ovenproof dish. Add a tortilla and then spread over half the salsa followed by half the meat mixture.

6 Repeat these layers, then add half the remaining cheese sauce and the final tortilla. Pour over the remaining cheese sauce and sprinkle the reserved cheese on top. Bake in the oven for 15–20 minutes until golden on top.

BEEF WITH PEPPERS AND BLACK BEAN SAUCE

A SPICY, RICH DISH WITH THE DISTINCTIVE TASTE OF BLACK BEAN SAUCE. THIS IS A RECIPE THAT WILL QUICKLY BECOME A FAVOURITE BECAUSE IT IS SO EASY TO PREPARE AND QUICK TO COOK.

SERVES FOUR

INGREDIENTS

350g/12oz rump (round) steak,
  trimmed and thinly sliced
20ml/4 tsp vegetable oil
300ml/½ pint/1¼ cups beef stock
2 garlic cloves, finely chopped
5ml/1 tsp grated (shredded) fresh
  root ginger
1 fresh red chilli, seeded and
  finely chopped
15ml/1 tbsp black bean sauce
1 green (bell) pepper, seeded and
  cut into 2.5cm/1in squares
15ml/1 tbsp dry sherry
5ml/1 tsp cornflour (cornstarch)
5ml/1 tsp granulated sugar
45ml/3 tbsp cold water
salt
cooked rice noodles, to serve

1 Place the rump steak in a bowl. Add 5ml/1 tsp of the oil and stir to coat.

VARIATIONS
• Use any chilli you like. Habanero, with its hint of apricot flavour, would be a good if very hot choice.
• For extra colour, use a red or orange (bell) pepper or even a yellow Hungarian wax chilli.

2 Bring the stock to the boil in a pan. Add the beef and cook for 2 minutes, stirring constantly to prevent the slices from sticking together. Drain the beef and set aside. Retain the stock for use in another recipe.

3 Heat the remaining oil in a wok. Stir-fry the garlic, ginger and chilli with the black bean sauce for a few seconds. Add the pepper squares and a little water. Cook for about 2 minutes more, then stir in the sherry. Add the beef slices to the pan, spoon the sauce over and reheat.

4 Mix the cornflour and sugar to a cream with the water. Pour the mixture into the pan. Cook, stirring, until the sauce has thickened. Season with salt. Serve immediately, with rice noodles.

COOK'S TIP
To make beef stock, brown 1kg/2¼lb beef or veal bones in an oven heated to 180°C/350°F/Gas 4 for 30 minutes. Put the bones in a pan with a bay leaf and some peppercorns. Cover with water. Add the washed skins of 2 onions, 2 chopped carrot and 1 celery stick. Bring to the boil, simmer for 40 minutes. Strain.

SHREDDED BEEF WITH CHILLIES

THE ESSENCE OF THIS RECIPE IS THAT THE BEEF IS CUT INTO VERY FINE STRIPS. THIS IS EASIER TO ACHIEVE IF THE MEAT IS PLACED IN THE FREEZER FOR 30 MINUTES BEFORE BEING SLICED.

3 Heat a wok and add half the oil. When it is hot, stir-fry the onion and ginger for 3–4 minutes, then lift out with a slotted spoon and set aside. Add the carrot, stir-fry for 3–4 minutes until slightly softened, then transfer to a plate and keep warm.

4 Heat the remaining oil in the wok, then quickly add the beef, with the marinade, followed by the chillies. Cook over high heat for 2 minutes, stirring all the time.

5 Return the fried onion and ginger to the wok and stir-fry for 1 minute more. Season with salt and pepper to taste, cover and cook for 30 seconds. Spoon the meat into 2 warmed bowls and add the carrot strips. Garnish with fresh chives and serve.

SERVES TWO

INGREDIENTS
225g/8oz rump (round) or fillet
   (tenderloin) of beef
15ml/1 tbsp each light and dark
   soy sauce
15ml/1 tbsp rice wine or
   medium-dry sherry
5ml/1 tsp dark brown soft sugar
90ml/6 tbsp vegetable oil
1 large onion, thinly sliced
2.5cm/1in piece fresh root ginger,
   peeled and grated (shredded)
1–2 carrots, cut into matchsticks
2–3 fresh chillies, halved, seeded
   (optional) and chopped
salt and ground black pepper
fresh chives, to garnish

1 With a sharp knife, slice the beef very thinly, then cut each slice into fine strips or shreds.

2 In a bowl, mix the light and dark soy sauces with the rice wine or sherry and sugar. Add the strips of beef and stir well to ensure that they are evenly coated with the marinade. Cover and marinate in a cool place for 30 minutes.

COOK'S TIPS
• Use dried chillies if you prefer. Snap them in half, shake out the seeds, then soak them in hot water for 20–30 minutes.
• If you enjoy your food really fiery, don't bother to remove the seeds from the chillies.

MADRAS CURRY <u>WITH</u> SPICY RICE

CHILLIES ARE AN INDISPENSABLE INGREDIENT OF A HOT MADRAS CURRY. AFTER LONG, GENTLE SIMMERING, THEY MERGE WITH THE OTHER FLAVOURINGS TO GIVE A DELECTABLE RESULT.

SERVES FOUR

INGREDIENTS
    30ml/2 tbsp vegetable oil
    25g/1oz/2 tbsp ghee or butter
    675g/1½lb stewing beef, cut into
        bitesize cubes
    1 onion, chopped
    3 green cardamom pods
    2 fresh green chillies, seeded and
        finely chopped
    2.5cm/1in piece of fresh root
        ginger, grated (shredded)
    2 garlic cloves, crushed
    15ml/1 tbsp Madras curry paste
    5ml/1 tsp ground cumin
    5ml/1 tsp ground coriander
    150ml/¼ pint/⅔ cup beef stock
    salt
For the rice
    225g/8oz/generous 1 cup
        basmati rice
    15ml/1 tbsp sunflower oil
    25g/1oz/2 tbsp ghee or butter
    1 onion, finely chopped
    1 garlic clove, crushed
    5ml/1 tsp ground cumin
    2.5ml/½ tsp ground coriander
    4 green cardamom pods
    1 cinnamon stick
    1 small red (bell) pepper, seeded
        and diced
    1 small green (bell) pepper, seeded
        and diced
    300ml/½ pint/1¼ cups chicken stock

1 Heat half the oil with half the ghee or butter in a large, shallow pan. Fry the meat, in batches if necessary, until browned on all sides. Transfer to a plate and set aside.

2 Heat the remaining oil and ghee or butter and fry the onion for about 3–4 minutes until softened. Add the cardamom pods and fry for 1 minute, then stir in the chillies, ginger and garlic, and fry for 2 minutes more.

3 Stir in the curry paste, ground cumin and coriander, then return the meat to the pan. Stir in the stock. Season with salt, bring to the boil, then reduce the heat and simmer very gently for 1–1½ hours, until the meat is tender.

4 When the curry is almost ready, prepare the rice. Put it in a bowl and pour over boiling water to cover. Set aside for 10 minutes, then drain, rinse under cold water and drain again. The rice will still be uncooked but should have lost its brittleness.

VARIATION
If you like, you can serve plain boiled rice with this curry. Put the rice in a sieve and rinse it under cold water. Place in a pan with 5ml/1 tsp salt, and add water to come 5cm/2in above the level of the rice. Bring to the boil and simmer for 9–12 minutes. Drain and serve.

5 Heat the oil and ghee or butter in a flameproof casserole and fry the onion and garlic gently for 3–4 minutes until softened and lightly browned.

6 Stir in the ground cumin and coriander, green cardamom pods and cinnamon stick. Fry for 1 minute, then add the diced peppers.

7 Add the rice, stirring to coat the grains in the spice mixture, and pour in the chicken stock. Bring to the boil, then reduce the heat, cover the pan tightly and simmer for about 8–10 minutes, or until the rice is tender and the stock has been absorbed. Spoon into a bowl and serve with the curry.

COOK'S TIPS
• The curry should be fairly dry, but take care that it does not catch on the base of the pan. If you want to leave it unattended, cook it in a heavy pan. Alternatively, cook it in a flameproof casserole, in an oven preheated to 180°C/350°F/Gas 4.
• Offer a little mango chutney, if you like, and if you want to cool the heat, a bowl of yogurt raita.

THAI GREEN BEEF CURRY

CHILLIES ARE THE MAIN INGREDIENT IN GREEN CURRY PASTE, WHICH IS USED FOR THIS FRAGRANT DISH. ALSO INCLUDED ARE THAI AUBERGINES.

SERVES FOUR TO SIX

INGREDIENTS

15ml/1 tbsp vegetable oil
45ml/3 tbsp green curry paste
600ml/1 pint/2½ cups coconut milk
450g/1lb beef sirloin, cut into long, thin slices
4 kaffir lime leaves, torn
15–30ml/1–2 tbsp Thai fish sauce (*nam pla*)
5ml/1 tsp palm sugar or soft light brown sugar
150g/5oz small Thai aubergines (eggplant), halved
a small handful of holy basil
2 fresh green chillies, to garnish

1 Heat the oil in a large pan or wok. Add the green curry paste and fry until fragrant.

2 Stir in half the coconut milk, a little at a time. Cook for about 5–6 minutes, until the milk separates and an oily sheen appears.

VARIATION
You can substitute thinly sliced chicken breast portions for the beef.

3 Add the beef to the pan with the kaffir lime leaves, Thai fish sauce, palm sugar and aubergines. Cook for 2–3 minutes, then stir in the remaining coconut milk.

4 Bring back to a simmer and cook until the meat and aubergines are tender. Stir in the basil just before serving. Finely shred the green chillies and use to garnish the curry.

COOK'S TIP
Thai aubergines look very like unripe tomatoes. Their virtue is that they will cook quickly in a recipe of this kind. They have a delicate flavour and are not so fleshy as the more common large purple-skinned variety. These small aubergines do not need peeling or salting. You may also find small yellow and purple ones.

CHILLI BEEF WITH BASIL

THIS IS A VERY EASY DISH THAT CHILLI LOVERS WILL ENJOY COOKING AND EATING. USE BIRD'S EYE CHILLIES IF YOU CAN AND FRAGRANT THAI JASMINE RICE TO SERVE WITH IT.

SERVES TWO

INGREDIENTS

16–20 large fresh basil leaves, plus
  30ml/2 tbsp finely chopped basil
about 90ml/6 tbsp groundnut
  (peanut) oil
275g/10oz rump (round) steak
30ml/2 tbsp Thai fish sauce
  (*nam pla*)
5ml/1 tsp soft dark brown sugar
2 fresh red chillies, sliced into rings
3 garlic cloves, chopped
5ml/1 tsp chopped fresh root ginger
1 shallot, thinly sliced
squeeze of lemon juice
salt and ground black pepper
Thai jasmine rice, to serve

1 Dry the basil leaves thoroughly, if necessary. Heat the oil in a wok. When it is hot, add the basil leaves and fry for about 1 minute until crisp and golden. Scoop out and drain on kitchen paper. Remove the wok from the heat and carefully pour off all but 30ml/2 tbsp of the oil.

2 Cut the steak across the grain into thin strips. In a bowl, mix together the fish sauce and sugar. Add the beef, mix well, then cover and set aside to marinate for about 30 minutes.

COOK'S TIP
Groundnut oil is widely used in Chinese cooking. Its ability to be heated to a high temperature without burning makes it ideal for stir-frying. It has a mild, pleasant taste.

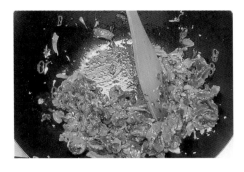

3 Reheat the oil until hot, add the chillies, garlic, ginger and shallot, and stir-fry for 30 seconds. Add the beef and chopped basil, and stir-fry for about 3 minutes more. Flavour with lemon juice and add salt and pepper to taste.

4 Transfer to a warmed serving platter, arrange the fried basil leaves over the top and serve immediately with rice. Good accompaniments would be lightly steamed green vegetables or a crisp green salad to provide contrast.

SPICY MEATBALLS

THESE SPICY LITTLE PATTIES COME FROM INDONESIA. SERVE THEM WITH BROAD EGG NOODLES AND FIERY CHILLI SAMBAL AS A DIPPING SAUCE.

SERVES FOUR TO SIX

INGREDIENTS
1cm/½in cube shrimp paste
1 large onion, roughly chopped
1–2 fresh red chillies, seeded
  and chopped
2 garlic cloves, crushed
15ml/1 tbsp coriander seeds
5ml/1 tsp cumin seeds
450g/1lb lean minced (ground) beef
10ml/2 tsp dark soy sauce
5ml/1 tsp soft dark brown sugar
juice of 1½ lemons
a little beaten egg
vegetable oil, for shallow frying
salt and ground black pepper
1 fresh green and 1–2 fresh red
  chillies, to garnish
Chilli Sambal (below), to serve

1 Wrap the shrimp paste in a piece of foil and gently warm it in a dry frying pan for 5 minutes, turning a few times. Unwrap the paste and put in a food processor or blender.

COOK'S TIP
When processing the shrimp paste, onion, chillies and garlic, do not run the machine for too long, or the onion will become too wet and spoil the consistency of the meatballs.

2 Add the onion, chillies and garlic to the food processor and process until finely chopped. Set aside. Dry-fry the coriander and cumin seeds in a hot frying pan for 1 minute, to release the aroma. Tip the seeds into a mortar and grind with a pestle.

3 Put the meat in a large bowl. Stir in the onion mixture. Add the ground spices, soy sauce, brown sugar, lemon juice and beaten egg. Season to taste.

4 Shape the meat mixture into small, even-size balls, and chill these for 5–10 minutes to firm them up.

5 Heat the oil in a wok or large frying pan and fry the meatballs for 4–5 minutes, turning often, until cooked through and browned. You may have to do this in batches.

6 Drain the meatballs on kitchen paper, and then pile them on to a warm serving platter or into a large serving bowl. Finely slice the green chilli and one of the red chillies, and sprinkle over the meatballs. Garnish with a whole red chilli, if you like. Serve with the sambal, spooned into a small dish.

VARIATION
Beef is traditionally used for this dish, but minced (ground) pork, lamb – or even turkey – would also be good.

CHILLI SAMBAL

THIS FIERCE CONDIMENT IS BOTTLED AS SAMBAL OELEK, BUT IT IS EASY TO PREPARE AND WILL KEEP FOR SEVERAL WEEKS IN A WELL-SEALED JAR IN THE REFRIGERATOR.

MAKES 450G/1LB

INGREDIENTS
450g/1lb fresh red chillies, seeded
10ml/2 tsp salt

COOK'S TIP
If any sambal drips on your fingers, wash well in soapy water *immediately*.

1 Bring a pan of water to the boil, add the seeded chillies and cook them for 5–8 minutes.

2 Drain the chillies and chop roughly. Grind the chillies in a food processor or blender, without making the paste too smooth. If you like, you can do this in batches.

3 Scrape into a screw-topped glass jar, stir in the salt and cover with a piece of greaseproof (waxed) paper or clear film (plastic wrap). Screw on the lid and store in the refrigerator. Wash all implements in soapy water. Spoon into dishes using a stainless-steel or plastic spoon. Serve as an accompaniment, as suggested in recipes.

Get into the habit of buying fresh chillies whenever you see them on sale, and you'll be surprised how often you'll use them in cooking, not necessarily as the principal ingredient, but for pungent punctuation. Chillies are great for highlighting other flavours, and nowhere is this more apparent than when they are added to vegetable and vegetarian dishes. Try Peppers filled with Spiced Vegetables, Pasta with Sugocasa and Chilli, or Mushrooms with Chipotle Chillies.

Vibrant Vegetarian and Side Dishes

PANCAKES STUFFED <u>WITH</u> LIGHTLY SPICED SQUASH

IN ORDER TO APPRECIATE THE INDIVIDUAL FLAVOURS OF THE BUTTERNUT SQUASH, LEEKS AND CHICORY IN THESE PANCAKES, IT IS IMPORTANT NOT TO OVERDO THE CHILLI.

SERVES FOUR

INGREDIENTS
- 115g/4oz/1 cup plain (all-purpose) flour
- 50g/2oz/generous ⅓ cup yellow corn meal
- 2.5ml/½ tsp salt
- 2.5ml/½ tsp chilli powder
- 2 large (US extra large) eggs
- 450ml/¾ pint/scant 2 cups milk
- 65g/2½oz/5 tbsp butter
- vegetable oil, for greasing
- 25g/1oz/⅓ cup freshly grated (shredded) Parmesan cheese

For the filling
- 30ml/2 tbsp olive oil
- 450g/1lb butternut squash (peeled weight), seeded
- large pinch of dried red chilli flakes
- 2 large leeks, thickly sliced
- 2.5ml/½ tsp chopped fresh or dried thyme
- 3 chicory (Belgian endive) heads, thickly sliced
- 115g/4oz full-flavoured goat's cheese, cut into cubes
- 90g/3½oz/scant 1 cup walnuts or pecan nuts, roughly chopped
- 30ml/2 tbsp chopped fresh flat leaf parsley
- salt and ground black pepper

2 When ready to cook the pancakes, melt 25g/1oz/2 tbsp of the butter and stir it into the batter. Heat a lightly greased 18cm/7in heavy frying pan or crêpe pan. Pour about 60ml/4 tbsp of the batter into the pan, tilt it so that the batter forms a pancake and cook for 2–3 minutes, until set and lightly browned underneath. Turn and cook the pancake on the other side for 2–3 minutes. Lightly grease the pan after every second pancake.

3 Make the filling. Heat the oil in a large pan. Add the squash and cook, stirring frequently, for 10 minutes, until almost tender. Add the chilli flakes and cook, stirring, for a further 1–2 minutes. Stir in the leeks and thyme, and cook for 4–5 minutes more.

5 Preheat the oven to 200°C/400°F/ Gas 6. Lightly grease an ovenproof dish. Either layer the pancakes with the filling to make a stack in the dish or stuff each pancake with 30–45ml/2–3 tbsp filling. Roll or fold the pancakes to enclose the filling and place in the dish.

6 Sprinkle the grated Parmesan over the pancakes. Melt the remaining butter and drizzle it over the layered or filled pancakes. Bake for 10–15 minutes, until the cheese is bubbling and the pancakes are piping hot. Serve immediately.

COOK'S TIP
This can all be prepared in advance, but make sure the filling is cold before adding to the pancakes.

VARIATIONS
- Fennel could be used instead of chicory, and pumpkin, other varieties of winter squash or courgette (zucchini) instead of butternut squash.
- If you like, you can add a fresh chilli, but make it a mild one, such as Anaheim. Roast and peel it first.

1 Sift the flour, corn meal, salt and chilli powder into a bowl. Make a well in the centre. Add the eggs and a little of the milk. Whisk the eggs and milk, gradually incorporating the dry ingredients and adding more milk to make a batter with a consistency like that of thick cream.

4 Add the chicory and cook, stirring frequently, for 4–5 minutes, until the leeks are cooked and the chicory is hot, but still with some bite to its texture. Cool slightly, then stir in the cheese, nuts and parsley. Season the mixture well with salt and pepper.

PASTA WITH SUGOCASA AND CHILLI

IT CAN BE DIFFICULT TO DETERMINE HOW MUCH CHILLI TO USE IN A DISH. THIS RECIPE PROVIDES A NEAT SOLUTION. BOTTLED SUGOCASA IS IDEAL FOR PASTA SAUCES, BEING FINER THAN CANNED CHOPPED TOMATOES AND COARSER THAN PASSATA. IT MAY BE LABELLED "CRUSHED ITALIAN TOMATOES".

SERVES FOUR

INGREDIENTS

500g/1¼lb sugocasa
2 garlic cloves, crushed
150ml/¼ pint/⅔ cup dry white wine
15ml/1 tbsp sun-dried tomato
   purée (paste)
1 fresh red chilli
300g/11oz/2¾ cups dried
   pasta shapes
60ml/4 tbsp finely chopped fresh
   flat leaf parsley
salt and ground black pepper
freshly grated (shredded) Pecorino
   cheese, to serve

1 Pour the sugocasa into a pan and add the crushed garlic, white wine, sun-dried tomato purée and whole chilli. Bring to the boil. Cover and simmer for about 15 minutes.

2 Bring a large pan of lightly salted water to the boil. Stir in the pasta shapes and cook for 10–12 minutes, or for the time suggested on the packet cooking instructions.

3 Remove the chilli from the sauce and stir in half the parsley. Taste for seasoning, adding salt and pepper as needed. If you prefer a hotter taste, chop some or all of the chilli and return it to the sauce and heat it through.

4 Drain the pasta and tip into a large heated bowl. Pour the sauce over the pasta and toss to mix. Serve at once, sprinkled with grated Pecorino and the remaining parsley.

SPAGHETTI WITH GARLIC, CHILLI AND OIL

PASTA DESCRIBED AS AL DENTE HAS A BIT OF BITE. THERE'S ANOTHER BITE THAT IS IMPORTANT, AND THAT'S ANY INGREDIENT GIVING A BIT OF AN EDGE TO A BLAND DISH. CHILLIES DO THE JOB SUPERBLY.

1 Bring a large pan of salted water to the boil and add the spaghetti, lowering it into the water gradually, as it softens. Cook for 10–12 minutes, or according to the packet instructions, until the strands are *al dente*.

2 Meanwhile, heat the oil very gently in a small pan. Add the crushed garlic and chopped dried chilli and stir over a low heat until the garlic is just beginning to brown. Remove the chilli and discard it.

3 Drain the pasta and tip it into a large heated bowl. Pour on the oil and garlic mixture, add the parsley and toss vigorously until the pasta glistens. Serve immediately, garnished with extra dried chillies.

SERVES FOUR

INGREDIENTS
 400g/14oz fresh or
  dried spaghetti
 90ml/6 tbsp extra virgin olive oil
 2–4 garlic cloves, crushed
 1 dried red chilli, chopped, plus
  extra dried chillies to garnish
 1 small handful fresh flat leaf
  parsley, roughly chopped
salt

COOK'S TIPS
• Use a fresh chilli, if you prefer.
• For extra heat, substitute chilli oil for some or all of the olive oil. Be careful when using chilli oil because the flavour becomes very concentrated, so use it sparingly.
• If you like, hand separately a bowl of freshly grated (shredded) Parmesan cheese. The delicious flavour of this cheese is better appreciated when fresh. A block will keep well in the refrigerator, wrapped in clear film (plastic wrap).

CHILLI, TOMATO AND SPINACH PIZZA

THIS RICHLY FLAVOURED TOPPING WITH A HINT OF SPICE MAKES A COLOURFUL AND SATISFYING PIZZA. ADDED TO A READY-MADE PIZZA BASE, IT MAKES THE COOK'S LIFE REALLY EASY.

SERVES THREE

INGREDIENTS
1–2 fresh red chillies
50g/2oz/½ cup sun-dried tomatoes in oil, drained, plus 45ml/3 tbsp oil from the jar
1 onion, chopped
2 garlic cloves, chopped
400g/14oz can chopped tomatoes
15ml/1 tbsp tomato purée (paste)
175g/6oz fresh spinach
1 ready-made pizza base, 25–30cm/10–12in in diameter
75g/3oz/¾ cup grated (shredded) smoked Bavarian cheese
75g/3oz/¾ cup grated (shredded) mature (sharp) Cheddar cheese
salt and ground black pepper

1 Slit the chillies, open them out and use a sharp knife to scrape out the seeds. Chop the flesh finely.

2 Heat 30ml/2 tbsp of the oil from the sun-dried tomatoes in a pan, add the chopped onion, garlic and chillies, and fry gently for about 5 minutes until the onions are soft. Do not let them brown.

3 Roughly chop the sun-dried tomatoes. Add them to the pan with the canned chopped tomatoes, tomato purée and seasoning. Simmer uncovered, stirring occasionally, for 15 minutes.

4 Preheat the oven to 220°C/425°F/ Gas 7. Remove the stalks from the spinach and wash the leaves in plenty of cold water. Drain well and pat dry with kitchen paper. Roughly chop the spinach.

5 Add the spinach to the sauce and stir gently. Cook, stirring, for a further 5–10 minutes until the spinach has wilted and no excess moisture remains.

6 Brush the pizza base with the remaining tomato oil, then spoon over the sauce. Sprinkle over the cheeses and bake for 15–20 minutes or for the time recommended on the packaging of the pizza base, until crisp and golden. Serve immediately.

JALAPEÑO AND ONION QUICHE

CANNED OR BOTTLED JALAPEÑO CHILLIES ARE USEFUL IN A RANGE OF DISHES, FROM DIPS AND SALADS TO SNACKS AND MAIN COURSES. THEY HAVE AN AFFINITY FOR EGGS AND CHEESE.

SERVES SIX

INGREDIENTS

15g/½oz/1 tbsp butter
2 onions, sliced
4 spring onions (scallions), cut in 1cm/½in pieces
2.5ml/½ tsp ground cumin
15–30ml/1–2 tbsp chopped canned or bottled jalapeño chillies
75g/3oz/¾ cup grated (shredded) Cheddar or Monterey Jack cheese
4 eggs
300ml/½ pint/1¼ cups milk
2.5ml/½ tsp salt
flat leaf parsley, to garnish
For the pastry
175g/6oz/1½ cups plain (all-purpose) flour
1.5ml/¼ tsp salt
1.5ml/¼ tsp cayenne pepper
75g/3oz/6 tbsp cold butter
75g/3oz/6 tbsp cold margarine
30–60ml/2–4 tbsp iced water

1 Make the pastry. Sift the flour, salt and cayenne pepper into a bowl. Rub in the butter and margarine until the mixture resembles coarse breadcrumbs.

2 Sprinkle in 30ml/2 tbsp iced water and mix until the dough holds together. If the dough is too crumbly, add a little more water, 15ml/1 tbsp at a time. Gather the dough into a ball and flatten slightly. Wrap in clear film (plastic wrap) and chill for at least 30 minutes.

3 Preheat the oven to 190°C/375°F/ Gas 5. Roll out the pastry to a thickness of about 3mm/⅛in. Use to line a 23cm/9in fluted quiche tin (tart pan) that has a removable base. Prick the base of the pastry case all over with a fork. Line the case with foil and fill with baking beans.

4 Bake for 12–15 minutes, until the pastry has just set. Remove from the oven and carefully lift out the foil and beans. Return it to the oven and bake for 5–8 minutes more, until golden.

5 While the pastry case is baking, melt the butter in a frying pan and cook the onions over a medium heat for 5 minutes, until softened. Add the spring onions and cook for 1 minute more. Stir in the cumin and jalapeños, and set aside.

6 Spoon the onion mixture into the pastry shell. Sprinkle with the cheese. In a bowl, whisk the eggs, milk and salt together. Pour the egg mixture into the pastry case. Bake for 30–40 minutes, until the filling has set. Serve warm or cold, garnished with parsley.

CHEESE AND LEEK SAUSAGES WITH CHILLI AND TOMATO SAUCE

A SPICY SAUCE, MADE USING FRESH OR DRIED CHILLI AND FLAVOURED WITH BALSAMIC OR RED WINE VINEGAR, PEPS UP THESE POPULAR VEGETARIAN SAUSAGES.

SERVES FOUR

INGREDIENTS
  25g/1oz/2 tbsp butter
  175g/6oz leeks, finely chopped
  90ml/6 tbsp cold mashed potato
  115g/4oz/2 cups fresh
    white breadcrumbs
  150g/5oz/1¼ cups grated
    (shredded) Caerphilly, Lancashire
    or Cantal cheese
  30ml/2 tbsp chopped fresh parsley
  5ml/1 tsp chopped fresh sage
    or marjoram
  2 large (US extra large) eggs, beaten
  good pinch of cayenne pepper
  65g/2½oz/scant 1 cup dry
    white breadcrumbs
  oil, for shallow frying
  salt and ground black pepper
For the sauce
  30ml/2 tbsp olive oil
  2 garlic cloves, thinly sliced
  1 fresh red chilli, seeded and finely
    chopped, or a good pinch of dried
    red chilli flakes
  1 small onion, finely chopped
  500g/1¼lb tomatoes, peeled, seeded
    and chopped
  a few fresh thyme sprigs
  10ml/2 tsp balsamic vinegar or red
    wine vinegar
  pinch of light muscovado
    (brown) sugar
  15–30ml/1–2 tbsp chopped fresh
    marjoram or oregano

1 Melt the butter in a pan and fry the leeks for 4–5 minutes, until softened but not browned. Mix with the mashed potato, fresh breadcrumbs, cheese, parsley and sage or marjoram. Add sufficient beaten egg (about two-thirds of the quantity) to bind the mixture. Season well and add the cayenne pepper to taste.

COOK'S TIP
These sausages are also delicious when they are served with chilli jam or a fruity chilli salsa.

2 Pat or roll the mixture between dampened hands to form 12 sausage shapes. Dip in the remaining egg, then coat in the dry breadcrumbs. Chill the coated sausages.

3 Make the sauce. Heat the oil in a pan and cook the garlic, chilli and onion over a low heat for 3–4 minutes. Add the tomatoes, thyme and vinegar. Season with salt, pepper and sugar.

4 Cook the sauce for 40–50 minutes, until considerably reduced. Remove the thyme and purée the sauce in a food processor or blender. Reheat with the marjoram or oregano and then adjust the seasoning.

5 Fry the sausages in shallow oil until golden brown on all sides. Drain on kitchen paper and serve with the sauce.

CHILLI CHEESE TORTILLA <u>WITH</u> FRESH TOMATO <u>AND</u> CORIANDER SALSA

Good warm or cold, this is like a sliced potato quiche without the pastry base, and is well spiked with chilli. It makes a satisfying lunch.

<u>SERVES FOUR</u>

INGREDIENTS
  45ml/3 tbsp sunflower or olive oil
  1 small onion, thinly sliced
  2–3 fresh green jalapeño chillies,
    seeded and sliced
  200g/7oz cold cooked potato,
    thinly sliced
  150g/5oz/1¼ cups grated
    (shredded) cheese
  6 eggs, beaten
  salt and ground black pepper
  fresh herbs and chilli, to garnish
For the salsa
  500g/1¼lb fresh, flavoursome tomatoes,
    peeled, seeded and finely chopped
  1 fresh mild green chilli, seeded and
    finely chopped
  2 garlic cloves, crushed
  45ml/3 tbsp chopped fresh
    coriander (cilantro)
  juice of 1 lime
  2.5ml/½ tsp salt

1 Make the salsa by mixing all the ingredients in a bowl. Mix well, cover and set aside.

2 Heat 15ml/1 tbsp of the oil in a large frying pan and gently fry the onion and jalapeños for 5 minutes, stirring until softened. Add the potato and cook for 5 minutes until lightly browned, keeping the slices whole. Using a slotted spoon, transfer the vegetables to a warm plate.

COOK'S TIP
Use a firm but not hard cheese, such as Double Gloucester or Monterey Jack.

3 Wipe the pan with kitchen paper, then add the remaining oil and heat until really hot. Return the vegetables to the pan. Sprinkle the cheese over the top and season.

4 Pour in the beaten egg, making sure that it seeps under the vegetables. Cook over a low heat, stirring, until set. Serve hot or cold, in wedges, with the salsa. Garnish with fresh herbs and chilli.

CUCUMBER AND ALFALFA TORTILLAS

SERVED WITH A PIQUANT CHILLI SALSA, THESE FILLED TORTILLAS ARE EXTREMELY EASY TO PREPARE AT HOME AND MAKE A MARVELLOUS LIGHT LUNCH OR SUPPER DISH.

SERVES FOUR

INGREDIENTS
  225g/8oz/2 cups plain
    (all-purpose) flour
  pinch of salt
  45ml/3 tbsp olive oil
  120–150ml/4–5fl oz/½–⅔ cup
    warm water
  lime wedges, to garnish
For the salsa
  1 red onion, finely chopped
  1 fresh red chilli, seeded and
    finely chopped
  30ml/2 tbsp chopped fresh dill
  ½ cucumber, peeled and chopped
  175g/6oz/3 cups alfalfa sprouts
For the avocado sauce
  1 large avocado, halved, peeled
    and stoned (pitted)
  juice of 1 lime
  25g/1oz/2 tbsp soft goat's cheese
  pinch of paprika

COOK'S TIP
When peeling the avocado, be sure to scrape off the bright green flesh from immediately under the skin as this gives the sauce its vivid colour.

1 Make the salsa. Put the onion and chilli in a bowl. Add the dill, cucumber and alfalfa sprouts, and mix well. Cover.

2 To make the sauce, place the avocado, lime juice and goat's cheese in a blender and process. Scrape into a bowl. Cover with clear film (plastic wrap).

3 To make the tortillas, place the flour and salt in a food processor or blender, add the oil and blend. Gradually add the water (the amount will vary depending on the flour). Stop adding water when a stiff dough has formed. Turn out on to a floured board and knead for about 5–10 minutes until smooth. Cover with a damp cloth.

4 Divide the mixture into 8 pieces. Knead each piece for a couple of minutes and form into a ball. Flatten and roll out each ball to form a 23cm/9in diameter circle.

5 Heat an ungreased heavy frying pan. Cook 1 tortilla at a time for about 30 seconds on each side. Wrap the cooked tortillas in a clean dishtowel. Make the 7 remaining balls of dough into tortillas in the same way.

6 Take the covering off the avocado sauce and dust the top with paprika. To serve, spread each tortilla with a spoonful of avocado sauce, top with salsa and roll up. Garnish with lime wedges. A green salad would be a good accompaniment.

BLACK BEAN AND CHILLI BURRITOS

TORTILLAS ARE A WONDERFULLY ADAPTABLE FOOD. HERE THEY ARE FILLED WITH BEANS, CHEESE AND SALSA, AND SPIKED WITH CHILLI. A SHORT PERIOD OF BAKING IN THE OVEN AND THEY'RE READY TO EAT.

SERVES FOUR

INGREDIENTS

225g/8oz/1¼ cups dried black
  beans, soaked in water overnight
1 bay leaf
45ml/3 tbsp coarse salt
1 small red onion, finely chopped
225g/8oz/2 cups grated (shredded)
  Cheddar cheese or Monterey Jack
45ml/3 tbsp chopped pickled
  jalapeño chillies
15ml/1 tbsp chopped fresh
  coriander (cilantro)
900ml/1½ pints/3¾ cups
  tomato salsa
8 wheat flour tortillas
salt and ground black pepper
diced avocado, to serve

1 Drain the beans and put them in a large pan. Add fresh cold water to cover and the bay leaf. Bring to the boil, then reduce the heat, cover and simmer for 30 minutes. Add the salt and continue simmering for about 30 minutes more, or until the beans are tender. Drain and tip into a bowl. Discard the bay leaf.

2 Grease a rectangular baking dish. Add the onion, half the cheese, the jalapeños, coriander and 250ml/8fl oz/ 1 cup of the salsa to the beans. Stir well and add salt and pepper if needed. Preheat the oven to 180°C/350°F/Gas 4.

3 Place 1 tortilla on a board. Spread a large spoonful of the filling down the middle, then roll up to enclose the filling. Place the burrito in the dish, seam side down. Repeat to make 7 more.

4 Sprinkle the remaining cheese over the burritos. Bake for 15 minutes, until all the cheese melts.

5 Serve the burritos immediately, with avocado and the remaining salsa.

COUSCOUS WITH EGGS AND SPICY RELISH

A RICHLY FLAVOURED ROASTED TOMATO SAUCE, SPIKED WITH CHILLI, IS AN IDEAL TOPPING FOR LIGHTLY COOKED EGGS IN A SAVOURY COUSCOUS NEST.

SERVES FOUR

INGREDIENTS

675g/1½lb plum tomatoes,
  roughly chopped
4 garlic cloves, chopped
75ml/5 tbsp olive oil
½ fresh red chilli, seeded
  and chopped
10ml/2 tsp soft light
  brown sugar
4 eggs
1 large onion, chopped
2 celery sticks, finely sliced
50g/2oz/⅓ cup sultanas
  (golden raisins)
200g/7oz/generous 1 cup ready-to-
  use couscous
about 350ml/12fl oz/1½ cups hot
  vegetable stock
salt and ground black pepper

1 Preheat the oven to 200°C/400°F/ Gas 6. Put the tomatoes and garlic in a roasting pan, drizzle with 30ml/2 tbsp of the oil, sprinkle with chopped chilli, sugar and salt and pepper, and roast for 20 minutes until soft.

VARIATION
Add a drained bottled pimiento or two to the tomato mixture before sieving it.

2 Lower the eggs carefully into boiling water and boil them for 4 minutes, then plunge them straight into cold water. When cold, shell them carefully.

3 Remove the tomatoes from the oven and push them through a sieve. Add 15ml/1 tbsp boiling water and 15ml/ 1 tbsp olive oil to the puréed tomatoes and blend to give a smooth, rich sauce. Season to taste with salt and pepper. Keep the sauce hot while you prepare the couscous.

4 Put 15–30ml/1–2 tbsp of the remaining olive oil in a large pan and gently fry the onion and celery until softened. Add the sultanas, couscous and hot stock, and set aside until all the liquid has been absorbed. This will take about 7 minutes. Stir gently, add extra hot stock if necessary and season to taste.

5 Spread out the couscous on to a large heated serving dish, half bury the eggs in it and spoon a little tomato sauce over the top of each egg. Serve immediately, with the rest of the sauce handed separately.

JAMAICAN BLACK BEAN POT

MOLASSES IMPARTS A RICH SYRUPY FLAVOUR TO THE SPICY SAUCE, WHICH MATCHES HOT CHILLI WITH BLACK BEANS, VIBRANT RED AND YELLOW PEPPERS AND ORANGE BUTTERNUT SQUASH.

SERVES FOUR

INGREDIENTS

225g/8oz/1¼ cups dried black beans, soaked overnight in water to cover
1 bay leaf
30ml/2 tbsp vegetable oil
1 large onion, chopped
1 garlic clove, chopped
½–1 Scotch bonnet chilli, seeded and finely chopped
5ml/1 tsp English mustard powder
15ml/1 tbsp blackstrap molasses
30ml/2 tbsp soft dark brown sugar
5ml/1 tsp dried thyme
5ml/1 tsp vegetable bouillon powder or 1 vegetable stock (bouillon) cube
1 red (bell) pepper, seeded and diced
1 yellow (bell) pepper, seeded and diced
675g/1½lb/5¼ cups butternut squash or pumpkin, seeded and cut into 1cm/½in dice
salt and ground black pepper
fresh thyme sprigs, to garnish

1 Drain the beans, rinse and drain again. Place in a large pan, cover with fresh water and add the bay leaf. Bring to the boil, then boil rapidly for 10 minutes. Reduce the heat, cover, and simmer for 30 minutes until tender. Drain, reserving the cooking water. Preheat the oven to 180°C/350°F/Gas 4.

VARIATIONS
• This dish is delicious served with cornbread or plain rice.
• If you like, you could substitute red kidney beans for the black beans, and still retain the authentic Caribbean flavour.

2 Heat the oil in the pan and sauté the onion, garlic and chilli for about 5 minutes, or until softened, stirring occasionally. Add the mustard powder, molasses, sugar and thyme. Cook for 1 minute, stirring. Stir in the black beans, mix well and spoon the mixture into a flameproof casserole.

3 Add enough water to the reserved cooking liquid to make 400ml/14fl oz/1⅔ cups, then mix in the bouillon powder or crumbled stock cube. Pour into the casserole and mix well. Bake in the oven for 25 minutes.

4 Add the peppers and squash or pumpkin to the casserole and mix well. Season to taste. Cover, then bake for 45 minutes more, or until the vegetables are tender. Serve garnished with thyme.

COOK'S TIP
The Scotch bonnet chilli, like its close relative, the habanero, is blisteringly hot. Handle it with great care (wearing gloves is wise) and use only as much as you dare. The uninitiated may find even half too much, and may prefer to substitute a milder variety, but it would be a shame to miss the chilli flavour.

CARIBBEAN RED BEAN CHILLI

WHEN PULSES PARTNER CHILLIES, THE HEAT SEEMS TO BE MODERATED SLIGHTLY, SO THIS LENTIL AND RED KIDNEY BEAN MIXTURE IS A GOOD VEHICLE FOR A HABANERO OR SCOTCH BONNET CHILLI.

3 Add the lentils, thyme, cumin, soy sauce, chilli, mixed spice and vegetarian oyster sauce, if using.

4 Cover and simmer for 40 minutes or until the lentils are cooked, stirring occasionally and adding more water if the lentils begin to dry out.

5 Stir in the red kidney beans and sugar and continue cooking for 10 minutes, adding a little extra stock or water if necessary. Season to taste with salt. Serve the chilli hot with boiled rice and sweetcorn.

VARIATION
You could substitute a can of black beans for the red kidney beans.

SERVES FOUR

INGREDIENTS
   30ml/2 tbsp vegetable oil
   1 onion, chopped
   400g/14oz can chopped tomatoes
   2 garlic cloves, crushed
   300ml/½ pint/1¼ cups white wine
   about 300ml/½ pint/1¼ cups stock
   115g/4oz/½ cup red lentils
   5ml/1 tsp dried thyme
   10ml/2 tsp ground cumin
   45ml/3 tbsp dark soy sauce
   ½–1 habanero or Scotch bonnet
     chilli, seeded and finely chopped
   5ml/1 tsp mixed (pumpkin pie) spice
   15ml/1 tbsp vegetarian oyster
     sauce (optional)
   225g/8oz can red kidney
     beans, drained
   10ml/2 tsp granulated sugar
   salt
   boiled rice and sweetcorn, to serve

1 Heat the oil in a large pan and fry the onion over a medium heat for a few minutes until slightly softened.

2 Add the tomatoes and garlic, cook for 10 minutes, then stir in the white wine and stock.

COOK'S TIP
It's a good idea to cut any surplus chillies in half, wrap the halves separately, and freeze them.

CHILLI BEANS WITH BASMATI RICE

RED KIDNEY BEANS, TOMATOES AND CHILLI MAKE A GREAT COMBINATION. SERVE WITH PASTA OR PITTA BREAD INSTEAD OF RICE, IF YOU PREFER.

SERVES FOUR

INGREDIENTS
  350g/12oz/1¾ cups basmati rice
  30ml/2 tbsp olive oil
  1 large onion, chopped
  1 garlic clove, crushed
  15ml/1 tbsp hot chilli powder
  15ml/1 tbsp plain (all-purpose) flour
  15ml/1 tbsp tomato purée (paste)
  400g/14oz can chopped tomatoes
  400g/14oz can red kidney beans,
    rinsed and drained
  150ml/¼ pint/⅔ cup hot
    vegetable stock
  salt and ground black pepper
  chopped fresh parsley, to garnish

3 Stir in the tomato purée, chopped tomatoes and kidney beans with the hot vegetable stock. Cover and cook for 12 minutes, stirring occasionally to prevent the beans from sticking.

4 Season the mixture with salt and pepper. Drain the rice and divide among serving plates. Ladle the chilli beans on to the plates, garnish with a sprinkling of chopped fresh parsley and serve.

1 Wash the rice several times under cold running water. Drain well. Bring a large pan of water to the boil. Add the rice and cook for 10–12 minutes, until tender. Meanwhile, heat the oil in a frying pan. Add the onion and garlic and cook for 2 minutes.

2 Stir the chilli powder and flour into the onion and garlic mixture. Cook gently for 2 minutes, stirring frequently to prevent the onions from browning.

PEPPERS FILLED WITH SPICED VEGETABLES

Jalapeño chillies and Indian spices season the vegetable stuffing in these colourful baked peppers. Serve these with plain rice, cucumber slices and a lentil dhal.

SERVES SIX

INGREDIENTS

- 6 large evenly shaped red or yellow (bell) peppers
- 500g/1¼lb potatoes, peeled, halved if large
- 1–2 jalapeños or other fresh green chillies, seeded and chopped
- 1 small onion, chopped
- 4–5 garlic cloves, chopped
- 5cm/2in piece of fresh root ginger, chopped
- 105ml/7 tbsp water
- 90–105ml/6–7 tbsp groundnut (peanut) oil
- 1 aubergine (eggplant), cut into 1cm/½in dice
- 10ml/2 tsp cumin seeds
- 5ml/1 tsp kalonji seeds
- 2.5ml/½ tsp ground turmeric
- 5ml/1 tsp ground coriander
- 5ml/1 tsp ground toasted cumin seeds
- 1–2 pinches of cayenne pepper
- about 30ml/2 tbsp lemon juice
- salt and ground black pepper
- 30ml/2 tbsp chopped fresh coriander (cilantro), to garnish

1 Cut the tops off the peppers and pull out the central core from each, keeping the shells intact. Shake out any remaining seeds. Cut a thin slice off the base of the peppers, if necessary, to make them stand upright.

2 Bring a large pan of lightly salted water to the boil. Add the peppers and cook for 5–6 minutes. Lift out and drain them upside down in a colander.

3 Bring the water in the pan back to the boil, add the potatoes and cook for 10–12 minutes, until just tender. Drain thoroughly, put on one side to cool, then cut into 1cm/½in dice.

4 Put the green chillies, onion, garlic and ginger in a food processor or blender with 60ml/4 tbsp of the water and process to a purée. Preheat the oven to 190°C/375°F/Gas 5.

5 Heat 45ml/3 tbsp of the oil in a large, deep frying pan and cook the aubergine, stirring occasionally, until browned on all sides. Remove from the pan and set aside. Add another 30ml/2 tbsp of the oil to the pan and sauté the potatoes until lightly browned. Remove from the pan and set aside.

6 If necessary, add another 15ml/1 tbsp oil to the pan, then add the cumin and kalonji seeds. Fry briefly until the seeds darken, then add the turmeric, coriander and ground cumin. Cook for 15 seconds. Stir in the chilli purée and fry, scraping the pan with a spatula, until the mixture begins to brown. Do not let it burn.

7 Return the potatoes and aubergines to the pan, and season with salt, pepper and 1–2 pinches of cayenne. Pour in the remaining measured water and 15ml/1 tbsp lemon juice. Cook, stirring, until the liquid evaporates.

8 Place the peppers on a baking tray and fill with the potato mixture. Brush the pepper skins with a little oil and bake for 30–35 minutes, until cooked. Allow to cool a little, then sprinkle with a little more lemon juice, garnish with the coriander and serve.

COOK'S TIPS

- Try using poblano chillies instead of the sweet peppers.
- The spice kalonji, also known as nigella, is a very tiny black seed that closely resembles the onion seed. It is available from most supermarkets and Indian foodstores.

VARIATIONS

- Instead of serving with rice and a lentil dhal, try Indian breads and a cucumber or mint yogurt raita.
- Substitute carrots and parsnips for the potatoes.

LENTIL DHAL WITH CHILLIES AND ROASTED GARLIC

FRESH AND DRIED CHILLIES FEATURE IN THIS SPICY LENTIL DHAL, WHICH MAKES A COMFORTING, STARCHY MEAL WHEN SERVED WITH BOILED RICE OR INDIAN BREADS.

SERVES FOUR TO SIX

INGREDIENTS

  40g/1½oz/3 tbsp butter or ghee
  1 onion, chopped
  2 fresh green chillies, seeded
    and chopped
  15ml/1 tbsp chopped fresh
    root ginger
  225g/8oz/1 cup yellow or red lentils
  900ml/1½ pints/3¾ cups water
  1 head of garlic
  5ml/1 tsp ground cumin
  5ml/1 tsp ground coriander
  2 tomatoes, peeled and diced
  a little lemon juice
  salt and ground black pepper
  30–45ml/2–3 tbsp fresh coriander
    (cilantro) sprigs, to garnish
For the whole spice mix
  30ml/2 tbsp groundnut (peanut) oil
  4–5 shallots, sliced
  2 garlic cloves, thinly sliced
  15g/½oz/1 tbsp butter or ghee
  5ml/1 tsp cumin seeds
  5ml/1 tsp mustard seeds
  3–4 small dried red chillies
  8–10 fresh curry leaves

1 Melt the butter or ghee in a large pan and gently cook the onion, chillies and ginger for 10 minutes, stirring the mixture occasionally until golden.

2 Stir in the lentils and water. Bring to the boil, then reduce the heat and partially cover the pan. Simmer, stirring occasionally, for 50–60 minutes, until the texture resembles that of a very thick soup.

3 Meanwhile, preheat the oven to 180°C/350°F/Gas 4. Put the whole head of garlic in a small baking dish and roast for 30–45 minutes until soft.

4 Slice the top off the head of garlic. Scoop the roasted flesh into the lentil mixture, then stir in the cumin and ground coriander. Cook for a further 10–15 minutes, stirring frequently. Stir in the tomatoes, then season the mixture, adding lemon juice to taste.

5 For the spice mix, heat the oil in a small, heavy pan and fry the shallots until crisp and browned. Add the garlic and cook, stirring, until it colours slightly. Remove with a slotted spoon and set aside.

6 Melt the butter or ghee in the same pan and fry the cumin and mustard seeds until the mustard seeds pop. Stir in the chillies, curry leaves and the shallot mixture, then swirl most of the hot mixture into the dhal. Season. Top with the remaining spice mixture, garnish with coriander sprigs and serve.

EGG AND GREEN LENTIL CURRY WITH GREEN CHILLIES AND GINGER

THIS SIMPLE AND NOURISHING CURRY CAN BE COOKED IN UNDER AN HOUR, FROM INGREDIENTS YOU MAY WELL HAVE IN YOUR REFRIGERATOR OR PANTRY. SERVE THE DISH WITH YOUR FAVOURITE CHUTNEY.

2 Boil the eggs for 10 minutes, then plunge them straight into cold water. When cool enough to handle, shell them and cut them in half lengthways.

3 Heat the oil in a large frying pan and fry the cloves and peppercorns for 2 minutes. Stir in the onion, chillies, garlic and ginger, and fry for a further 5–6 minutes, stirring frequently.

4 Stir in the curry paste and fry for a further 2 minutes, stirring constantly. Add the chopped tomatoes, sugar and water. Simmer for about 5 minutes until the sauce thickens, stirring occasionally. Add the boiled eggs, drained lentils and garam masala. Cover and simmer for 10 minutes, then serve.

SERVES FOUR

INGREDIENTS
- 75g/3oz/scant ½ cup green lentils
- 750ml/1¼ pints/3 cups stock
- 6 eggs
- 30ml/2 tbsp oil
- 3 cloves
- 1.5ml/¼ tsp black peppercorns
- 1 onion, finely chopped
- 2 fresh green chillies, finely chopped
- 2 garlic cloves, crushed
- 2.5cm/1in piece fresh root ginger, peeled and chopped
- 30ml/2 tbsp curry paste
- 400g/14oz can chopped tomatoes
- 2.5ml/½ tsp granulated sugar
- 175ml/6fl oz/¾ cup water
- 2.5ml/½ tsp garam masala

1 Wash the lentils thoroughly under cold running water. Drain and check for small stones. Put the lentils in a large, heavy pan. Pour in the stock. Bring to the boil, then reduce the heat, cover and simmer gently for about 15 minutes or until the lentils are soft. Drain and set aside.

COOK'S TIPS
• If you haven't got any fresh chillies, substitute dried ones. Reconstitute them by soaking in hot water for at least 20 minutes.
• A little sugar is often added to chilli beans, to soften the flavour. If you have any, try stirring in a spoonful of chilli jam instead, or a dash of Tabasco sauce.

PARSNIPS AND CHICKPEAS IN A CHILLI PASTE

*THE SWEET FLAVOUR OF PARSNIPS GOES VERY WELL WITH THE SPICES IN THIS INDIAN-STYLE
VEGETABLE STEW. SERVE IT WITH PLAIN YOGURT AND OFFER INDIAN BREADS TO MOP UP THE SAUCE.*

SERVES FOUR

INGREDIENTS
  200g/7oz/scant 1 cup dried
    chickpeas, soaked overnight in cold
    water, then drained
  7 garlic cloves, finely chopped
  1 small onion, chopped
  5cm/2in piece fresh root
    ginger, chopped
  2 fresh green chillies, such as
    jalapeños or serranos, seeded and
    finely chopped
  550ml/18fl oz/2½ cups water
  60ml/4 tbsp groundnut (peanut) oil
  5ml/1 tsp cumin seeds
  10ml/2 tsp ground coriander seeds
  5ml/1 tsp ground turmeric
  2.5–5ml/½–1 tsp mild chilli powder
  50g/2oz/½ cup cashew nuts, toasted
    and ground
  250g/9oz tomatoes, peeled
    and chopped
  900g/2lb parsnips, cut into chunks
  5ml/1 tsp ground toasted
    cumin seeds
  juice of ½–1 lime
  salt and ground black pepper
To serve
  fresh coriander (cilantro) leaves
  a few cashew nuts, toasted

1 Put the chickpeas in a pan, cover
with cold water and bring to the boil.
Boil vigorously for 10 minutes, then
reduce the heat so that the water boils
steadily and cook for 1–1½ hours, or
until tender. The cooking time will
depend on how long the chickpeas have
been stored.

2 Meanwhile, for the sauce, set 10ml/
2 tsp of the garlic aside, and place the
remainder in a food processor or
blender. Add the onion, ginger and half
the chillies. Pour in 75ml/5 tbsp of the
water and process to a smooth paste.

COOK'S TIP
For a milder result, use Anaheim chillies
and mild paprika instead of chilli powder.

3 Heat the oil in a large, deep frying
pan and cook the cumin seeds for
30 seconds. Stir in the coriander seeds,
turmeric, chilli powder and ground
cashew nuts. Add the ginger and chilli
paste and cook, stirring frequently, until
the water begins to evaporate. Add the
tomatoes and stir-fry until the mixture
begins to turn red-brown in colour.

4 Drain the chickpeas and add them
to the pan, with the parsnips and
remaining water. Season with 5ml/1 tsp
salt and plenty of black pepper. Bring to
the boil, stir, then simmer, uncovered,
for 15–20 minutes, until the parsnips
are completely tender.

5 Reduce the liquid, if necessary, by
boiling fiercely until the sauce is thick.
Add the ground toasted cumin with
lime juice to taste. Stir in the reserved
garlic and chilli, and cook for a final
1–2 minutes. Sprinkle the coriander
leaves and toasted cashew nuts over
and serve immediately.

VARIATIONS
Substitute red kidney beans for chickpeas
or use carrots and butter (lima) beans.

SWEET RICE WITH HOT SOUR CHICKPEAS

CONTRASTING FLAVOURS CAN BE JUST AS INTERESTING AS COMPLEMENTARY ONES. CHICKPEAS, SPICED WITH CHILLIES AND SOURED WITH LEMON, TASTE REMARKABLY GOOD WITH SWEET RICE.

SERVES SIX

INGREDIENTS
  350g/12oz/1⅔ cups dried chickpeas, soaked overnight in water
  60ml/4 tbsp vegetable oil
  1 large onion, very finely chopped
  2 tomatoes, peeled and finely chopped
  15ml/1 tbsp ground coriander
  15ml/1 tbsp ground cumin
  5ml/1 tsp ground fenugreek
  5ml/1 tsp ground cinnamon
  1–2 fresh hot green chillies, seeded and finely sliced
  2.5cm/1in piece of fresh root ginger, grated (shredded)
  60ml/4 tbsp lemon juice
  15ml/1 tbsp chopped fresh coriander (cilantro)
  salt and ground black pepper
For the rice
  40g/1½oz/3 tbsp ghee or butter
  4 green cardamom pods
  4 cloves
  650ml/22fl oz/2¾ cups water
  350g/12oz/1¾ cups basmati rice (see Cook's Tip)
  5–10ml/1–2 tsp granulated sugar
  5–6 saffron threads, soaked in warm water

2 Heat the oil in a pan. Reserve about 30ml/2 tbsp of the chopped onion and add the remainder to the pan. Fry over a medium heat for 4–5 minutes, stirring. Add the tomatoes. Cook over a low to medium heat for 5–6 minutes.

3 Stir in the ground coriander, cumin, fenugreek and cinnamon. Cook for 30 seconds, then add the chickpeas and 350ml/12fl oz/1½ cups of the reserved cooking liquid. Season with salt, then cover and simmer very gently for 15–20 minutes, stirring occasionally and adding more liquid if necessary.

4 For the rice, melt the ghee or butter in a pan and fry the cardamom and cloves for a few minutes. Pour in the water, then add the rice. Bring to the boil, reduce the heat to very low and cover tightly. Cook for 15 minutes or until the liquid has been absorbed. Stir the sugar and saffron liquid into the rice. Replace the lid.

5 Mix the reserved onion with the sliced chilli(es), ginger and lemon juice, and stir the mixture into the chickpeas. Add the chopped coriander, adjust the seasoning and serve with the rice.

1 Drain the chickpeas well and place them in a large pan. Pour in water to cover, bring to the boil, then lower the heat, cover and simmer for 1–1¼ hours until tender. Drain, reserving the cooking liquid.

COOK'S TIP
Soak the rice in 1.2 litres/2 pints/5 cups water for 30 minutes. Drain.

BEANCURD AND GREEN BEAN RED CURRY

THE CHILLIES ARE STIRRED INTO THIS CURRY JUST BEFORE SERVING, SO CHOOSE A VARIETY WHOSE HEAT WILL BE TOLERABLE TO ALL YOUR GUESTS, OR OFFER THE CHILLIES SEPARATELY.

SERVES FOUR TO SIX

INGREDIENTS

600ml/1 pint/2½ cups coconut milk
15ml/1 tbsp red curry paste
45ml/3 tbsp Thai fish sauce
    (*nam pla*)
10ml/2 tsp palm sugar or soft dark
    brown sugar
225g/8oz/3 cups button
    (white) mushrooms
115g/4oz green beans, trimmed
175g/6oz firm beancurd (tofu),
    rinsed and cut into 2cm/¾in cubes
4 kaffir lime leaves, torn
2 fresh red chillies, seeded
    and sliced
coriander (cilantro) leaves, to garnish

3 Add the green beans and cubes of beancurd, and simmer gently for a further 4–5 minutes.

4 Stir in the kaffir lime leaves and chillies. Serve garnished with the coriander leaves.

1 Pour about one-third of the coconut milk into a pan. Cook until it starts to separate and an oily sheen appears.

2 Add the red curry paste, fish sauce and sugar to the coconut milk. Mix together thoroughly, then stir in the mushrooms and cook for 1 minute. Stir in the rest of the coconut milk and bring back to the boil.

COOK'S TIP
Firm beancurd is suitable for stir-frying, braising and poaching. You can keep it in the refrigerator for up to 5 days by changing the water daily.

VARIATION
This works equally well with aubergines (eggplant), cauliflower, broccoli, bamboo shoots or a mixture of vegetables.

FIVE-SPICE VEGETABLE NOODLES

THE MELLOW WARMTH OF FIVE-SPICE POWDER PROVIDES AN EXCELLENT COUNTERPOINT TO THE RAW HEAT OF THE CHILLIES IN THIS SUPERB STIR-FRY.

2 Cut the carrots and celery into matchstick strips. Cut the fennel bulb in half and cut out the hard core. Cut into slices, then cut the slices into matchstick strips.

3 Cut both chillies in half and scrape out the seeds with a sharp knife. Cut 1 chilli into slices and chop the remaining chilli finely.

4 Heat the remaining oil in a wok until very hot. Add all the vegetables, with the chopped chilli, and stir-fry for about 7–8 minutes.

5 Add the ginger and garlic, and stir-fry for 2 minutes, then stir in the spices. Cook for 1 minute. Add the spring onions and stir-fry for 1 minute. Pour in the warm water and cook for 1 minute.

SERVES TWO TO THREE

INGREDIENTS
  225g/8oz dried egg noodles
  30ml/2 tbsp sesame oil
  2 carrots
  1 celery stick
  1 small fennel bulb
  2 fresh red chillies
  2 courgettes (zucchini), halved
    and sliced
  2.5cm/1in piece of fresh root ginger,
    peeled and grated (shredded)
  1 garlic clove, crushed
  7.5ml/1½ tsp Chinese
    five-spice powder
  2.5ml/½ tsp ground cinnamon
  4 spring onions (scallions), sliced
  60ml/4 tbsp warm water

1 Bring a large pan of lightly salted water to the boil. Add the noodles and cook for 2–3 minutes until just tender. Drain the noodles thoroughly in a colander, return them to the pan and toss in a little of the oil. Set aside. Tossing them in oil in this way will keep them from sticking together as they cool.

6 Stir in the noodles and toss over the heat until the noodles have heated through. Serve sprinkled with the sliced red chilli.

COOK'S TIP
A cleaver is the preferred cutting tool used in Chinese cooking.

CHINESE CHILLI NOODLES

THERE ARE PLENTY OF CONTRASTING TEXTURES IN THIS SPICY STIR-FRY. CRISP GREEN BEANS AND BEANSPROUTS VERSUS NOODLES AND OMELETTE STRIPS MAKES FOR AN INTERESTING DISH.

SERVES FOUR

INGREDIENTS

2 eggs
5ml/1 tsp chilli powder
5ml/1 tsp ground turmeric
60ml/4 tbsp vegetable oil
1 large onion, finely sliced
2 fresh red chillies, seeded and
  finely sliced
15ml/1 tbsp soy sauce
2 large cooked potatoes, cut into
  small cubes
6 pieces fried beancurd
  (tofu), sliced
225g/8oz/4 cups beansprouts
115g/4oz green beans, blanched
350g/12oz fresh thick
  egg noodles
salt and ground black pepper
sliced spring onions (scallions),
  to garnish

1 Beat the eggs lightly, then strain them through a fine sieve into a bowl. Heat a lightly greased omelette pan. Pour in half of the beaten egg and tilt the pan quickly to cover the base thinly. When the egg is just set, turn the omelette over, using chopsticks or a spatula, and fry the other side.

2 Slide the omelette on to a plate, blot with kitchen paper, roll up and cut into narrow strips. Make a second omelette in the same way and slice. Set the omelette strips aside for the garnish.

3 In a cup, mix together the chilli powder and turmeric. Form a paste by stirring in a little water.

4 Heat the oil in a wok or frying pan. Fry the onion until soft. Reduce the heat and stir in the chilli paste, chillies and soy sauce. Fry for 2 minutes.

5 Add the potatoes and fry for about 2 minutes, mixing well with the chillies. Add the beancurd, the beansprouts, green beans and noodles.

6 Gently stir-fry until the noodles are evenly coated and heated through. Take care not to break up the potatoes or the beancurd. Season with salt and pepper. Serve hot, garnished with the reserved omelette strips and spring onion slices.

COOK'S TIPS

• When making this dish for non-vegetarians, or for vegetarians who eat fish, add a piece of shrimp paste. A small chunk about the size of a stock (bouillon) cube, mashed with the chilli paste, will add a rich, aromatic flavour.
• Most chilli powder we buy is actually a blended mixture of ground dried red chillies, cumin, oregano and salt, often with a little garlic powder mixed in. For a pure powder, you'll need to find a specialist food store or order by mail.

THAMIN LETHOK

THIS IS BASED ON THE BURMESE WAY OF DEALING WITH LEFTOVERS. THE NOODLES AND RICE ARE ARRANGED ON PLATTERS WITH THE ACCOMPANIMENTS. IT IS PERFECT FOR A SUMMER PARTY.

SERVES SIX

INGREDIENTS
175g/6oz/scant 1 cup long grain rice
1–2 red chillies, seeded and
  roughly chopped
1 small onion, roughly chopped
115g/4oz egg noodles, soaked for
  30 minutes in cold water to cover
115g/4oz rice noodles, soaked for
  at least 10 minutes in cold water
  to cover
50g/2oz cellophane noodles, soaked
  for 15 minutes in warm water
225g/8oz spinach leaves
175g/6oz/3 cups beansprouts
chilli sambal or chilli jam
25ml/1½ tbsp tamarind pulp or
  concentrate, soaked in 200ml/
  7fl oz/scant 1 cup warm water,
  or 6 lemon wedges
salt
For the accompaniments
3 spring onions (scallions),
  finely shredded
crisp fried onion
50g/2oz cellophane noodles, fried
  until crisp

1 Bring a large pan of lightly salted water to the boil and cook the rice for 12–15 minutes until tender. Drain, tip into a bowl and set aside. Mix the chillies and onion in a bowl and set aside too.

2 Drain all the noodles and cook them in separate pans of boiling, salted water until tender. The egg noodles will need 3–4 minutes and the rice and cellophane noodles will be ready when the water boils again. Drain, refresh under cold water and drain again.

VARIATIONS
• To add some protein to this dish, you could include some beancurd (tofu), stir-fried with a little light soy sauce.
• Omit the cellophane noodles and increase the quantity of egg or rice noodles.

3 Put the spinach into a large pan with just the water that clings to the leaves after washing. Cover the pan and cook over a medium heat for 2 minutes until the leaves are starting to wilt. Drain well. When cool enough to handle, squeeze the remaining moisture out with your hands. Cook the beansprouts in the same way. Leave both to get cold.

COOK'S TIP
If you prefer your chillies cooked, fry the chillies and onion in about 15ml/1 tbsp oil and either stir the mixture into the rice or serve it separately.

4 Arrange the cold rice, noodles, spinach and beansprouts attractively on a large serving platter. Add the bowl containing the chilli and onion mixture, and a second bowl holding chilli sambal or jam. Set out the range of accompaniments.

5 Strain the tamarind juice, if using, into a jug (pitcher) or put the lemon wedges on a plate. Each guest takes a little of whichever main ingredients they like, adds some accompaniments and drizzles over a little tamarind juice or a squeeze of lemon juice to taste.

CHILLI AND PAK CHOI OMELETTE PARCELS

COLOURFUL STIR-FRIED VEGETABLES AND CORIANDER IN BLACK BEAN SAUCE MAKE A REMARKABLY GOOD OMELETTE FILLING, WHICH IS QUICK AND EASY TO PREPARE.

SERVES FOUR

INGREDIENTS

130g/4½oz broccoli, cut into
 small florets
30ml/2 tbsp groundnut (peanut) oil
1cm/½in piece fresh root ginger,
 finely grated (shredded)
1 large garlic clove, crushed
2 fresh red chillies, seeded and
 finely sliced
4 spring onions (scallions),
 diagonally sliced
175g/6oz/3 cups pak choi
 (bok choy), shredded
50g/2oz/2 cups fresh coriander
 (cilantro) leaves, plus extra
 to garnish
115g/4oz/2 cups beansprouts
45ml/3 tbsp black bean sauce
4 eggs
salt and ground black pepper

1 Bring a pan of lightly salted water to the boil and blanch the broccoli for 2 minutes. Drain, then refresh under cold running water, and drain again.

2 Heat 15ml/1 tbsp of the oil in a frying pan and stir-fry the ginger, garlic and half the chilli for 1 minute. Add the spring onions, broccoli and pak choi, and toss the mixture over the heat for 2 minutes more.

3 Chop three-quarters of the coriander and add to the frying pan. Add the beansprouts and stir-fry for 1 minute, then add the black bean sauce and heat through for 1 minute more. Remove the pan from the heat and keep warm.

4 Mix the eggs lightly with a fork and season well. Heat a little of the remaining oil in a small frying pan and add one-quarter of the beaten egg. Tilt the pan so that the egg covers the base, then sprinkle over one-quarter of the reserved coriander leaves. Cook until set, then turn out the omelette on to a plate and keep warm while you make 3 more omelettes.

5 Spoon one-quarter of the stir-fry on to each omelette and roll up. Cut in half crossways and serve, garnished with coriander leaves and chilli slices.

COOK'S TIP
If you overdo the chilli, don't reach for a glass of water. Drinking it will simply spread the discomfort. Instead, eat something starchy, such as a piece of bread, or try a spoonful of yogurt.

SPICY ROOT VEGETABLE GRATIN

SUBTLY SPICED WITH CURRY POWDER, TURMERIC, CORIANDER AND MILD CHILLI POWDER, THIS RICH GRATIN IS SUBSTANTIAL ENOUGH TO SERVE ON ITS OWN.

2 Preheat the oven to 180°C/350°F/Gas 4. Heat half the butter in a heavy pan, and add the curry powder, turmeric and coriander. Stir in half the chilli powder. Cook for 2 minutes, then put aside to cool slightly.

3 Drain the vegetable slices, then pat them dry with kitchen paper. Place in a bowl, add the spice mixture and the shallots, and mix well.

SERVES FOUR

INGREDIENTS
 2 large potatoes, total weight
   about 450g/1lb
 2 sweet potatoes, total weight
   about 275g/10oz
 175g/6oz celeriac
 15ml/1 tbsp unsalted
   (sweet) butter
 5ml/1 tsp curry powder
 5ml/1 tsp ground turmeric
 2.5ml/½ tsp ground coriander
 5ml/1 tsp mild chilli powder
 3 shallots, chopped
 150ml/¼ pint/⅔ cup single
   (light) cream
 150ml/¼ pint/⅔ cup milk
 salt and ground black pepper
 chopped fresh flat leaf parsley,
   to garnish

1 Thinly slice the potatoes, sweet potatoes and celeriac, using a sharp knife or the slicing attachment in a food processor. Immediately place the slices in a bowl of cold water to prevent discolouring. Set aside.

VARIATION
Substitute parsnips or carrots for the sweet potatoes, and turnips for the celeriac.

4 Arrange the vegetables in a gratin dish, adding salt and pepper to each layer. Mix together the cream and milk, pour the mixture over the vegetables, then sprinkle the remaining chilli powder on top.

5 Cover with baking parchment and bake for about 45 minutes. Remove the parchment, dot with the remaining butter and bake for 50 minutes more until the top is golden. Serve garnished with the chopped fresh parsley.

COOK'S TIP
A salad of mixed leaves could be served separately with the gratin then some fresh fruit, such as mango, to follow.

THAI MIXED VEGETABLE CURRY WITH LEMON GRASS RICE

FRAGRANT JASMINE RICE, SUBTLY FLAVOURED WITH LEMON GRASS AND CARDAMOM, IS THE PERFECT ACCOMPANIMENT TO THIS VEGETABLE CURRY.

SERVES FOUR

INGREDIENTS
  10ml/2 tsp vegetable oil
  400ml/14fl oz/1⅔ cups coconut milk
  300ml/½ pint/1¼ cups
    vegetable stock
  225g/8oz new potatoes, halved or
    quartered if large
  130g/4½oz baby corn cobs
  5ml/1 tsp granulated sugar
  185g/6½oz/generous 1 cup
    broccoli florets
  1 red (bell) pepper, seeded and
    sliced lengthways
  115g/4oz spinach, tough stalks
    removed, leaves shredded
  30ml/2 tbsp chopped fresh
    coriander (cilantro)
  salt and ground black pepper
For the spice paste
  1 fresh red chilli, seeded and
    roughly chopped
  3 fresh green chillies, seeded and
    roughly chopped
  1 lemon grass stalk, outer layers
    removed and lower 5cm/
    2in chopped
  2 shallots, chopped
  finely grated rind of 1 lime
  2 garlic cloves, chopped
  5ml/1 tsp ground coriander
  2.5ml/½ tsp ground cumin
  1cm/½in fresh galangal,
    chopped (optional)
  30ml/2 tbsp chopped fresh
    coriander (cilantro)
For the rice
  225g/8oz/generous 1 cup jasmine
    rice, rinsed and drained
  1 lemon grass stalk, outer leaves
    removed, cut into 3 pieces
  6 cardamom pods, bruised
  475ml/16fl oz/2 cups water

1 Make the spice paste by grinding all the ingredients to a coarse paste in a food processor or blender. Scrape the paste out of the food processor or blender into a bowl, using a plastic spatula.

2 Heat the oil in a large heavy pan and fry the spice paste for 1–2 minutes, stirring constantly.

3 Pour in the coconut milk and stock, stir well and bring to the boil. Reduce the heat, add the potatoes and simmer for 15 minutes.

4 Meanwhile, prepare the rice. Tip the rice into a large pan and add the lemon grass and cardamom pods. Pour over the measured water.

COOK'S TIP
Save preparation time by making the spice paste the day before it is required. Cover and refrigerate.

5 Bring to the boil, then reduce the heat, cover, and cook for 10–15 minutes until the water has been absorbed and the rice is tender and slightly sticky. Season with salt, and leave to stand, covered, for 10 minutes.

6 Add the baby corn to the potatoes in the pan, with salt and pepper to taste, and cook for 2 minutes. Stir in the sugar, broccoli and red pepper, and cook for 2 minutes or until the vegetables are tender. Stir in the shredded spinach and half the fresh coriander. Cook for 2 minutes.

7 Remove the whole spices from the rice, fluff up the grains with a fork, then spoon into heated bowls. Top with the curry, sprinkled with the remaining fresh coriander.

VARIATIONS
• Substitute Thai aubergines (eggplant) for the potatoes.
• Use baby carrots instead of corn cobs.
• For non-vegetarians, add cooked prawns (shrimp) and just heat through.
• For protein, add toasted cashew nuts.

OKRA, CHILLI AND TOMATO TAGINE

THE WORD "TAGINE" USUALLY CONJURES UP AN IMAGE OF A SPICY LAMB AND APRICOT STEW, BUT THIS VEGETARIAN VERSION IS EQUALLY AUTHENTIC.

SERVES FOUR

INGREDIENTS
  350g/12oz okra
  5–6 tomatoes
  2 small onions
  2 garlic cloves, crushed
  1 fresh green chilli, seeded
  5ml/1 tsp paprika
  small handful of fresh
    coriander (cilantro)
  175ml/6fl oz/¾ cup water
  30ml/2 tbsp sunflower oil
  juice of 1 lemon

1 Trim the okra and then cut into 1cm/½in lengths. Peel and seed the tomatoes and chop roughly.

2 Roughly chop 1 of the onions and place in a food processor or blender with the garlic, chilli, paprika, coriander and 60ml/4 tbsp of the water. Blend to a paste.

COOK'S TIP
A tagine is an earthenware dish with a tall conical lid, which has given its name to slowly simmered stews. It is used in North African cooking.

3 Heat the sunflower oil in a large pan. Thinly slice the second onion in rings and fry in the oil for 5–6 minutes until golden brown. Using a slotted spoon, transfer the fried onion rings to a plate lined with crumpled kitchen paper. Set aside.

4 Reduce the heat and scrape the onion and coriander mixture into the pan. Cook for 1–2 minutes, stirring frequently, and then add the okra, tomatoes, lemon juice and remaining water. Stir well to mix, cover tightly and simmer over a low heat for about 15 minutes until the okra is tender.

5 Transfer the tagine to a warmed serving dish, sprinkle with the fried onion rings and serve immediately while hot.

VARIATION
To make this more substantial, add extra vegetables, such as aubergine (eggplant), carrots and leeks.

CHEESE COURGETTES WITH GREEN CHILLIES

THIS IS A VERY TASTY WAY TO SERVE COURGETTES, WHICH CAN TASTE A BIT BLAND, AND THE DISH LOOKS GOOD TOO. SERVE IT AS A VEGETARIAN MAIN DISH OR AN UNUSUAL SIDE DISH.

2 Cut a cross in the base of each tomato. Place in a heatproof bowl and pour over boiling water to cover. Leave in the water for 30 seconds then lift out on a slotted spoon and plunge into a bowl of cold water. Drain. The skins will have begun to peel back from the crosses. Remove the skins, cut the tomatoes in half and squeeze out the seeds. Chop the flesh into strips.

3 Trim the courgettes, then cut them lengthways into 1cm/½in wide strips. Slice the strips into matchsticks.

4 Stir the courgettes into the onion mixture and fry for 10 minutes, stirring occasionally, until just tender. Add the tomatoes and chopped jalapeños, and cook for 2–3 minutes more.

SERVES SIX

INGREDIENTS
 30ml/2 tbsp vegetable oil
 ½ onion, thinly sliced
 2 garlic cloves, crushed
 5ml/1 tsp dried oregano
 2 tomatoes
 500g/1¼lb courgettes (zucchini)
 50g/2oz/⅓ cup drained pickled
  jalapeño chilli slices, chopped
 115g/4oz/½ cup cream
  cheese, cubed
 salt
 fresh oregano sprigs, to garnish

1 Heat the oil in a frying pan. Add the onion, garlic and dried oregano. Fry over gentle heat for 3–4 minutes, stirring frequently, until the onion is soft and translucent.

5 Add the cream cheese. Reduce the heat to the lowest setting. As the cheese melts, stir gently to coat the courgettes. Season with salt, pile into a heated dish and serve, garnished with oregano. If serving as a main dish, warm, crusty, bread makes a good accompaniment. Alternatively, serve with boiled rice, or mixed into chunky pasta.

COURGETTES <u>WITH</u> CHILLI SAUCE

CRUNCHY COATED COURGETTES ARE GREAT SERVED WITH A FIERY TOMATO SAUCE. VEGETARIANS WILL LIKE THIS AS A MAIN DISH; MEAT AND FISH EATERS WILL APPRECIATE IT AS AN ACCOMPANIMENT.

SERVES TWO

INGREDIENTS
    15ml/1 tbsp olive oil
    1 onion, finely chopped
    1 fresh red chilli, seeded and
        finely diced
    10ml/2 tsp hot chilli powder
    400g/14oz can chopped tomatoes
    1 vegetable stock (bouillon) cube
    60ml/4 tbsp hot water
    450g/1lb courgettes (zucchini)
    150ml/¼ pint/⅔ cup milk
    50g/2oz/½ cup plain
        (all-purpose) flour
    oil for deep-frying
    salt and ground black pepper
    fresh thyme sprigs, to garnish
To serve
    lettuce leaves
    watercress sprigs (optional)
    slices of seeded bread

1 Heat the oil in a pan and fry the onion for 2–3 minutes. Stir in the chilli and chilli powder, and cook for 30 seconds.

2 Add the tomatoes. Crumble in the stock cube and stir in the water. Season to taste, cover and cook for 10 minutes.

VARIATION
Substitute baby leaf spinach for the watercress sprigs.

3 Meanwhile, trim the courgettes and cut them into 5mm/¼in slices.

4 Pour the milk into a shallow dish and spread out the flour in another. Dip the courgette slices in the milk, then into the flour, until well coated.

5 Heat the oil for deep-frying to 180°C/350°F or until a cube of day-old bread, added to the oil, browns in 30–45 seconds. Add the courgettes in batches and deep-fry for 3–4 minutes until crisp. Drain on kitchen paper.

6 Mix the courgettes with the sauce and place on warmed plates. Garnish with thyme sprigs and serve with lettuce, watercress, if using, and seeded bread.

CHILLI BEANS WITH LEMON AND GINGER

AN EXTREMELY QUICK AND DELICIOUS MEAL, MADE WITH CANNED BEANS FOR SPEED. YOU CAN USE ANY RED CHILLI, SUCH AS FRESH CAYENNES OR RED FRESNO, OR REHYDRATE A DRIED PASILLA OR TWO.

4 Stir in the ginger and garlic paste from the blender or food processor and cook for another minute.

5 Pour in the remaining water, then add the lemon juice and fresh coriander, stir well and bring to the boil. Cover the pan tightly and cook gently over a low heat for 5 minutes.

6 Stir in all the beans and cook for a further 5–10 minutes, until piping hot. Season with pepper and serve.

SERVES FOUR

INGREDIENTS

5cm/2in piece fresh ginger root, peeled and roughly chopped
3 garlic cloves, roughly chopped
250ml/8fl oz/1 cup cold water
15ml/1 tbsp sunflower oil
1 large onion, thinly sliced
1 fresh red chilli, seeded and finely chopped
1.5ml/¼ tsp cayenne pepper
10ml/2 tsp ground cumin
5ml/1 tsp ground coriander
2.5ml/½ tsp ground turmeric
30ml/2 tbsp lemon juice
75g/3oz/1½ cups chopped fresh coriander (cilantro)
400g/14oz can black-eyed beans, (peas) drained and rinsed
400g/14oz can aduki beans, drained and rinsed
400g/14oz can haricot (navy) beans, drained and rinsed
ground black pepper

1 Place the ginger, garlic and 60ml/ 4 tbsp of the cold water in a blender or food processor and whizz until smooth.

2 Heat the oil in a pan. Add the onion and chilli, and cook gently for 5 minutes until softened.

3 Add the cayenne, cumin, coriander and turmeric, and stir-fry for 1 minute.

VARIATION

Substitute chickpeas or butter (lima) beans for the haricot beans.

COOK'S TIPS

• If time allows, make this the day before you intend to serve it, so that the flavours have time to blend and become absorbed by the beans.
• Chillies in a dish such as this one sometimes have a mellower taste after standing, so what may have seemed explosive at the onset may become less so. You can't count on this result, however!
• Don't add extra salt to the beans: canned ones tend to be ready-salted.
• Cooked in this way, these beans are very good served cold in a three-bean salad.
• Add any leftovers to soup.

POTATOES WITH AUBERGINES AND CHILLIES

USING BABY POTATOES ADDS TO THE ATTRACTIVENESS OF THIS DISH. CHOOSE THE SMALLER VARIETY OF AUBERGINES TOO, AS THEY ARE FAR TASTIER THAN THE LARGE ONES.

SERVES FOUR

INGREDIENTS
    10–12 waxy baby potatoes
    6 small aubergines (eggplant)
    1 medium red (bell) pepper
    1 fresh red chilli
    15ml/1 tbsp corn oil
    2 medium onions, sliced
    4–6 curry leaves
    2.5ml/½ tsp kalonji seeds
    5ml/1 tsp crushed coriander seeds
    2.5ml/½ tsp cumin seeds
    5ml/1 tsp grated (shredded) fresh
      root ginger
    5ml/1 tsp crushed garlic
    5ml/1 tsp crushed dried red chillies
    15ml/1 tbsp chopped fresh fenugreek
      leaves (see Cook's Tip)
    5ml/1 tsp chopped fresh
      coriander (cilantro)
    15ml/1 tbsp natural (plain) yogurt
    fresh coriander (cilantro) leaves,
      to garnish

1 Bring a pan of lightly salted water to the boil, add the baby potatoes and cook for 10–15 minutes until just soft. Drain and set aside.

2 Cut the aubergines into quarters, leaving the stems attached.

COOK'S TIPS
• Fresh fenugreek leaves, called *methi*, are widely used in Indian cooking, particularly with potatoes, spinach and yam. If you can't find fresh leaves, use dried, or increase the quantity of fresh coriander.
• Small aubergines, with their stem, are readily available from Asian grocers.

3 Cut the pepper in half, remove the seeds, then slice the flesh into strips. Slit the chilli and scrape out the seeds with a sharp knife. Chop the flesh finely.

4 Heat the oil in a wok or frying pan and fry the onions, pepper strips, chopped fresh chillies, curry leaves, kalonji seeds, crushed coriander seeds and cumin seeds until the onions are a soft golden brown. (You may need to be careful when frying the curry leaves and seeds because they spit, sizzle and pop.)

5 Mix in the ginger, garlic, crushed chillies and fenugreek, followed by the aubergines and potatoes. Cover with a lid. Lower the heat and cook for 5–7 minutes.

6 Remove the lid, stir in the fresh coriander, then swirl in the yogurt. Serve immediately, garnished with the coriander leaves.

COOK'S TIP
Curry leaves are small and almond-shaped. They can be found in Asian food stores.

BENGALI-STYLE VEGETABLES

THIS HOT DRY CURRY USES SPICES THAT DO NOT REQUIRE LONG SLOW COOKING. YOU CAN PREPARE AND PARTIALLY COOK THE VEGETABLES IN ADVANCE AND COMPLETE THE DISH QUICKLY LATER IN THE DAY.

SERVES FOUR

INGREDIENTS

½ cauliflower, broken into florets
1 large potato, peeled and cut into 2.5cm/1in dice
115g/4oz green beans, trimmed
2 courgettes (zucchini), halved lengthways and sliced
2 fresh green chillies
2.5cm/1in piece of fresh root ginger, peeled
120ml/4fl oz/½ cup natural (plain) yogurt
10ml/2 tsp ground coriander
2.5ml/½ tsp ground turmeric
25g/1oz/2 tbsp ghee
2.5ml/½ tsp garam masala
5ml/1 tsp cumin seeds
10ml/2 tsp granulated sugar
pinch each of ground cloves, ground cinnamon and ground cardamom
salt and ground black pepper

1 Bring a large pan of water to the boil. Add the cauliflower florets and diced potato, and cook for 5 minutes. Add the beans and courgettes, and cook for 2–3 minutes.

2 Meanwhile, cut the chillies in half, then scrape out and discard the seeds using a very sharp knife. Roughly chop the flesh. Finely chop the ginger. Mix the chillies and ginger together in a small bowl.

3 Drain the vegetables and tip them into a bowl. Add the chilli and ginger mixture, with the yogurt, ground coriander and turmeric. Season with plenty of salt and pepper, and mix well.

4 Heat the ghee in a large frying pan. Add the vegetable mixture and cook over a high heat for 2 minutes, stirring from time to time.

5 Stir in the garam masala and cumin seeds, and cook for 2 minutes. Stir in the sugar, ground cloves, cinnamon and cardamom, and cook for 1 minute or until all the liquid has evaporated. Serve at once.

COOK'S TIPS
• Ghee has a burning point higher than the best oils, so it is very good for frying and searing.
• An alternative to ghee is to add a little groundnut (peanut) oil to ordinary butter. It allows the frying temperature to be reached without burning.

BALTI-STYLE VEGETABLES WITH CASHEW NUTS

IT IS THE PREPARATION THAT TAKES THE TIME HERE. DO IT IN ADVANCE AND EVERYONE WILL BE IMPRESSED AT THE SPEED WITH WHICH YOU'LL BE ABLE TO PRODUCE A DELICIOUS MEAL.

SERVES FOUR

INGREDIENTS
2 carrots
1 red (bell) pepper, seeded
1 green (bell) pepper, seeded
2 courgettes (zucchini)
115g/4oz green beans, trimmed
1 medium bunch spring
  onions (scallions)
15ml/1 tbsp extra virgin olive oil
4–6 curry leaves
2.5ml/½ tsp white cumin seeds
4 dried red chillies
10–12 cashew nuts
5ml/1 tsp salt
30ml/2 tbsp lemon juice
fresh mint leaves, to garnish
cooked rice, to serve (optional)

1 Prepare the vegetables: cut the carrots, peppers and courgettes into matchsticks, halve the beans and chop the spring onions. Set aside.

VARIATION
Use peanuts instead of cashew nuts, and baby leeks for spring onions.

2 Heat the oil in a wok or frying pan and fry the curry leaves, cumin seeds and dried chillies for about 1 minute, until aromatic. Be careful with the timing, as curry leaves quickly burn.

3 Add the vegetables and nuts, and stir-fry for 3–4 minutes. Add the salt and lemon juice. Toss the vegetables over the heat for 3–5 minutes more, until they are crisp-tender.

4 Lift out and discard the curry leaves. Spoon the fragrant stir-fry on to a heated serving dish and garnish with mint leaves. Serve immediately, with boiled rice, if you like.

BALTI URAD DHAL WITH GREEN AND RED CHILLIES

URAD DHAL, OFF-WHITE HULLED, SPLIT PEAS, IS JUST ONE OF MANY DIFFERENT PULSES SOLD IN INDIAN FOOD STORES. THE FLAVOUR IS ENLIVENED WHEN COOKED WITH CHILLIES AND OTHER SPICES.

2 Heat the oil in a wok or frying pan over a medium heat. Fry the bay leaf with the onions and cinnamon bark.

3 Add the ginger, whole garlic cloves and half the green and red chillies.

4 Drain almost all the water from the split peas. Add to the wok or frying pan, followed by the remaining green and red chillies and finally the fresh mint. Heat through briefly and serve.

SERVES FOUR

INGREDIENTS
   115g/4oz/½ cup urad dhal or
      yellow split peas
   30ml/2 tbsp corn oil
   1 bay leaf
   2 onions, sliced
   1 piece cinnamon bark
   15ml/1 tbsp grated (shredded)
      fresh root ginger
   2 garlic cloves
   2 fresh green chillies, seeded and
      sliced lengthways
   2 fresh red chillies, seeded and
      sliced lengthways
   15ml/1 tbsp chopped
      fresh mint

1 Put the dhal or split peas in a bowl and pour in enough cold water to cover by at least 2.5cm/1in. Cover and leave to soak overnight. Next day, drain the dhal and boil it in water until the individual grains are soft enough to break into two. Set aside.

COOK'S TIP
For a milder curry, replace some of the chillies with green or red (bell) peppers which will also add colour to the dish.

MUSHROOMS <u>WITH</u> CHIPOTLE CHILLIES

CHIPOTLE CHILLIES ARE JALAPEÑOS THAT HAVE BEEN SMOKE-DRIED. THEIR SMOKY FLAVOUR IS THE PERFECT FOIL FOR THE MUSHROOMS IN THIS SIMPLE SALAD.

SERVES SIX

INGREDIENTS
    2 chipotle chillies
    450g/1lb/6 cups button
      (white) mushrooms
    60ml/4 tbsp vegetable oil
    1 onion, finely chopped
    2 garlic cloves, crushed or chopped
    salt
    small bunch of fresh coriander
      (cilantro), to garnish

VARIATION
Use cascabel instead of chipotle chillies. The name "cascabel" means "little rattle" and accurately describes the sound they make when shaken. Cascabel's nutty flavour is best appreciated when the skin is removed. Soak as for chipotle chillies, scoop out the flesh and add it to the onion and garlic.

1 Put the dried chillies in a heatproof bowl and pour over hot (not boiling) water to cover. Leave to stand for 20–30 minutes until they have softened. Drain, cut off the stalks, then slit the chillies and scrape out the seeds. Chop the flesh finely.

2 Trim the mushrooms, then clean them with a damp cloth or kitchen paper. If they are large, cut them in half.

3 Heat the oil in a large frying pan. Add the onion, garlic, chillies and mushrooms, and stir until evenly coated in the oil. Fry for 6–8 minutes, stirring occasionally, until the onion and mushrooms are tender.

4 Season with salt and spoon into a serving dish. Chop some of the coriander, leaving some whole leaves, and use to garnish. Serve hot.

RED HOT CAULIFLOWER

VEGETABLES ARE SELDOM SERVED PLAIN IN MEXICO. THE CAULIFLOWER HERE IS FLAVOURED WITH A SIMPLE SERRANO AND TOMATO SALSA AND FRESH CHEESE.

SERVES SIX

INGREDIENTS

1 small onion
1 lime
1 medium cauliflower
400g/14oz can chopped tomatoes
4 fresh serrano chillies, seeded and
   finely chopped
1.5ml/¼ tsp granulated sugar
75g/3oz feta cheese, crumbled
salt
chopped fresh flat leaf parsley,
   to garnish

1 Chop the onion very finely and place in a bowl. With a zester or sharp knife, peel away the zest of the lime in thin strips. Add the lime zest to the finely chopped onion.

2 Cut the lime in half and use a reamer or citrus squeezer to extract the juice from each half in turn, adding it to the onion and lime zest mixture. Set aside for the lime juice to soften the onion.

COOK'S TIP
A zester enables you to pare off tiny strips of lime rind with no pith.

3 Cut the cauliflower into florets. Tip the tomatoes into a pan and add the chillies and sugar. Heat gently. Meanwhile, bring a pan of water to the boil, add the cauliflower florets and cook gently for 5–8 minutes until tender.

4 Add the chopped onion mixture to the tomato salsa, with salt to taste. Stir and heat through, then spoon about one-third of the salsa into a serving dish.

5 Arrange the drained cauliflower florets on top of the salsa and spoon the remaining salsa on top.

6 Sprinkle with the feta, which should soften a little on contact. Serve immediately, sprinkled with chopped fresh flat leaf parsley.

SICHUAN SIZZLER

THIS DISH IS ALSO KNOWN AS FISH-FRAGRANT AUBERGINE, AS THE FLAVOURINGS OFTEN ACCOMPANY FISH. IF YOU USE TINY AUBERGINES, OMIT THE SALTING PROCESS, HALVE AND DEEP-FRY THEM.

SERVES FOUR

INGREDIENTS

2 medium aubergines (eggplant)
5ml/1 tsp salt
3 dried red chillies
groundnut (peanut) oil, for
 deep-frying
3–4 garlic cloves, finely chopped
1cm/½ in piece fresh root ginger,
 finely chopped
4 spring onions (scallions), cut into
 2.5cm/1in lengths (white and green
 parts kept separate)
15ml/1 tbsp Chinese rice wine or
 medium-dry sherry
15ml/1 tbsp light soy sauce
5ml/1 tsp granulated sugar
1.5ml/¼ tsp ground roasted
 Sichuan peppercorns
15ml/1 tbsp Chinese rice vinegar
5ml/1 tsp sesame oil

1 Trim the aubergines and cut them into strips, about 4cm/1½ in wide and 7.5cm/3in long. Place the aubergines in a colander and sprinkle over the salt. Leave for 30 minutes, then rinse them thoroughly under cold running water. Pat dry with kitchen paper.

2 Meanwhile, soak the chillies in a bowl of warm water for 20–30 minutes. Then drain and pat dry with kitchen paper.

3 Cut each chilli into 3–4 pieces, discarding the seeds.

4 Half-fill a wok with oil and heat to 180°C/350°F. Deep-fry the aubergine pieces until golden brown. Drain on kitchen paper. Pour off most of the oil from the wok.

5 Reheat the oil left in the wok and add the garlic, ginger, chillies and the white spring onion. Stir-fry for 30 seconds.

6 Add the aubergine and toss over the heat for 1–2 minutes. Stir in the rice wine or sherry, soy sauce, sugar, ground peppercorns and rice vinegar. Stir-fry for 1–2 minutes. Sprinkle over the sesame oil and green spring onion, and serve.

FIERY VEGETABLES IN COCONUT MILK

EIGHT CHILLIES MAY SEEM A BIT EXCESSIVE, ESPECIALLY IF YOU CHOOSE A SUPER-HOT VARIETY SUCH AS BIRD'S EYES, BUT REMEMBER THAT THE COCONUT MILK WILL PACIFY YOUR PALATE SOMEWHAT.

SERVES FOUR TO SIX

INGREDIENTS
450g/1lb mixed vegetables, such as aubergines (eggplant), baby sweetcorn, carrots, green beans, asparagus and patty pan squash
8 fresh red chillies, seeded
2 lemon grass stalks, tender portions chopped
4 kaffir lime leaves, torn
30ml/2 tbsp vegetable oil
250ml/8fl oz/1 cup coconut milk
30ml/2 tbsp Thai fish sauce (*nam pla*)
salt (optional)
15–20 fresh holy basil leaves, to garnish

COOK'S TIP
If you are unsure about the heat, use fewer chillies or mix hot with mild Anaheims or sweet (bell) peppers.

1 Trim the vegetables, then, using a sharp knife, cut them into pieces. They should all be more or less the same shape and thickness. Set aside.

2 Chop the fresh red chillies roughly and put them in a mortar. Add the lemon grass and kaffir lime leaves and grind to a paste. This can be done using a small blender, if you have one, or in the small bowl attachment of a food processor.

3 Heat the oil in a wok or large deep frying pan. Add the chilli mixture and fry over a medium heat for 2–3 minutes, stirring continuously.

4 Stir in the coconut milk and bring to the boil. Add the vegetables and cook for about 5 minutes or until they are all crisp-tender. Season with the fish sauce, and salt if needed. Spoon on to heated plates, garnish with holy basil leaves, and serve.

CHILLI CHIVE RICE WITH MUSHROOMS

WHILE COOKING, THIS RICE DISH DEVELOPS A WONDERFUL AROMA, WHICH IS MATCHED BY THE COMPLEMENTARY FLAVOURS OF CHILLI, GARLIC CHIVES AND FRESH CORIANDER.

3 Add the rice to the onions and fry over a low heat, stirring frequently, for 4–5 minutes. Pour in the stock mixture, then stir in the salt and a good grinding of black pepper.

4 Bring to the boil, stir and reduce the heat to very low. Cover tightly and cook for 15–20 minutes, until the rice has absorbed all the liquid.

5 Remove from the heat. Lay a clean, folded dishtowel over the open pan and press on the lid, jamming it firmly in place. Leave to stand for 10 minutes. The towel will absorb the steam while the rice becomes completely tender.

6 Meanwhile, heat the remaining oil in a frying pan and cook the mushrooms for 5–6 minutes, until tender and browned. Add the remaining chives and cook for a further 1–2 minutes.

7 Stir the mixed, sliced mushrooms and chopped fresh coriander leaves into the cooked rice. Adjust the seasoning, transfer to a warmed serving dish and serve immediately, sprinkled with the cashew nuts.

SERVES FOUR

INGREDIENTS
    350g/12oz/1¾ cups long grain rice
    60ml/4 tbsp groundnut (peanut) oil
    1 small onion, finely chopped
    2 fresh green chillies, seeded and
        finely chopped
    a handful of garlic chives, chopped
    15g/½oz/¼ cup fresh
        coriander (cilantro)
    600ml/1 pint/2½ cups vegetable or
        mushroom stock
    5ml/1 tsp salt
    250g/9oz/3–3½ cups mixed
        mushrooms, thickly sliced
    50g/2oz/½ cup cashew nuts, fried in
        15ml/1 tbsp oil until golden brown
    ground black pepper

1 Wash and drain the rice. Heat half the oil in a pan and cook the onion and chillies over a low heat, stirring occasionally, for 10–12 minutes, until soft, but not browned.

2 Set half the garlic chives aside. Cut the stalks off the coriander and set the leaves aside. Purée the remaining chives and the coriander stalks with the stock in a blender or food processor.

COOK'S TIP
Wild mushrooms are often expensive, but they do have distinctive flavours. Mixing them with cultivated mushrooms is an economical way of using them. Look for ceps, chanterelles, oyster, morels and horse mushrooms.

MEXICAN RICE

CHILLIES PLAY A SUPPORTING ROLE IN THIS SOUTH AMERICAN RECIPE. LEAVING THEM WHOLE LIMITS THEIR IMPACT, BUT STILL MAKES A CONTRIBUTION TO THE FINISHED DISH.

SERVES SIX

INGREDIENTS
 200g/7oz/1 cup long grain rice
 200g/7oz can chopped tomatoes in
   tomato juice
 ½ onion, roughly chopped
 2 garlic cloves, roughly chopped
 30ml/2 tbsp vegetable oil
 450ml/¾ pint/scant 2 cups
   vegetable stock
 2.5ml/½ tsp salt
 3 fresh green fresno chillies or other
   fresh green chillies
 150g/5oz/1 cup frozen peas
 ground black pepper

1 Put the rice in a large heatproof bowl and pour over boiling water to cover. Stir once, then leave to stand for 10 minutes. Drain, rinse under cold water, then drain again. Leave in the sieve and set aside to dry slightly.

2 Meanwhile, pour the tomatoes and juice into a food processor or blender, add the onion and garlic, and process until smooth.

3 Heat the oil in a large, heavy pan, add the rice and cook over a medium heat until it becomes a delicate golden brown. Stir occasionally to ensure that the rice does not stick to the base of the pan. Reduce the heat if the rice begins to darken too much.

4 Add the tomato mixture and stir over a medium heat until all the liquid has been absorbed. Stir in the stock, salt, whole chillies and peas.

5 Continue to cook the mixture, stirring occasionally, until all the liquid has been absorbed and the rice is just tender. Season with pepper.

6 Remove the pan from the heat, cover it with a tight-fitting lid and leave it to stand in a warm place for 5–10 minutes. Remove the chillies, fluff up the rice lightly and serve, sprinkled with black pepper. The chillies can be used as a garnish, if you like.

COOK'S TIP
Do not stir the rice too often after you add the stock or the grains will break down and the mixture will quickly become starchy.

POTATOES <u>WITH</u> RED CHILLIES

IF YOU LIKE CHILLIES, YOU'LL LOVE THESE POTATOES! THE RED CHILLIES ADD COLOUR, FLAVOUR AND FIRE TO THE FINISHED DISH, WHICH IS FRAGRANCED WITH WARMING SPICES.

<u>SERVES FOUR</u>

INGREDIENTS
    12–14 small new or salad
      potatoes, halved
    30ml/2 tbsp vegetable oil
    2.5ml/½ tsp crushed dried
      red chillies
    2.5ml/½ tsp white cumin seeds
    2.5ml/½ tsp fennel seeds
    2.5ml/½ tsp crushed coriander seeds
    5ml/1 tsp salt
    1 onion, sliced
    1–4 fresh red chillies, chopped
    45ml/3 tbsp chopped fresh
      coriander (cilantro)

COOK'S TIP
After draining the cooked potatoes, cover with kitchen paper and put on the lid. The paper will absorb the steam and leave the potatoes dry.

1 Bring a pan of lightly salted water to the boil and cook the potatoes for about 15 minutes until tender but still firm. Remove from the heat and drain off the water. Set aside until needed.

2 Heat the oil in a deep frying pan and add the crushed chillies, cumin, fennel and coriander seeds. Sprinkle the salt over and fry, stirring continuously, for 30–40 seconds.

3 Add the sliced onion and fry until golden brown. Tip in the dry potatoes, add the chopped red chillies and 15ml/ 1 tbsp of the chopped coriander and stir well.

4 Reduce the heat to very low, then cover and cook for 5–7 minutes. Serve the potatoes hot, on a heated dish, garnished with the remaining chopped fresh coriander.

BOMBAY POTATOES

THIS CLASSIC GUJERATI (INDIAN VEGETARIAN) DISH OF POTATOES IS SLOWLY COOKED IN A RICHLY FLAVOURED CURRY SAUCE WITH FRESH CHILLIES FOR AN ADDED KICK.

SERVES FOUR TO SIX

INGREDIENTS

> 450g/1lb new or small salad potatoes
> 5ml/1 tsp ground turmeric
> 60ml/4 tbsp vegetable oil
> 2 dried red chillies
> 6–8 curry leaves
> 2 onions, finely chopped
> 2 fresh green chillies, finely chopped
> 50g/2oz/1 cup coriander (cilantro)
>   leaves, coarsely chopped
> 1.5ml/¼ tsp asafoetida
> 2.5ml/½ tsp each cumin, mustard,
>   onion, fennel and kalonji seeds
> lemon juice, to taste
> salt
> fried fresh curry leaves, to garnish

VARIATION
This works very well with cauliflower florets. Just reduce the cooking time.

1 Chop the potatoes into small chunks. Bring a pan of lightly salted water to the boil and add the potatoes with half the turmeric. Cook for 15–20 minutes, or until tender. Drain and set aside a few, then coarsely mash the rest. Set aside.

2 Heat the oil in a large heavy pan and fry the red chillies and curry leaves until the chillies begin to char. Do not let them burn or they will taste bitter.

3 Add the onions, fresh green chillies, coriander, remaining turmeric, asafoetida and spice seeds, and cook, stirring, until the onions are tender.

4 Fold in the potatoes and add a few drops of water. Cook over a low heat for about 10 minutes, stirring gently so that the potatoes absorb the spices without starting to break up. Remove the dried chillies and curry leaves.

5 Serve the potatoes hot, with lemon juice squeezed or poured over, and seasoned with salt. Garnish with the fried fresh curry leaves, if you like.

COOK'S TIP
Asafoetida is a spice with a pungent, rather unpleasant odour, which vanishes when it is cooked. It is widely used in Indian vegetarian cooking.

Chillies taste great in all sorts of salads, from a simple mixture of spinach and serranos to the colourful combination of fruit and vegetables that is known as Gado-gado. Not surprisingly, they have a great affinity for sweet peppers, but also work well with shellfish, especially squid. Some fresh chillies are tender enough to use as they are, seeded and sliced, but others benefit from being roasted so that the flesh takes on a smoky flavour. Do this over a flame or under the grill, or use a culinary blow torch so that only the outer skin is charred.

Piquant
Salads

PINK <u>AND</u> GREEN SALAD

THERE'S JUST ENOUGH CHILLI IN THIS STUNNING SALAD TO BRING A ROSY BLUSH TO YOUR CHEEKS.

SERVES FOUR

INGREDIENTS
225g/8oz/2 cups dried farfalle or
   other pasta shapes
juice of ½ lemon
1 small fresh red chilli, seeded and
   very finely chopped
60ml/4 tbsp chopped fresh basil
30ml/2 tbsp chopped fresh
   coriander (cilantro)
60ml/4 tbsp extra virgin olive oil
15ml/1 tbsp mayonnaise
250g/9oz peeled cooked
   prawns (shrimp)
1 avocado
salt and ground black pepper

1 Bring a large pan of lightly salted water to the boil and cook the pasta for 10–12 minutes, folllowing the packet instructions, or until it is *al dente*.

2 Meanwhile, put the lemon juice and chilli in a bowl with half the basil and coriander. Add salt and pepper to taste. Whisk well to mix, then whisk in the oil and mayonnaise until thick. Add the prawns and stir to coat in the dressing.

3 Drain the pasta in a colander, and rinse under cold running water until cold. Leave to drain and dry, shaking the colander occasionally.

4 Halve, stone (pit) and peel the avocado, then cut the flesh into dice. Add to the prawns and dressing with the pasta, toss well to mix and taste for seasoning. Serve immediately, sprinkled with the remaining basil and coriander.

COOK'S TIP
Keep a few chillies in the freezer and you'll never need to worry about getting fresh supplies just when you want them.

SCALLOP CONCHIGLIE

SCALLOPS, PASTA AND ROCKET ARE FLAVOURED WITH ROASTED PEPPER, CHILLI AND BALSAMIC VINEGAR.

2 Make the vinaigrette. Put the vinegar in a bowl and stir in the honey until dissolved. Add the chopped pepper, chillies and garlic, then whisk in the oil.

3 Bring a large pan of lightly salted water to the boil and cook the pasta for 10–12 minutes, or until *al dente*.

4 Meanwhile, heat the oil and butter in a frying pan until sizzling. Add half the scallops and toss over a high heat for 2 minutes. Remove with a slotted spoon and keep warm. Cook the remaining scallops in the same way.

5 Add the wine to the liquid remaining in the pan and stir over a high heat until the mixture has reduced to a few tablespoons. Remove from the heat and keep warm.

6 Drain the pasta and tip it into a warmed bowl. Add the rocket, scallops, the reduced cooking juices and the vinaigrette, and toss well to combine.

SERVES FOUR

INGREDIENTS
 8 large fresh scallops
 300g/11oz/2¾ cups dried conchiglie
  or other pasta shapes
 15ml/1 tbsp olive oil
 15g/½oz/1 tbsp butter
 120ml/4fl oz/½ cup dry white wine
 90g/3½oz/1½–2 cups rocket
  (arugula) leaves, stalks trimmed
 salt and ground black pepper
For the vinaigrette
 15ml/1 tbsp balsamic vinegar
 5–10ml/1–2 tsp clear honey,
  to taste
 1 piece bottled roasted (bell) pepper,
  drained and finely chopped
 1–2 fresh red chillies, seeded
  and chopped
 1 garlic clove, crushed
 60ml/4 tbsp extra virgin olive oil

1 Unless the fishmonger has already done so, remove the dark beard-like fringe and tough muscle from the scallops. Cut each of the scallops into 2–3 pieces. If the corals are attached, pull them off and cut each piece in half. Season with salt and pepper.

VARIATION
Use prawns (shrimp) instead of scallops.

COOK'S TIP
This is best prepared using fresh scallops, which look creamy-grey. If pure white they will have been frozen.

THAI SHELLFISH SALAD WITH CHILLI DRESSING AND FRIZZLED SHALLOTS

IN THIS INTENSELY FLAVOURED SALAD, SWEET PRAWNS AND MANGO ARE PARTNERED WITH A SWEET-SOUR GARLIC DRESSING HEIGHTENED WITH THE HOT TASTE OF CHILLI.

SERVES FOUR TO SIX

INGREDIENTS

675g/1½lb raw prawns (shrimp),
   shelled and deveined, with
   tails on
finely shredded rind of 1 lime
½ fresh red chilli, seeded and
   finely chopped
30ml/2 tbsp olive oil, plus extra
   for brushing
1 ripe but firm mango
2 carrots, cut into long
   thin shreds
10cm/4in piece cucumber, sliced
1 small red onion, halved and
   thinly sliced
45ml/3 tbsp roasted peanuts,
   roughly chopped
salt and ground black pepper

For the dressing
1 large garlic clove, chopped
10–15ml/2–3 tsp granulated sugar
juice of 1½–2 limes
15–30ml/1–2 tbsp Thai fish sauce
   (*nam pla*)
1 fresh red chilli, seeded
5–10ml/1–2 tsp light rice vinegar

For the frizzled shallots
30ml/2 tbsp groundnut
   (peanut) oil
4 large shallots, thinly sliced

COOK'S TIPS
• Crisp frizzled shallots are a traditional addition to Thai salads.
• For an authentic flavour, use Pacific shrimp, which are a wonderful brownish blue when raw. If they are frozen, make sure they are thawed before using.
• When searing the prawns, make sure that they have all turned pink, as undercooked prawns are unpleasant to eat and may be harmful. However, do not overcook, which spoils the texture.
• Mangoes vary considerably. Some are ripe when the skin is green flushed with red; others when they are red-gold or yellow. Ripe mangoes give gently when squeezed lightly in the palm of the hand.

1 Place the prawns in a glass or china dish and add the lime rind and chilli. Season with salt and pepper, and spoon the oil over. Toss to mix, cover and leave to marinate for 30–40 minutes.

2 Make the dressing. Place the garlic in a mortar with 10ml/2 tsp sugar. Pound until smooth, then work in the juice of 1½ limes and 15ml/1 tbsp of the fish sauce.

3 Transfer the dressing to a jug (pitcher). Finely chop half the fresh red chilli, and add it to the dressing. Taste the mixture and add more sugar, lime juice, fish sauce and the rice vinegar to taste.

4 Cut through the mango lengthwise 1cm/½in from each side of the centre to free the stone (pit). Remove all the peel and cut the flesh away from the stone. Cut all the flesh into fine strips. Set the mango aside. Make the frizzled shallots by heating the oil in a wok or frying pan and frying them until crisp. Drain on kitchen paper and set aside.

5 In a bowl, toss the mango, carrots, cucumber and onion with half the dressing. Arrange the salad on individual plates or in bowls.

6 Heat a ridged, cast-iron griddle pan or heavy frying pan until very hot. Brush the prawns with a little oil, then sear them for 2–3 minutes on each side, until they turn pink and are patched with brown on the outside. Arrange the prawns on the salads.

7 Sprinkle the remaining dressing over the salads. Finely shred the remaining chilli and sprinkle it over the salads with the crisp-fried shallots. Serve, with the peanuts handed around separately.

VARIATIONS
• Use scallops or chicken breast portions instead of prawns.
• Chop cashew nuts in place of peanuts.
• Substitute finely sliced baby leeks for the shallots.
• Make into a more substantial meal by mixing with cooked pasta shapes.

SPICY SQUID SALAD

THIS TASTY, COLOURFUL SALAD IS A REFRESHING WAY OF SERVING SQUID. THE GINGER AND CHILLI DRESSING IS ADDED WHILE THE SQUID IS STILL HOT, AND FLAVOURS THE SHELLFISH AND BEANS.

SERVES FOUR

INGREDIENTS

  450g/1lb squid
  300ml/½ pint/1¼ cups fish stock
  175g/6oz green beans, trimmed
    and halved
  45ml/3 tbsp fresh coriander
    (cilantro) leaves
  10ml/2 tsp granulated sugar
  30ml/2 tbsp rice vinegar
  5ml/1 tsp sesame oil
  15ml/1 tbsp light soy sauce
  15ml/1 tbsp vegetable oil
  2 garlic cloves, finely chopped
  10ml/2 tbsp finely chopped fresh
    root ginger
  1 fresh chilli, seeded and chopped
salt

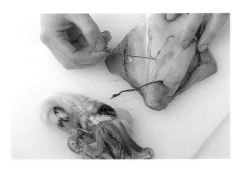

1 Prepare the squid. Holding the body in one hand, gently pull away the head and tentacles. Discard the head then trim and reserve the tentacles. Remove the transparent "quill" from inside the body of the squid and peel off the purplish skin on the outside.

2 Cut the body of the squid open lengthways and wash thoroughly. Score criss-cross patterns on the inside, taking care not to cut through the flesh completely, then cut into 7.5 × 5cm/ 3 × 2in pieces.

COOK'S TIPS
• If you hold your knife at an angle when scoring the squid, there is less of a risk of cutting right through it.
• Always make sure your knives are kept sharp to make cutting easier.

3 Bring the fish stock to the boil in a wok or pan. Add all the squid pieces, then lower the heat and cook for about 2 minutes until they are tender and have curled. Drain.

4 Bring a pan of lightly salted water to the boil, add the beans and cook them for 3–5 minutes, until they are crisp-tender. Drain, refresh under cold water or turn into a bowl of iced water, then drain again. Mix the squid and beans in a serving bowl.

5 In a bowl, mix the coriander leaves, sugar, rice vinegar, sesame oil and soy sauce. Pour the mixture over the squid and beans, and toss lightly, using a spoon, to coat.

6 Heat the vegetable oil in a wok or small pan. When it is very hot, stir-fry the garlic, ginger and chilli for a few seconds, then pour the dressing over the squid mixture. Toss gently and leave for at least 5 minutes. Add salt to taste and serve warm or cold.

CHICKEN, VEGETABLE AND CHILLI SALAD

THIS VIETNAMESE SALAD IS FULL OF SURPRISING TEXTURES AND FLAVOURS. SERVE AS A LIGHT LUNCH DISH OR FOR SUPPER WITH CRUSTY FRENCH BREAD.

SERVES FOUR

INGREDIENTS

225g/8oz Chinese leaves
   (Chinese cabbage)
2 carrots, cut in matchsticks
½ cucumber, cut in matchsticks
2 fresh red chillies, seeded and cut
   into thin strips
1 small onion, sliced into fine rings
4 pickled gherkins, sliced into fine
   rings, plus 45ml/3 tbsp of the
   liquid from the jar
50g/2oz/½ cup peanuts, lightly ground
225g/8oz cooked chicken, sliced
1 garlic clove, crushed
5ml/1 tsp granulated sugar
30ml/2 tbsp cider or white
   wine vinegar
salt

COOK'S TIP
Add extra cider or white wine vinegar to
the dressing for a sharper taste.

1 Discard any tough, outer leaves from the Chinese leaves, then stack the remainder on a board. Using a sharp knife, cut them into shreds that are about the same width as the carrot matchsticks. Put the Chinese leaves and carrot matchsticks in a salad bowl.

2 Spread out the cucumber matchsticks in a colander and sprinkle with salt. Stand the colander on a plate and set aside for 15 minutes, to extract the excess liquid.

3 Mix the chillies and onion rings in a small bowl. Add the sliced gherkins and peanuts. Rinse the salted cucumber thoroughly, drain well and pat dry with kitchen paper.

4 Add the cucumber matchsticks to the salad bowl and toss together lightly. Stir in the chilli mixture. Arrange the chicken on top. In a bowl, whisk the gherkin liquid with the garlic, sugar and vinegar. Pour over the salad, toss lightly and serve.

LARP OF CHIANG MAI

ANYONE WHO HAS TRAVELLED THROUGH NORTH-EASTERN THAILAND IS LIKELY TO HAVE ENCOUNTERED THIS TRADITIONAL DISH, IN WHICH CHICKEN IS COATED IN A HOT AND SHARP CHILLI SAUCE.

SERVES FOUR TO SIX

INGREDIENTS
 450g/1lb minced (ground) chicken
 1 lemon grass stalk, trimmed
 3 kaffir lime leaves, finely chopped
 4 fresh red chillies, seeded
   and chopped
 60ml/4 tbsp lime juice
 30ml/2 tbsp Thai fish sauce
   (*nam pla*)
 15ml/1 tbsp roasted ground rice
   (see Cook's Tip)
 2 spring onions (scallions), chopped
 30ml/2 tbsp fresh coriander
   (cilantro) leaves
 thinly sliced kaffir lime leaves, mixed
   salad leaves and fresh mint sprigs,
   to garnish

1 Heat a large non-stick frying pan. Add the chicken and moisten with a little water. Stir constantly over a medium heat for 7–10 minutes until it is cooked.

2 While the chicken is cooking, cut off the lower 5cm/2in of the lemon grass stalk and chop finely.

3 Transfer the cooked chicken to a bowl and add the chopped lemon grass, lime leaves, chillies, lime juice, fish sauce, ground rice, spring onions and coriander leaves. Mix thoroughly.

4 Spoon the chicken mixture into a salad bowl. Sprinkle sliced kaffir lime leaves over the top and garnish with salad leaves and sprigs of mint.

COOK'S TIP
Use glutinous rice (a short to medium grain rice) for the roasted ground rice. Put in a frying pan and dry-roast it until golden brown. Remove and grind to a powder, using a mortar and pestle or a food processor. When the rice is cold, store it in a glass jar in a cool, dry place.

THAI BEEF SALAD

A HEARTY MAIN MEAL SALAD, THIS COMBINES TENDER STRIPS OF STEAK WITH A WONDERFUL CHILLI AND LIME DRESSING. SERVE IT WITH WARM CRUSTY BREAD OR A BOWL OF RICE.

SERVES FOUR

INGREDIENTS
 oil, for frying
 2 sirloin steaks, each
   about 225g/8oz
 1 lemon grass stalk, trimmed
 1 red onion, finely sliced
 ½–1 fresh red chilli,
   finely chopped
 ½ cucumber, cut into strips
 30ml/2 tbsp chopped spring
   onion (scallion)
 juice of 2 limes
 15–30ml/1–2 tbsp Thai fish sauce
   (*nam pla*)
 Chinese mustard cress, or fresh
   herbs, to garnish

COOK'S TIP
Look out for gui chai leaves in Thai groceries. These look like very thin spring onions and are often used as a substitute for the more familiar vegetable.

1 Heat a large frying pan until hot, add a little oil and pan-fry the steaks for 6–8 minutes for medium-rare. If you prefer, cook the steaks under a preheated medium grill (broiler). Allow to rest for 10–15 minutes.

2 Cut off the lower 5cm/2in of the lemon grass stalk and chop it finely.

3 When the meat is cool, slice it thinly on a cutting board and put the slices in a large bowl.

4 Add the sliced onion, chilli, cucumber, lemon grass and chopped spring onion to the meat slices.

5 Toss the salad and flavour with the lime juice and fish sauce. Transfer to a serving bowl or plate and serve at room temperature or chilled, garnished with Chinese mustard cress or fresh herbs.

VARIATION
Instead of beef, use pork, chicken or meaty tuna steaks.

BEEF <u>AND</u> SWEET POTATO SALAD <u>WITH</u> MILD CHILLI DRESSING

THIS SALAD MAKES A GOOD MAIN DISH FOR A SUMMER BUFFET. IT IS DELICIOUS WITH A SIMPLE POTATO SALAD AND SOME PEPPERY LEAVES.

SERVES SIX TO EIGHT

INGREDIENTS

800g/1¾lb fillet (tenderloin) of beef
15ml/1 tbsp black peppercorns, lightly crushed
10ml/2 tsp chopped fresh thyme
60ml/4 tbsp olive oil
450g/1lb orange-fleshed sweet potatoes, peeled
salt and ground black pepper

For the dressing

1 garlic clove, chopped
60ml/4 tbsp fresh flat leaf parsley
30ml/2 tbsp chopped fresh coriander (cilantro)
15ml/1 tbsp small salted capers, rinsed and drained
½–1 fresh green chilli, seeded and chopped
10ml/2 tsp Dijon mustard
10–15ml/2–3 tsp white wine vinegar
75ml/5 tbsp extra virgin olive oil
2 shallots, finely chopped

1 Roll the beef in the crushed peppercorns and thyme. Cover and set aside for 2–3 hours. Preheat the oven to 200°C/400°F/Gas 6.

2 Heat half the olive oil in a heavy frying pan. Add the beef and brown it all over, turning frequently, to seal it. Place in a roasting pan and cook in the oven for 15–20 minutes.

COOK'S TIP
Choose a mild chilli such as Italia, if you can locate it. An Anaheim would also be good, but peel before chopping.

3 Remove the beef from the oven, cover with foil, allow to rest for 10–15 minutes.

4 Meanwhile, preheat the grill (broiler). Cut the sweet potatoes into 1cm/½in slices. Brush with the remaining olive oil, season to taste with salt and pepper, and grill (broil) for about 5–6 minutes on each side, until tender and browned. Cut the sweet potato slices into strips and place them in a bowl.

5 Cut the beef into slices or strips and toss with the sweet potato, then set the bowl aside.

6 Make the dressing. Put the garlic, parsley, coriander, capers, chilli, mustard and 10ml/2 tsp of the vinegar in a food processor or blender and process until chopped. With the motor still running, gradually pour in the oil to make a smooth dressing. Season with salt and pepper, and add more vinegar, to taste. Stir in the shallots.

7 Toss the dressing with the sweet potatoes and beef, and leave to stand for up to 2 hours before serving.

VARIATIONS
• Use pork or ham joints instead of beef.
• Try Bordeaux mustard instead of Dijon. It has a mild aromatic flavour.

SALAD OF ROASTED SHALLOTS, CHILLIES AND BUTTERNUT SQUASH WITH FETA

THIS IS ESPECIALLY GOOD SERVED WITH A SALAD BASED ON RICE OR COUSCOUS. SERVE THE DISH WITH PLENTY OF GOOD, WARM, CRUSTY BREAD.

SERVES FOUR TO SIX

INGREDIENTS
  75ml/5 tbsp olive oil
  15ml/1 tbsp balsamic vinegar, plus
    a little extra if needed
  15ml/1 tbsp sweet soy sauce
  350g/12oz shallots, peeled but
    left whole
  3 fresh red chillies
  1 butternut squash, peeled, seeded
    and cut into chunks
  5ml/1 tsp finely chopped fresh thyme
  60ml/4 tbsp chopped fresh flat
    leaf parsley
  1 small garlic clove, finely chopped
  75g/3oz/¾ cup walnuts or pecan
    nuts, chopped
  150g/5oz feta cheese
  salt and ground black pepper

1 Preheat the oven to 200°C/400°F/ Gas 6. Beat the oil, vinegar and soy sauce together in a large bowl.

2 Toss the shallots and 2 of the chillies in the oil mixture and turn into a large, shallow roasting pan or ovenproof dish. Season with salt and pepper. Roast, uncovered, for 25 minutes, stirring once or twice.

3 Add the butternut squash and roast for a further 35–40 minutes, stirring once, until the squash is tender and browned. Remove from the oven, stir in the chopped thyme and set the vegetable mixture aside to cool.

4 Mix the parsley and garlic together and stir in the nuts. Seed and finely chop the remaining chilli.

5 Stir the parsley, garlic and nut mixture into the cooled vegetables. Add chopped chilli to taste and adjust the seasoning, adding a little extra balsamic vinegar if you like. Crumble the feta cheese and add it to the salad, tossing together lightly. Transfer to a serving dish and serve immediately, at room temperature rather than chilled.

ROASTED PEPPER AND TOMATO SALAD

CHILLIES DO NOT NEED TO DOMINATE TO MAKE THEIR PRESENCE FELT IN A DISH. HERE THEY ARE USED TO ACCENTUATE THE FLAVOUR OF THEIR MILDER RELATIONS, THE SWEET PEPPERS.

SERVES FOUR

INGREDIENTS

- 3 red (bell) peppers
- 6 large plum tomatoes
- 2.5ml/½ tsp dried red chilli flakes
- 1 red onion, finely sliced
- 3 garlic cloves, finely chopped
- grated rind and juice of 1 lemon
- 45ml/3 tbsp chopped fresh flat leaf parsley
- 30ml/2 tbsp extra virgin olive oil or chilli oil
- salt
- black and green olives and extra chopped flat leaf parsley, to garnish

COOK'S TIPS

• Peppers roasted this way will keep for several weeks. After peeling off the skins, place the pepper pieces in a jar with a tight-fitting lid. Pour over olive oil to cover. Store in the refrigerator.

• For an intense flavour, roast fresh red chillies with the peppers and tomatoes.

1 Preheat the oven to 220°C/425°F/ Gas 7. Place the peppers on a baking tray and roast, turning occasionally, for 10 minutes or until the skins are almost blackened. Add the tomatoes to the baking tray, return to the oven and roast for 5 minutes more.

2 Place the roasted peppers in a plastic bag, close the top loosely, trapping in the steam to loosen the skins, and then set them aside, with the tomatoes, until they are cool enough to handle, which should take about 15 minutes.

3 Carefully pull off the skin from the peppers. Remove the seeds, then chop the peppers and tomatoes roughly and place in a mixing bowl.

4 Add the chilli flakes, onion slices, chopped garlic, lemon rind and juice. Sprinkle over the parsley. Mix well, then transfer to a serving dish.

5 Sprinkle with a little salt, drizzle over the olive oil or chilli oil and sprinkle olives and extra parsley over the top. Serve at room temperature.

SPINACH AND SERRANO CHILLI SALAD

YOUNG SPINACH LEAVES MAKE A WELCOME CHANGE FROM LETTUCE AND ARE EXCELLENT IN SALADS.
THE ROASTED GARLIC IS AN INSPIRED ADDITION TO THE DRESSING.

SERVES SIX

INGREDIENTS
    500g/1¼lb baby spinach leaves
    50g/2oz/⅓ cup sesame seeds
    50g/2oz/¼ cup butter
    30ml/2 tbsp olive oil
    6 shallots, sliced
    8 fresh serrano chillies, seeded and
        cut into strips
    4 tomatoes, sliced
For the dressing
    6 smoked or roasted garlic cloves
    120ml/4fl oz/½ cup white
        wine vinegar
    2.5ml/½ tsp ground white pepper
    1 bay leaf
    2.5ml/½ tsp ground allspice
    30ml/2 tbsp chopped fresh thyme,
        plus extra sprigs, to garnish

1 Pull any coarse stalks from the spinach leaves, rinse the leaves and dry them in a salad spinner or clean dishtowel. Put them in a plastic bag in the refrigerator.

2 Make the dressing. Remove the skins from the garlic, then chop the flesh and put it in a jar that has a screw-top lid. Add the vinegar, pepper, bay leaf, allspice and chopped thyme. Close tightly, shake well, then set aside.

COOK'S TIP
You can buy smoked garlic from most supermarkets. If you prefer to use roasted garlic, place the cloves in a roasting pan in an oven preheated to 180°C/350°F/Gas 4 and cook for about 15 minutes until soft.

3 Toast the sesame seeds in a dry frying pan, shaking frequently over a medium heat until golden. Set aside.

4 Heat the butter and oil in a frying pan. Fry the shallots for 4–5 minutes, until softened, then stir in the chilli strips and fry for 2–3 minutes more.

5 In a large bowl, layer the spinach with the shallot and chilli mixture, and the tomato slices. Pour over the dressing. Sprinkle with sesame seeds and serve, garnished with thyme sprigs.

VARIATION
For a crunchy salad, use finely sliced red or white cabbage instead of spinach.

COUSCOUS AND CHILLI SALAD

THIS IS A SPICY VARIATION ON A CLASSIC TABBOULEH, TRADITIONALLY MADE WITH BULGUR WHEAT AND NOT COUSCOUS, WHICH IS ACTUALLY A FORM OF SEMOLINA GRAIN.

SERVES FOUR

INGREDIENTS
   45ml/3 tbsp olive oil
   5 spring onions (scallions), chopped
   1 garlic clove, crushed
   5ml/1 tsp ground cumin
   350ml/12fl oz/1½ cups
      vegetable stock
   175g/6oz/1 cup couscous
   2 tomatoes, peeled and chopped
   60ml/4 tbsp chopped fresh parsley
   60ml/4 tbsp chopped fresh mint
   1 fresh green chilli, seeded and
      finely chopped
   30ml/2 tbsp lemon juice
   salt and ground black pepper
   crisp lettuce leaves, to serve
   toasted pine nuts and grated lemon
      rind, to garnish

1 Heat the oil in a pan. Add the spring onions and garlic. Stir in the cumin and cook over a medium heat for 1 minute. Pour in the stock and bring to the boil.

2 Remove the pan from the heat, stir in the couscous, cover the pan tightly and leave to stand for 10 minutes, until all the liquid has been absorbed.

3 Tip the couscous into a bowl. Stir in the tomatoes, parsley, mint, chilli and lemon juice, and season. Leave to stand for 1 hour for the flavours to develop.

4 To serve, line a bowl with lettuce leaves and spoon the couscous salad into the centre. Sprinkle toasted pine nuts and lemon rind over, to garnish.

VARIATIONS
• You can use fine bulgur wheat instead of couscous. Follow the packet instructions for its preparation.
• It is very important for the flavour of the salad to use fresh mint. If it is not available, substitute fresh coriander. The flavour will not be quite the same but dried or freeze-dried mint are not suitable alternatives.

GADO-GADO WITH PEANUT AND CHILLI SAUCE

A BANANA LEAF, WHICH CAN BE BOUGHT FROM ASIAN FOOD STORES, CAN BE USED AS WELL AS THE MIXED SALAD LEAVES TO LINE THE PLATTER FOR A SPECIAL OCCASION.

SERVES SIX

INGREDIENTS
  ½ cucumber
  2 pears (not too ripe) or 175g/6oz
    wedge of yam bean (jicama)
  1–2 eating apples
  juice of ½ lemon
  mixed salad leaves
  6 small tomatoes, cut in wedges
  3 slices fresh pineapple, cored and
    cut in wedges
  3 eggs, hard-boiled (hard-cooked)
    and shelled
  175g/6oz egg noodles, cooked,
    cooled and chopped
  deep-fried onions, to garnish
For the peanut sauce
  2–4 fresh red chillies, seeded
    and ground, or 15ml/1 tbsp
    chilli sambal
  300ml/½ pint/1¼ cups coconut milk
  350g/12oz/1¼ cups crunchy
    peanut butter
  15ml/1 tbsp dark soy sauce or soft
    dark brown sugar
  5ml/1 tsp tamarind pulp, soaked in
    45ml/3 tbsp warm water
  coarsely crushed peanuts
  salt

1 Make the peanut sauce. Put the chillies or chilli sambal in a pan. Pour in the coconut milk. Stir in the peanut butter. Heat gently, stirring, until mixed.

COOK'S TIP
To make your own peanut butter, process roasted peanuts in a food processor, slowly adding vegetable oil to achieve the right texture. Add salt to taste.

2 Simmer gently until the sauce thickens, then stir in the soy sauce or sugar. Strain in the tamarind juice, add salt to taste and stir well. Spoon into a bowl and sprinkle with a few coarsely crushed peanuts.

VARIATION
Quail's eggs can be used instead of hen's eggs and look very attractive in this dish. Hard-boil for 3 minutes, shell, then halve or leave whole.

3 To make the salad, core the cucumber and peel the pears or yam bean. Cut them into matchsticks. Finely shred the apples and sprinkle them with the lemon juice. Spread a bed of salad leaves on a flat platter, then pile the fruit and vegetables on top.

4 Add the sliced or quartered hard-boiled eggs, the chopped noodles and the deep-fried onions. Serve at once, with the sauce.

HOT HOT CAJUN POTATO SALAD

IN CAJUN COUNTRY, WHERE TABASCO ORIGINATES, HOT MEANS REALLY HOT, SO YOU CAN GO TO TOWN WITH THIS SALAD IF YOU THINK YOU CAN TAKE IT!

SERVES SIX TO EIGHT

INGREDIENTS

    8 waxy potatoes
    1 green (bell) pepper, seeded
      and diced
    1 large gherkin, chopped
    4 spring onions (scallions), shredded
    3 eggs, hard-boiled (hard-cooked),
      shelled and chopped
    250ml/8fl oz/1 cup mayonnaise
    15ml/1 tbsp Dijon mustard
    Tabasco sauce, to taste
    pinch or 2 of cayenne
    salt and ground black pepper
    fanned, sliced gherkin, to garnish
    salad leaves, to serve

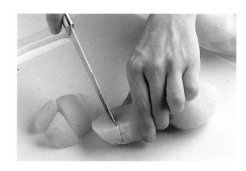

1 Put the unpeeled potatoes in a pan of cold salted water, bring to the boil and cook for 20–30 minutes, until tender. Drain. When the potatoes are cool enough to handle, peel them and cut into large chunks.

2 Place the potatoes in a large bowl and add the green pepper, gherkin, spring onions and eggs. Mix gently.

3 In a separate bowl, mix the mayonnaise with the mustard and season with salt, black pepper and Tabasco sauce to taste.

4 Add the dressing to the potato mixture, toss gently to coat, then sprinkle a pinch or 2 of cayenne on top. Garnish with fanned, sliced gherkin.

COOK'S TIP
To hard-boil eggs, pierce the round end so air can escape to prevent cracking. Place in boiling water for 8 minutes. Remove into cold water, then peel.

SWEET POTATO, PEPPER AND CHILLI SALAD

THIS SALAD IS COMPOSED OF A DELICIOUS BLEND OF INGREDIENTS AND HAS A TRULY TROPICAL TASTE.
IT IS IDEAL SERVED WITH ASIAN OR CARIBBEAN DISHES.

2 Meanwhile, mix the dressing ingredients together in a bowl and season to taste.

3 Put the red pepper in a large bowl and add the celery and onion. Tip in the finely chopped chilli and mix with a wooden spoon.

4 Remove the sweet potatoes from the oven. When they are cool enough to handle, peel them. Cut them into cubes and add them to the large bowl. Drizzle the dressing over and toss carefully. Season again to taste and serve, garnished with fresh coriander.

VARIATION
This would work well with potatoes.

SERVES FOUR TO SIX

INGREDIENTS
   1kg/2¼lb sweet potatoes
   1 red (bell) pepper, seeded and
    finely diced
   3 celery sticks, finely diced
   ¼ red skinned onion, finely chopped
   1 fresh red chilli, finely chopped
   salt and ground black pepper
For the dressing
   45ml/3 tbsp chopped fresh coriander
    (cilantro), plus extra to garnish
   juice of 1 lime
   150ml/¼ pint/⅔ cup natural
    (plain) yogurt

1 Preheat the oven to 200°C/400°F/ Gas 6. Wash the potatoes and pat dry with kitchen paper, pierce them all over and bake in the oven for 40 minutes or until tender.

SPICY VEGETABLE RIBBONS

FEW SALADS LOOK PRETTIER THAN THIS COMBINATION OF CUCUMBER, CARROT AND MOOLI RIBBONS, TOSSED WITH BEANSPROUTS AND SPIKED WITH CHILLI.

2 Wash the beansprouts and drain them thoroughly in a colander. Pat them dry with kitchen paper.

3 Peel the cucumber, cut it in half lengthwise and scoop out and discard the seeds. Peel the cucumber flesh into long ribbon strips, using a swivel vegetable peeler or mandoline.

4 Peel the carrots and mooli into ribbons as for the cucumber.

5 Place the carrots, mooli and cucumber ribbons in a large shallow serving dish, add the beansprouts, onion, ginger, chilli and coriander or mint and toss to mix. Pour the dressing over the salad just before serving.

SERVES FOUR

INGREDIENTS
    225g/8oz/4 cups beansprouts
    1 cucumber
    2 carrots
    1 small mooli (daikon)
    1 small red onion, thinly sliced
    2.5cm/1in fresh root ginger, peeled
      and cut into thin matchsticks
    1 small fresh red chilli, seeded and
      thinly sliced
    handful of fresh coriander (cilantro)
      leaves or fresh mint leaves
For the dressing
    15ml/1 tbsp rice vinegar
    15ml/1 tbsp light soy sauce
    15ml/1 tbsp Thai fish sauce
      (*nam pla*)
    1 garlic clove, finely chopped
    15ml/1 tbsp sesame oil
    45ml/3 tbsp groundnut (peanut) oil
    30ml/2 tbsp sesame seeds,
      lightly toasted

1 First make the dressing by mixing all the ingredients in a bottle or screw-top jar and shaking vigorously.

COOK'S TIPS
• Keep beansprouts refrigerated and use within a day of purchase.
• Mooli, which looks like a white parsnip, has a fresh, peppery taste. Eat it raw or cooked, but as it has a high water content it needs to be salted before cooking.
• Refrigerated, the dressing will keep for a couple of days.

GREEN PAPAYA AND CHILLI SALAD

THIS SALAD APPEARS IN MANY GUISES IN SOUTH-EAST ASIA. AS GREEN PAPAYA IS NOT EASY TO FIND, FINELY SHREDDED CARROTS, CUCUMBER OR GREEN APPLE CAN BE USED INSTEAD.

SERVES FOUR

INGREDIENTS

1 green papaya
4 garlic cloves, roughly chopped
15ml/1 tbsp chopped shallots
3–4 fresh red chillies, seeded and
  sliced, plus extra sliced fresh red
  chillies to garnish (optional)
2.5ml/½ tsp salt
2–3 snake beans or 6 green beans,
  cut into 2cm/¾in lengths
2 tomatoes, cut into thin wedges
45ml/3 tbsp Thai fish sauce
  (*nam pla*)
15ml/1 tbsp granulated sugar
juice of 1 lime
30ml/2 tbsp crushed roasted peanuts

3 Add the sliced beans and wedges of tomato to the mortar and crush them lightly with the pestle.

VARIATION
Use cashew nuts instead of peanuts.

4 Flavour the mixture with the fish sauce, sugar and lime juice – you will not need extra salt. Transfer the salad to a serving dish and sprinkle with crushed peanuts. Garnish with the extra sliced red chillies, if using, and serve.

1 Cut the papaya in half lengthways. Scrape out the seeds with a spoon, then peel, using a swivel vegetable peeler or a small sharp knife. Shred the flesh finely using a food processor or grater.

2 Put the garlic, shallots, sliced chillies and salt in a large mortar and grind to a paste with a pestle. Add the shredded papaya, a little at a time, pounding until it becomes slightly limp and soft.

INDEX